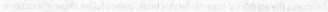
ESL
DeMYSTiFieD®

Ed Swick

Mc
Graw
Hill
Education

New York   Chicago   San Francisco   Athens   London   Madrid
Mexico City   Milan   New Delhi   Singapore   Sydney   Toronto

428.24
S976d

4 5 6 7 8 9 QVS/QVS 21 20 19 18 17

ISBN   978-0-07-182077-6 (book and CD set)
MHID   0-07-182077-9 (book and CD set)

ISBN   978-0-07-182075-2 (book for set)
MHID   0-07-182075-2 (book for set)

e-ISBN 978-0-07-182078-3
e-MHID 0-07-182078-7

Library of Congress Cataloging-in-Publication Data

Swick, Edward.
      ESL Demystified/Ed Swick.
                p. cm.
    ISBN 0-07-182077-9   ISBN 978-0-07-182077-6 (book and cd set)
    ISBN 978-0-07-182075-2 (book for set)
    1. English language—Textbooks for foreign speakers.   2. English language—
    Grammar—Problems, exercises, etc.
    PE 1128.S9773   2014
    428.2'4
                                                            2013026954

McGraw-Hill Education products are available at special quantity discounts to use as premiums and sales promotions or for use in corporate training programs. To contact a representative, please visit the Contact Us pages at www.mhprofessional.com.

This book is printed on acid-free paper.

ADDITIONAL MATERIAL

To access the additional material for this book, please follow these instructions:

1. Go to mhprofessional.com/mediacenter.

2. Enter this book's ISBN: 978-0-07-182077-6 and select the Find Product button.

3. Enter your e-mail address to receive a link to the downloadable file.

Contents

Introduction

All languages have rules that govern how the grammar of those languages functions. In all languages, the rules of grammar are sometimes broken, and if a rule is broken often enough and by enough people, a new rule replaces the original one that conforms to the new pattern the people have accepted.

For example, for centuries the verb **dive** was considered an irregular verb in the past tense (**dove**) and a regular verb as a past participle (**has dived**). No one knows for sure why it happened, but the past tense also became **dived** in North America over the last two centuries.

Another such verb is **dream**. Its past tense and past participle appear in two forms: **dreamt** and **dreamed.** You will hear both in most English-speaking countries, and both are considered correct.

Why does this occur? The answer is simple: these are the patterns that the speakers of a language use and accept as correct. Those who learn this language must accept these patterns and learn to use them as well. There is no other concrete answer to *why does this occur* because other explanations have been obscured by the passage of a great deal of time.

How and why a language functions in one way or another is often *mysterious.* This book will guide you in *demystifying* a variety of structures and linguistic patterns as you set about improving your English language skills.

The first chapter of this book is different from the others. It is a guide to vowel and consonant pronunciation and is provided because the key to speaking and understanding well is pronouncing words correctly. If you develop the habit of pronouncing a word or phrase incorrectly, not only will you be hard to understand, you will also not understand a familiar word or phrase when you hear it pronounced correctly. This is an important chapter for you if you are determined to improve your accent.

Most other chapters describe and illustrate elements of English that often require *demystifying*. For example, the word **his** is both a possessive adjective and a pronoun. What is the difference? How is each used? Those questions are answered, and numerous examples are provided. The patterns that are described are then put into practical exercises. The basis of language is speech, so all concepts are practiced not only in written exercises but also in oral exercises.

Each chapter ends with a quiz that will help you to evaluate your understanding of the material covered. The quizzes are open-book quizzes—you should use the content of the chapter as a resource for determining the correct answers. A good suggestion is to achieve a score of at least 80 percent before going on the next chapter.

After every five chapters, you will find a Part Test. Its goal is to check whether you have achieved the basics of the content of the five chapters and to give you a way to measure your progress. It is suggested that you consider these tests closed-book tests in order to check your comprehension of the concepts in each part. You should get a score of at least 75 percent in a Part Test before moving on to the next part.

In most chapters, you will encounter a section called Idioms Demystified. The idioms provided are not selected at random but rather because they conform to the concepts of the chapter they are in. The idioms are explained and include several examples of their use. You'll also find sections called Take Note. These boxes highlight important information for your study.

The last chapter of the book is a culmination of the other chapters. The main goal is to give you an abundance of writing practice and opportunities to write creatively. The writing exercises provide guidance on how you should write, but you will be the author of your sentences.

The book ends with the Final Exam. This is your measuring tool to determine how much you have improved and how well you can manipulate the concepts that have been *demystified*. This exam contains fifty questions, and a good score on the Final Exam would be 75 percent or above.

An audio recording accompanies this book. On it you will find oral exercises from each chapter. Use the audio tracks to imitate the pronunciation and intonation you hear. Losing an accent is not just improving the pronunciation of words but also the *melody*, with which a sentence is said.

At the end of the book you will find an appendix that contains the International Phonetic Alphabet (IPA). Use this as your guide for improving your pronunciation. As a download from the McGraw-Hill Education website, you will find a second appendix that provides a complete list of irregular verbs in their simple past and past participial forms. This is your resource for conjugating verbs correctly. Refer to it to maintain accuracy in speaking and writing. (Please see the copyright page for details on how to access this material.)

Language learning does not have to be a tedious chore, so approach the use of this book as a pleasant task. It is your personal tool for developing your language skills, improving what you already know, and becoming a fluent speaker of English.

Part One

Getting Started

chapter 1

Improving Your Accent

In this chapter you will find the guidelines for improving your accent in order to make you sound more like a native speaker of English. The nuances of consonants and vowels will be presented, and some tricks for demystifying the English spelling system are also included.

CHAPTER OBJECTIVES

In this chapter you will learn about:

- The different pronunciations of consonants
- The different pronunciations of vowels
- Consonant combinations
- Vowel combinations
- Spelling difficulties

Part of knowing English well is pronouncing it properly to achieve an authentic accent. A good accent not only makes you sound more like a native, it also improves comprehension. A person who pronounces words incorrectly is likely not to understand them immediately when they are used by native speakers. Therefore, a good accent is essential.

There are a variety of English accents, all of them derived from the mother language in England. North America has its own pronunciation, and that is the accent discussed in this chapter. However, no matter which accent you use, all of them are understood by all speakers of English, although sometimes with a bit of extra-careful listening and knowledge of some vocabulary differences.

Consonants

English consonants are pronounced much like the consonants of other European languages. The few exceptions will be explained here. The greatest problem with consonants comes from spelling, not pronunciation. English speakers gradually came to accept the fact that the way they write English words is not always in conformity with how they pronounce English words. Spelling is based on tradition and habit, not on phonetics. Little effort has been made to modernize English spelling, so newcomers to the language have to learn not only how to speak English but also how to use the various formulas for spelling. Where necessary, the International Phonetic Alphabet (IPA) will be used to describe consonant sounds. (You can find a complete chart of the IPA in the Appendix.)

Some consonants have two forms: the *voiced consonant* and the *voiceless consonant*. Voiced consonants require a resonation in the throat to pronounce them. Voiceless consonants do not. Let's look at these consonants.

Voiced Consonants	Voiceless Consonants
b	p
d	t
g	k
v	f
z	s

One consonant combination is unique in that it has both a voiced and voiceless form. That consonant combination is **th**.

Voiced Consonant	Voiceless Consonant
th (ð)	th (θ)

Unlike many other European languages, English pronounces voiced consonants at the beginning of a word, in the middle of a word, and at the end of a word. Most of the voiceless consonants are treated the same. However, the voiceless consonant **t** is often pronounced like **d** in the middle of a word when it follows a vowel. The voiceless consonant **s** is sometimes pronounced like **z**, especially when forming a plural or a third personal singular present tense verb with **-es** or when preceded by a voiced consonant.

Oral Practice

Read each string of words aloud, with the correct pronunciation.

Voiced Consonants
boy, tobacco, tub
do, window, nod
get, biggest, wig
van, wavy, love (silent *e*)
zoo, buzzing, quiz
the (ð), mother (ð), breathe (ð)

Voiceless Consonants
pat, upon, lip
kiss, baking, rake (silent *e*)
fat, safest, puff
sat, master, fuss
still, casing, less
both (θ), filthy (θ), breath (θ)

Voiceless Consonants Pronounced Like Voiced Consonants
(s pronounced like z) laser, busy, houses
noisy, wise, rods
marries, finds, feeds

(t pronounced like d in the middle of a word)
tip, water, wait
tan, better, sit
task, fitting, hate (silent *e*)

? Still Struggling

Practice saying the following phrase until you can say it rapidly and with the correct pronunciation. Notice that both the voiced and voiceless consonant combinations are in the phrase.

He thanked (θ) the (ð) both (θ) of them (ð).

Written Practice 1-1

Choose the IPA symbol that represents the pronunciation of **th** in each of the following words.

1. father	θ	ð		6. bath	θ	ð
2. faith	θ	ð		7. bathe	θ	ð
3. think	θ	ð		8. mother	θ	ð
4. thumb	θ	ð		9. thank	θ	ð
5. together	θ	ð		10. mathematics	θ	ð

The Consonants c, k, and q

The consonant **c** is the written symbol for two sounds: **k** and **s**. When **c** is followed by a consonant or the vowels **a**, **o**, and **u**, it is pronounced like **k**. When it is followed by **e**, **i**, and **y**, it is most often pronounced like **s**.

cat, come, cup	cell, center, certain
clear, close, clip	city, circus, citrus
crab, creek, crust	cycle, cylinder, cymbal

The letters **ck**, **ch**, **que**, and **q** can be pronounced like **k**. **Ck** does not begin a word. **Que** is at the end of words, and **q** is found primarily in words of Arabic origin. **K** itself is pronounced like **k** and can be used at the beginning a word, in the middle of a word, or at the end of a word.

neck, pick, rock	Iraq, al Qaeda, Quran
psychology, chorus, character	kind, hiker, book
physique, mystique, boutique	

The combination of the consonant **q** and the vowel **u** precedes vowels and is pronounced like **kw**.

quite	acquire
queer	requisition
quaint	

When **k** begins a word and is followed by the consonant **n**, the **k** is silent. The **n** is the initial sound for that word. For example:

knapsack	know
knee	knuckle

Oral Practice

 Track 1

Read each sentence aloud, with the correct pronunciation.

The little kitten drank cold milk.
Cecilia quit work at three o'clock.
The theater was filled with enthusiastic theater-goers.
What kind of candy do Karen and Clark like?
In winter, my brother thoroughly enjoys skiing and ice skating.
Kevin knew that the knight that guards the king carries a knife.
A mouse sits under the bookcase carelessly close to the three cats.
Susan's father puts butter on a slice of hot toast.

Written Practice 1-2

Indicate whether the consonants in bold type are voiced (V) or voiceless (VL).

1. gather _____   6. size   _____
2. bags   _____   7. most   _____
3. bitter _____   8. quiz   _____
4. clocks _____   9. special   _____
5. pace   _____   10. painter   _____

The Consonant g

The consonant **g** is most frequently pronounced as a hard **g** (see the Appendix, which lists the consonants in the International Phonetic Alphabet), as in the word **go**. If a consonant follows **g**, **g** is pronounced hard, as in the word **glass**. When it precedes **e**, **i**, or **y**, it is often pronounced like **j (dʒ)**, as in the words **gem** and **gin**. At the end of a word, **g** is pronounced hard, unless it is followed by **e**. For example:

Hard g   **(dʒ)**
log   cage
big   page

Oral Practice

Read each pair of words aloud. A hint on their pronunciation is given on the right.

sage, rage	(dʒ)	gymnasium, gyroscope	(dʒ)
mug, slug	hard **g**	ghost, grow	hard **g**
general, gesture	(dʒ)	gentle, huge	(dʒ)
tiger, begging	hard **g**	giggle, get	hard **g**

TAKE NOTE *When **g** follows **d**, it is always pronounced like (dʒ). For example:*

fudge	**nudge**	**hedge**	**lodge**
edge	**wedge**	**judgment**	**pudgy**

Oral Practice

🔘 Track 2

Read each sentence aloud, with the correct pronunciation.

The gentleman got up and gave his guests a warm greeting.
A large gray goose sat on the ledge and gazed down at the gathering
   seagulls.
George gets good grades in geography and gold stars in language.
The gymnast grabs the rings and uses his strength to perform a
   great move.
Give your grandfather the good golf clubs and Gene the old ones.

The Consonant Combination *gh*

Numerous words that come from Old English have a pesky combination of two consonants: **g** and **h**. Not a single word that has this consonant combination still has the sound of the original pronunciation. Old English evolved from the Germanic language that the Anglo-Saxons brought to England. And in that language, as with the Modern German **ch**, the **gh** had a guttural sound similar to **ch** in Scottish or German. Compare some English vocabulary with the Modern German spelling of similar words.

English	German
knight	Knecht
light	Licht
night	Nacht
right	Recht
sight	Sicht

In 1066 the Norman French conquered England. And they brought with them their language and culture. Because the French and the Saxons took many decades to assimilate, many experts believe that this was part of the cause of the change in English pronunciation. When the French began to use English, they had difficulty with the **gh** sound. They mispronounced it and often just omitted it. As the two cultures of England grew together, these mispronunciations became widely accepted in England and have lasted until the present day.

The spelling of words with **gh** is based on a very old tradition and has nothing to do with actual pronunciation. Therefore, native speakers of English as well as newcomers to the language have to learn how to say the words in one fashion and spell them in another.

A few words are pronounced with the sound f where the **gh** is written. Even though many of the words have the same vowel combination, they often have a different pronunciation of those vowels. For example:

cough	(ɔːf)	laugh	(æf)
draught	(æf)	rough	(ʌf)
enough	(ʌf)	tough	(ʌf)

Many other words are pronounced as if the **gh** were silent. For example:

bought	light	sought
brought	night	taught
daughter	ought	thought
fight	sigh	tight
high	sight	

TAKE NOTE *When a word begins with gh, it is pronounced as g. For example:*

ghost

ghastly

ghoul

There are fewer than fifteen such words in English.

Oral Practice

🔘 Track 3

Read each sentence aloud, with the correct pronunciation.

How was your flight from Chicago last night?
You have no right to act so tough and pick a fight with him.
I thought your daughter had lost some weight.
That's not enough milk. I ought to go out for more.
The sun is high in the sky and far too bright for me.
Is his height six feet, and does he weigh more than 200 pounds?
Their laughter over my suit brought a tear to my eye as I let out a deep sigh.

Written Practice 1-3

Indicate whether the consonants in bold type are silent, S, or pronounced as the consonant f or k.

1. laughing _____   6. rougher _____
2. kneel   _____   7. slaughter _____
3. bought   _____   8. kept   _____
4. flight   _____   9. although _____
5. knead   _____   10. kicking _____

The Consonant h

The consonant h has the sound of a quiet aspiration at the back of the throat. It is pronounced at the beginning and in the middle of words. At the end of a word, unless it is in a combined form (th, gh, ch, sh, and so on), it is not pronounced. For example: house, mohair, shah. Forms of the words honest and honor begin with a silent h.

The Consonant j

Although j is found primarily at the beginning of words, it sometimes appears in the middle (as in major) or at the end of a foreign word. It is pronounced (dʒ). For example: jet, rajah, haj (or hajj).

The Consonant *l*

The North American l is pronounced by gently tapping the alveolar ridge on the roof of the mouth with the tip of the tongue. At the same time, there is resonation in the throat. Careful. If the tongue is pressed against the upper teeth, the l is more similar to the Slavic l. If the tongue is pressed to the roof of the mouth behind the alveolar ridge, the l is more west-central European (French or German l).

Oral Practice

Read each pair of words aloud, with the correct pronunciation.

heavy, behold	behave, hope
just, Ouija board	jam, adjust
look, allow	doll, silly

The Consonants *m* and *n*

The sound of these two consonants begins with resonation in the throat with the vowel sound (**ɑ:**). To say **m** touch the lips together. To say **n** keep the mouth slightly open and touch the tongue between the upper front teeth and the alveolar ridge. These consonants can be found at the beginning, the middle, and the end of words. For example:

mother, sometime, room
small, dimmer, warm
nice, winner, fun
snack, wonder, line (silent *e*)

When n is followed by **g**, a slightly new sound is made. It is pronounced as (**ŋ**) in the IPA. For example: **singing, long, finger.**

The Consonant *r*

The North American r causes difficulty for many newcomers to English. It is best to start learning the pronunciation of this consonant in the final position of a word, for example, the word **her** (**3:ʳ**). Pronounce the vowel e in that word and at the same time purse the lips to pronounce u. This is the start of the sound of a final r. Exaggerate that sound and jut the jaw out slightly with the tongue pointing to a spot between the alveolar ridge and the upper teeth. This pronunciation is also used when another consonant follows r at the end of a word.

Oral Practice

Read each string of words aloud, with the correct pronunciation.

for, sir, more, beer	mark, park, smirk, Turk
better, longer, taller, wider	bird, arm, barb, sharp
turn, learn, barn, born	caring, hearing, pouring, daring
short, start, part, hurt	

When r begins a word or is in the middle of a word, the same sound as the final r is made. However, the vowel sound e must be omitted.

Oral Practice

Read each string of words aloud, with the correct pronunciation.

red, bread, friend	rule, true, enrage
roast, bring, arrange	strange, present, crowd

Oral Practice

 Track 4

Read each sentence aloud, with the correct pronunciation.

A large, brown bear roared at the crowd of tourists.
My brother and sister brought a friend from France to dinner.
Her red dress looks rather worn and frayed.
The children are learning several words in German and Russian.
Harry ordered a better dessert for our relatives.
Are Richard and Claire really running in Friday's marathon?

The Consonant w

This consonant is never pronounced like a v. An initial w sound begins with the tight pursing of the lips with the tip of the tongue on the lower teeth. Say oo (u:). Immediately follow the sound oo with the vowel sound (a:). Practice saying these two vowel sounds together as a diphthong: (u:)-(a:), (u:)-(a:). (u:)-(a:). Once you have mastered w followed by (a:), you are ready to practice with other vowel sounds.)

Oral Practice

Read each string of words aloud, with the correct pronunciation.

win, wait, wise	was, were, went
will, water, wore	wonder, western, welcome

When the consonant r follows w, its normal pronunciation is used. However, when h follows w, the h is silent. Some English speakers still voice the h and pronounce words that begin with wh as if the h *preceded* w: what (*h*wat), where (*h*were). This pronunciation sounds a bit dated but may be heard when someone wishes to pronounce precisely or sound formal.

Oral Practice

Read each string of words aloud, with the correct pronunciation.

write, wrote, written	whip, whelp, whale
wrist, wrestle, wrap	when, which, why
wrangle, wren, wrong	whine, wheel, white

TAKE NOTE *There are a couple exceptions to the pronunciation of w. In these cases, the initial sound of the words is h instead of w. The exceptions occur in the following words.*

	Pronunciation
whole	**hoʊl**
who	**hu:**
whom	**hu:m**
whose	**hu:z**

The consonant w has its normal pronunciation when it is in the middle of a word: **always, unwind, forward**. But at the end of a word, w is pronounced quickly and resembles a diphthong composed of the accompanying vowel and w. For example:

Pronunciation of Diphthong

allow	(ɑ:-u:)
fellow	(oʊ-u:)
flew	(u-u)
now	(ɑ:-u:)
show	(oʊ-u:)

This also occurs when w is followed by another consonant or syllable.

town	(ɑ:-u:)	sewing	(oʊ-u:)
crowd	(ɑ:-u:)	lowest	(oʊ-u:)

Oral Practice

🔘 Track 5

Read each sentence aloud, with the correct pronunciation.

Which window needs washing?

While I was in Washington, I wanted to see the West Wing of the White House.

Who showed Wendy the wristwatch we bought for her wedding?

Now that Walter is away in Wyoming, we will borrow his car without his knowing.

Do you ever wonder what would happen if the world suddenly ended?

The frown on that clown's face was enough to make me wince.

The Consonant x

The consonant x is pronounced x in the middle or at the end of a word. For example: **box, fix, toxic, relax**. At the beginning of a word, it is pronounced like z: **Xerox, xylophone, xenophobia**. In the word **x-ray**, it is pronounced like x, because it is the pronunciation of that letter attached to the word **ray**.

Written Practice 1-4

Indicate whether the consonants in bold type are silent, S, or if they are not silent, give the letter that represents the pronunciation of the consonant. For example:

write _____R_____

1. tou**gh** _____
2. ro**w** _____
3. whi**te** _____
4. **w**ho _____
5. **wh**en _____

6. fi**x** _____
7. throu**gh** _____
8. to**w**er _____
9. s**t**ore _____
10. **wh**y _____

Consonant Combinations

You have already encountered consonant combinations that have their own sound (**th**, **gh**, **wh**). There are others consonants that combine to represent yet other sounds. One of the most significant is the sound for **sh** (ʃ). The common representation of this sound is **sh**, and it is found at the beginning, the middle, and the end of words: **she**, **shall**, **usher**, **mashed**, **wish**, **push**. The letters **sch** can also represent (ʃ), but words with this consonant combination tend to come from a foreign word or name: **Schiller**, **schmaltz**, **schnauzer**. Be aware, as well, that this consonant combination is also pronounced as **sk: schism**, **schedule**, **school**. When in doubt about the pronunciation of **sch**, check it in a dictionary.

The combinations of **si**, **ci**, and **ti** also often represent the sound (ʃ), particularly at the end of a word in a syllable formed by **-ion** or **-ous**. For example:

compulsion, revulsion, impression
conscious, delicious, luscious, precious
cautious, position, constitution, notion

The consonants **ch** can also represent (ʃ). For example: **machine**, **panache**, **touché**. Most words that use this pronunciation of **ch** come from foreign words.

Oral Practice

Read each string of words aloud, with the correct pronunciation.

fishing, shower, bushes
Schopenhauer, scholastic, schnapps

machinery, papier-mâché, machete

suspicious, caption, situation

The common pronunciation of **ch** is (tʃ), as in the word **church**. This is a high-frequency sound in English and is found in a large number of words. In the middle or at the end of a word, it often follows **t**. For example:

Beginning of Word	Middle of Word	End of Word
chip	archer	touch
change	coaching	watch
charming	poached	rich
cheek	butcher	sketch

Oral Practice

🔘 Track 6

Read each sentence aloud, with the correct pronunciation.

Why did the children chuckle at the overflowing washing machine?

Sharon wished she could listen to a Chinese radio station.

The watchman shoved at the door until it was shut tight.

Please don't touch the dishes that Chad just washed.

Who questioned the shy coachman about the condition of the team's horseshoes?

She cherishes the precious gems she purchased in Washington last March.

❓ Still Struggling

Practice saying the following phrase until you can say it rapidly and with the correct pronunciation.

She sells seashells at the seashore.

The sound (ʒ) sometimes occurs in a word with the syllable **-sure**, after a **z**, or after **si**. For example: **pleasure, leisure, azure, vision, provision**. The sound (ʒ) is sometimes used in place of (dʒ) in a few words that end in **-ge**. This can occur when the stress is on the last syllable of the word, as in, for example, **garage, mirage, corsage**.

Oral Practice

Read each string of words aloud, with the correct pronunciation.

luggage, measure, barrage
illusion, confusion, baggage
treasure, carriage, occasion

Vowels

English vowels are no less complex in their pronunciation than English consonants. Each vowel can have more than one pronunciation, but it is only a slight *shading* or *nuance* of that pronunciation.

The Vowel *a*

The vowel **a**, for example, has the alphabetic name **a** (**eɪ**) but it is pronounced that way only when it is combined with other letters. The most common combination is **a + consonant + e**. For example:

(**eɪ**)
concentrate
game
haze
late
made
phrase
shade
tape

The same sound is used when **a** is followed by **y**.

laying   play
maybe   relay

The same sound is also used when **a** is followed by **i**.

detail   sail
mail   wait

A few words have a different combination of vowels but are still pronounced as (eɪ). For example: **eight**, **great**, **weight**.

Another pronunciation of **a** is (ɑː). However, there are no distinct spelling clues to help to decide whether (ɑː) is the required pronunciation of this vowel. One indicator is that (ɑː) *tends* to precede a double consonant. This vowel sound can be heard in words such as the following.

(ɑː)
arm
bark
father
wand

The vowel **a** is also pronounced (æ). Once again, there are no distinct clues that indicate that this is the required pronunciation of the vowel **a**. For example:

(æ)
cat
program
rank
shack

The **schwa** sound is also used to pronounce **a**. Its IPA is (ə). This occurs most frequently in an unstressed syllable. Let's look at some examples.

(ə)
about
along
arithmetic
cinema

The vowel **a** is pronounced (ɔː) in words that contain **all** and **aw**. For example:

(ɔː)
falling
small
crawl
withdraw

Oral Practice

Read each string of words aloud, with the correct pronunciation.

track, stall, again   stale, pail, barn

straw, can, brand   dilemma, afraid, debate

Dane, plain, mall

The Vowel *e*

The vowel **e** is pronounced like its alphabetic name (i:) when in the vowel combinations of **ee, ea, ei, ie,** and **y** at the end of a word. The sound (i:) is also found in the combination of **e + consonant + e.**

For example:

(i:)

feet	steal	ceiling	believe	delete	hurry
meet	meat	receive	retrieve	scene	funny
steep	treat	receipt	grief	serene	trophy

The short **e** sound (e) is commonly used when it precedes a consonant. For example:

(e)

better

forget

met

slept

wedding

TAKE NOTE *Note that **e** has two pronunciations in the definite article **the**.
When it precedes a consonant, it is pronounced with a **schwa** sound: (ð ə). If it
precedes a vowel, it is pronounced like **e**: (ð i:). For example:*

(ð ə)	**(ð i:)**
the dog	the apple
the house	the island
the shoe	the oven

The Vowel *i*

The vowel **i** is sometimes pronounced like its alphabetic name: (aɪ). This occurs most frequently in the combination **i + consonant + e**. For example:

(aɪ)
fine
pie
rise
stripe

As a short vowel, **i** is pronounced as (ɪ). This sound is frequently heard when **i** precedes a consonant or a double consonant. For example:

(ɪ)
equip
hiss
nibble
sit

Oral Practice

Read each string of words aloud, with the correct pronunciation.

eager, file, messy   deep, scheme, divine
kill, precise, relieve   ceiling, ripen, extra

The Vowel *o*

The vowel **o** is pronounced like its alphabetic name (oʊ) when it is the last letter in a word, when it is in the combination **o + consonant + e**, when it precedes **a**, and sometimes when it precedes **w**. For example:

(oʊ)

Last letter	o + consonant + e	oa	ow
ago	home	goat	low
piano	drone	soap	flow
hobo	stove	coat	slow
alto	joke	poach	know

The short vowel sound of o (ɒ) is found mostly when it precedes a consonant or double consonant in a word or syllable. For example:

(ɒ)
top
rocket
doll
potter

When o precedes u or sometimes w, it is pronounced as (aʊ).

(aʊ)
about
shout
cow
towel

And followed by i or y, o is pronounced as (ɔɪ).

(ɔɪ)
soil
boiler
boy
destroy

A double o (oo) is a frequently used for the sound (uː). But be aware that this sound is pronounced both *long* and *short*. Its short pronunciation tends to be in a syllable ending in k (ook). Let's compare the two pronunciations of oo.

Long oo (uː)	Short oo (ʊ)
mood	look
soon	book
loop	shook
zoo	took

Oral Practice

🔘 Track 7

Read each sentence aloud, with the correct pronunciation.

The winner of the tennis match had an early lead in the first set.
Every person in the room noticed the presence of a lovely maiden.

It was too hot in the backyard, so I took off my glasses and jumped in the
   pool.
We decided to join the archery team, but the equipment is so expensive.
On a hot evening in July, Bob feared the roses might wilt and die.
Lillian went home at ten and toyed with the idea of ordering a pizza.

The Vowel *u*

The alphabetic name of **u** (ʊə) is heard in such words as **pure** and **fury**. In
such words there is an audible y-sound (**pyure, fyury**). Many other words
in the combination **u + consonant + e** do not have an audible y-sound. For
example:

Audible y-Sound (ʊə)	No Audible y-Sound (uː)
cute	true
muse	glue
fuse	sue
abuse	ruse

The sound (uː) is also spelled with **ew**. For example: **grew, knew, chew,** and
brew.

The short **u** is represented by (ʌ). This sound can be heard in a large number
of words, some of which are:

(ʌ)
buzz
cup
knuckle
luck

The short **u** (ʊ) is most frequently spelled with **oo** but is also spelled **ou** in
the following auxiliary verbs.

(ʊ)
could
should
would

(The **l** is always silent in these auxiliary verbs.)

The letter combination **ur** occurs in several words and is pronounced as (ɜːʳ). For example:

(ɜːʳ)
burn
churn
occur
urn

The Vowel *y*

The letter **y** is sometimes called a *semivowel*, because it functions as both a vowel and at times as a consonant. When used as a vowel, **y** most often is pronounced like (iː), particularly at the end of a word.

(iː)
ability
funny
honey
sorry

The letter **y** is pronounced as a consonant (j) at the beginning of a word or sometimes the beginning of a syllable. For example:

(j)
beyond
yawn
yes
young

Oral Practice

Read each string of words aloud, with the correct pronunciation.

flew, nut, butter
yellow, under, angry
yours, mute, brute
messy, memory, year
curb, cute, alley

There is a special sound that is represented by the IPA (ʒ). This sound is often heard to represent a few words that have **z** in them but more frequently in words with the syllable **-sure**. For example:

b(ʒ)
azure
leisure
measure
pleasure

Oral Practice

🔘 Track 8

Read each sentence aloud, with the correct pronunciation.

A young boy stood in a grove of oak trees and took pictures with a small camera.
The pirates located the treasure in a sandy mound not far from their boat.
The baby's upper teeth were finally coming in, which made the little boy whimper in pain.
You should brush your hair twice a day and use a good conditioner.
A youthful girl in a yellow dress turned to see who was whistling at her.
My uncle said that he has a special gift for me in the living room.

? Still Struggling

If you feel frustrated that there are few concrete rules to help you to pronounce English words correctly, remember that native speakers have the same frustration. They spend many years of their education learning to spell with accuracy and to relate that spelling to the actual pronunciation of words.

QUIZ

Select the word that contains the sound of the IPA symbol. For example:

(**u:**)	close	(true)	sell	make

1. (**dʒ**)	build	spend	judge	cart
2. (**ð**)	then	ripe	both	yellow
3. (**eɪ**)	snake	fool	write	think
4. (**ɜːʳ**)	little	chip	funny	father
5. (**ʊ**)	style	book	thought	now
6. (**ʃ**)	victory	sharp	dumb	borrow
7. (**ɒ**)	rock	spell	down	cute
8. (**æ**)	China	nap	spin	breathe
9. (**ŋ**)	dine	mummy	machine	sing
10. (**ɪ**)	Mary	Tim	John	Susan

Names, Definite and Indefinite Articles, and Determiners

In this chapter you will find a discussion of how speakers of English use names. In addition, the chapter provides a careful look at articles and determiners, showing how these words modify nouns and affect the meaning of a sentence.

CHAPTER OBJECTIVES

In this chapter you will learn about:

- First names, middle names, surnames, and how they are used
- The meaning and use of definite articles
- The meaning and use of indefinite articles
- When to omit articles
- The kinds of determiners and their use

Names

All languages use names. There is nothing new or mysterious about that. But how names are used in languages does require explanation and practice.

First names used in English are exactly that: the names given by parents that appear first in a person's name in contrast to the family name. For example:

First Name	Family Name
John	Jones
Hillary	Clinton
Benjamin	Franklin
Rosa	Parks

Some first names are traditional. Many might say that they are old-fashioned, because they have been used for centuries but are not popular any longer. For example:

Tradition Male Names	Traditional Female Names
Harold	Alice
Lancelot	Guinevere
Herbert	Agatha
Julius	Martha

Other first names that have been used for a long time are still in vogue.

Male Names	Female Names
James	Mary
John	Sophia
Joseph	Barbara
David	Sara
William	Elizabeth

Each generation seems to develop a list of old and new names that is unique to that generation. A few of these that are presently considered the most popular are:

Male Names	Female Names
Christopher	Jessica
Matthew	Ashley
Justin	Tiffany
Derek	Kimberly

Because North America is a continent populated by immigrants from around the world, English speakers encounter many first names that are popular in other lands, such as **Boris**, **Kim**, **Jean-Claude**, **Fernando**, **Hussein**, and **Katsumi**.

No matter what the first name is, it is used almost exclusively when someone is addressing children or when two children address one another. When you ask a child his or her name, you can expect the response to be a first name unless the child has been coached to give a full name.

What's your name, little boy?
My name is Robert.
What's your name, little girl?
My name is Erica.
Who's your friend, Erica?
His name is Daniel.

In most grade schools and high schools, teachers regularly address their students by their first names, even on first meeting them. The relationship of an adult with a child is customarily informal, and addressing a child by his or her first name is appropriate.

Middle names are often given to children for religious reasons. The names of saints are popular for middle names. But in North America, middle names are also given in honor of a family member or just to be fashionable.

Male Middle Names of Saints	**Female Middle Names of Saints**
Michael **Joseph**	Jessica **Mary**
Richard **Peter**	Nancy **Ann**

If a grandfather's first name is **George**, his grandson might be called **Phillip George**. If a favorite aunt's first name is **Joanne**, her niece might be called **Natalie Joanne**. Or children will have middle names that their parents find attractive: **John Nathan** and his sister, **Kelli Heather**.

It is rare to call a child by both the first and middle names. Some parents do so to sound stern.

Robert Andrew, come here immediately!
Brianna Diane, turn down that radio!

A teacher might use both names to distinguish between two students who have the same first name: **John William** and **John Steven**.

Last names or surnames used by English speakers come in every variety. Some are very short, such as some Asian names: **Lu**. Some are very long, like

Indian or Slavic names: **Swieczkowski**. Last names reflect the many cultures that make up the population of Canada and the United States. You can probably guess what part of the world the people come from who bear the following last names.

Chávez	Rhee
Gandhi	Schmidt
Ling	Tanaka
Maloney	Zafrani
Obama	

Oral Practice

Read each sentence out loud.

What is your name?
My name is Daniel.
His name is Brad.
Her name is Jennifer.
What is the little boy's name?
The little boy's name is Jeffrey.
What is the little girl's middle name?
Her middle name is Sara.
What is your last name?
My last name is Larson.

In formal situations or when two adults first meet, it is appropriate to use a title with a last name. The basic gender titles are:

Mr.	married or single men
Ms.	married or single women
Miss	single women; but this title is considered sexist

Some professional titles or titles of a political or business office are as follows:

Professor	university educator
Dr.	physician or anyone holding a doctoral degree
Mayor	official of a municipality
President	official of a political unit or business
Chairman	leader of an organization or business

A first name is usually not used with a title and last name unless you are making an introduction: **This is our guest from Spain, Professor Enrique Rodriguez.** It also appears in the address on an envelope or in a business letter.

Dr. Helen Richardson
290 N. Brighton Road
Chicago, Illinois 60601

Oral Practice

🔘 Track 9

Read each sentence aloud, using the titles and last names provided.

Mr. Smith, please have a seat in the waiting room.
Ms. Marconi will show you the way out.
Maria Lopez has been crowned Miss America.
The lecture was given by Professor Wilson.
Have you met Dr. Laski?
Governor Phillips signed the bill into law.
Senator Snow left her notes in her office.
I received a letter from President Obama.
Detective Onassis will handle the investigation.

Written Practice 2-1

Complete each sentence with any appropriate name.

1. My name is _____.

2. The little girl's name is _____.

3. The little boy's name is _____.

4. My neighbor's first name and middle name are _____ _____.

5. This woman's last name is _____.

6. Dr. _____ works in that large hospital.

7. Do you know Chairman _____?

8. His full name is _____ _____ _____.

9. My last name is _____.

10. President _____ was born in Hawaii.

AMERICAN PRESIDENTIAL NAMES DEMYSTIFIED

It is common to refer to a president by his or her last name alone. The practice is not disrespectful. For example:

Clinton was president for eight years.
Was **McKinley** president at the end of the nineteenth century?

But when presidents have the same last name, their middle names or initials are used to prevent confusion.

John Adams was our third president.
His son was **John Quincy Adams**.
Andrew Johnson was vice president when Lincoln was assassinated.
Lyndon Johnson/LBJ came to the presidency in 1963.
Theodore/Teddy Roosevelt/TR was born in 1858.
Franklin Roosevelt/FDR died in 1945.
George H. W. Bush led the country during the first Gulf War.
Former **president George W. Bush** now lives in Texas.

Nicknames

North Americans frequently use nicknames. They often reflect a close relationship between two people. Or a person may prefer to be called by his or her nickname in order to be more informal. Some nicknames are alternative forms of first names. For example:

First Name	Alternative
Ann	Annie
Barbara	Barb, Barbie
Elizabeth	Betty, Liz, Beth
John	Jack, Jackie
Joseph	Joe, Joey
Katherine	Kathy, Kate, Kitty
Michael	Mike, Mikey, Mickey
Richard	Rich, Richie, Dick, Dickie
Thomas	Tom, Tommy

It is a friendly gesture to offer your nickname as your preferred form of address when meeting people. Consider the following little dialogue.

Robert Smith: I'm so glad I finally met you, Mr. Jones.

John Jones: I've been looking forward to meeting you, too. And please call me **Jack**.

Robert Smith: **Jack** it is. And you can call me **Bob**.

Young people often prefer the alternative form of their names in social situations, although the full first name is also correct.

Bill, would you like another beer? (William)

Ask **Jimmy** to play the piano. (James)

Franny, do you want to order a pizza? (Francis)

There are also some alternative forms for family members.

Dad, can I borrow the car tonight? (father)

Did **Mom** get the promotion she wanted? (mother)

Sis, can you take the dog out for a walk? (sister)

Some people even use nicknames as a way of identifying a specific characteristic of a person. For example:

Hey, **Stretch**, why aren't you on the basketball team? (someone tall)

I saw **Red** at the mall last night. (someone with red hair)

The notorious Prohibition-Era gangster Al Capone was known as **Scarface**. (facial scars)

And some nicknames are pejorative; that is, their purpose is to demean or insult someone.

Try to wake **Sleepyhead** up to go to class. (someone sleeping or lazy)

Tell **Loudmouth** to let someone else talk. (someone who talks loudly or too much)

Written Practice 2-2

Give the full first name from which the nickname in bold comes. For example:

Did **Tommy** go to work yet. _Thomas_

1. **Jim** caught another cold. _____

2. What time is **Billy** coming home? _____

3. My friend would like to dance with **Judy**. _____

4. Does **Ronnie** have a job now? _____

5. **Sammy** and his wife live in that big, white house.

_____

Definite and Indefinite Articles

English has only one definite article (**the**). It is used to introduce a noun and gives that noun the meaning of *specificity*. It shows that the noun refers to a specific person or object.

the man	*not just any man*
the newspaper	*not just any newspaper*
the crime	*not just any crime*

The indefinite articles (**a** and **an**) introduce a noun but do not give that noun specificity. This means that the noun is mentioned *in general* or is being introduced into a narrative for the first time.

a woman	*any woman*
an airplane	*any airplane*
a flower	*any flower*

The indefinite article is used when someone or something is first brought into a conversation or mentioned in a statement. After the person or thing has been mentioned, it becomes specific. Thereafter, that noun is introduced by the definite article. For example:

"There is **a policeman** over there. Do you see him?" (**policeman** is now specific)
"Yes, I see **the policeman**."

All references to **the policeman** from here on will use **the**. Let's look at another example.

"I want **a car**. Which one should I buy?" (**car** is now specific)

"Buy **the** red **car**."

All further references to **the car** will use **the**. Let's look at a longer dialogue to see how the definite article continues to be used as the conversation progresses.

"My wife needs **a** new **coat**, but I'm not sure what I should buy her."

"I like **the** woolen **coat** on that mannequin."

"But **the** woolen **coat** is dark brown. She hates brown."

"Think again. **The** woolen **coat** is on sale."

"I'll take **the** woolen **coat**!"

If you respond to a question about **a** person or thing in general in the negative, the outcome is different. For example:

"There's **a** large **dog** on my porch. Do you see it?"

"**A dog**? Where? I don't see **a dog**."

"Look. It's staring right at us."

"Yes, I see **the dog** now. And **the dog** is quite large, as you said."

Oral Practice

Track 10

Read each line in the dialogues aloud.

Susan: There's a bug sitting on your shoe.
Maria: Do you think the bug is dangerous?
Susan: I don't think so. The bug looks dead.
Maria: Oh! Get the bug off me!

Tom: Look at the girl at the next table.
Rick: I don't see a girl there.
Tom: Look at the girl at the table on your right.
Rick: Very pretty. Do you know the girl? I want to
    meet her.

Written Practice 2-3

Complete the sentence with the appropriate article: **the** or **a/an**.

1. I need _____ cup of coffee. I'm cold.

2. Bill said that Mary has _____ new boyfriend.

3. We saw a good movie last night. _____ movie was called *Home Alone*.

4. Ashley needs _____ pencil. Do you have _____ extra one?

5. It's snowing! I love _____ snow. I like to go skiing.

INDEFINITE PLURALS

Definite articles are used with either singular or plural nouns. The indefinite articles (**a, an**) are used only with singular nouns. No article is used with plural nouns to give the indefinite meaning.

Singular	Plural
a boy	boys (*any boys in general*)
an argument	arguments (*any arguments in general*)
a problem	problems (*any problems in general*)

Determiners

The definite and indefinite articles are called *determiners*. Determiners are adjectives that have a specific purpose. For example, the definite and indefinite articles are used to show that a noun is depicted as specific or general. There are four other types of determiners, and each one also has a specific function.

Interrogative Determiners

The *interrogative determiners* are adjectives that are used to ask three questions: **what?**, **which?**, and **whose?** As adjectives, they modify a noun. For an interrogative determiner to function as an adjective, it must be preceded by a noun. If the determiner stands alone, it is a pronoun. For example:

Adjectives	Pronouns
What house does she live in?	**What** is under the bed?
Which dress did Tina buy?	**Which** belongs to you?
Whose parents are those?	**Whose** parents speak English well?

TAKE NOTE *Both **what** and **which** modify nouns in the same way and seem similar in meaning. But **what** is used to ask general questions: **what time?**, **what color blouse?**, **what road?** **Which** asks for a choice: **which shirt (blue or red)?**, **which house (the big one or the little one)?**, **which symphony (number four or number five)?***

Oral Practice

Read each line out loud.

What time is the concert?
In what year did men first fly to the moon?
At what time should I meet you?
Which tie goes with this shirt?
In which movie did Brad Pitt star—*Troy* or *Home Alone?*
Which boy did she dance with?
Whose children are making so much noise?
With whose puppies are they playing?
Whose child did Jimmy catch a cold from?

TAKE NOTE *Notice in the preceding Oral Practice that a preposition that accompanies an interrogative determiner stands at the beginning of the question in formal style. A question is casual and less formal when it ends with a preposition.*

With whose puppies are they playing? (*formal*)
Whose child did Jimmy catch a cold **from**? (*casual*)

Written Practice 2-4

Complete the sentence with the correct interrogative determiner: **what**, **which**, or **whose**.

1. _____ dog bit you? Ours?

2. _____ suit will you wear? The blue one or the brown one?

3. _____ husband is dancing with my wife?

4. _____ book are you reading?

5. _____ month was your son born in?

6. _____ store has put that CD on sale?

7. _____ car is in front of the house? Yours?

8. _____ time should I pick you up?

9. _____ kind of cheese is that?

10. _____ wallet is this?

Demonstrative Adjectives

Another category of determiners consists of the *demonstrative adjectives*. The demonstrative adjectives are **this** and **that**, which modify singular nouns, and **these** and **those**, which modify plural nouns. **This** and **that** refer to someone or something nearby, and **these** and **those** refer to people and things in the distance.

Singular	Plural
This boy is my son.	**These** boys are my sons.
That gift is for you.	**Those** gifts are for you.

If the demonstrative adjectives are used without an accompanying noun, they are used as pronouns.

Adjectives	Pronouns
This book is mine.	**This** is mine.
That book must be yours.	**That** must be yours.
These keys don't fit in the lock	**These** don't fit in the lock.
Those dishes were made in Mexico.	**Those** were made in Mexico.

The noun **one** is frequently used together with a demonstrative adjective to act as a replacement for the pronominal use. The plural **ones** (**these ones**, **those ones**) is a correct form but sounds awkward, and most English speakers would avoid it. Other numbers work perfectly well in the plural with **these** and **those**. For example:

Adjectives	Pronouns
This book is mine.	**This one** is mine.
That book must be yours.	**That one** must be yours.
These keys don't fit in the lock	**These two** don't fit in the lock.
Those dishes were made in Mexico.	**Those four** were made in Mexico.

Oral Practice

Read each line out loud.

This man is a good friend of mine.
Is that cake gluten-free?
These cream puffs are delicious.
I don't like those spicy meatballs.
Which ones do you like?
I like these.
Which one did she buy?
She bought that one.
This cookbook looks very interesting.
But these two are on sale.
Does that one have a lot of dessert recipes?

Written Practice 2-5

Complete the sentence with the demonstrative adjective that makes the most sense: **this**, **that**, **these**, or **those**.

1. Is _____ seat mine or is it that one?

2. Those look old, but _____ two look much newer.

3. I don't want this one. I want _____ one.

4. Are _____ gloves yours?

5. _____ men now have jobs, but those are still looking for work.

6. Can you see _____ two large houses down the street?

7. _____ woman that you met in Spain last year is an actress.

8. Please send me _____ wonderful recipe for fudge I had at your house last week.

9. I received _____ very same birthday card last year.

10. Would you mail _____ letters that I left on my desk?

Possessive Adjectives

The *possessive adjectives* are the possessive form of the personal pronoun. They should not be confused with the pronominal form of the personal pronouns, which cannot modify nouns.

Personal Pronoun	Possessive Adjective	Possessive Pronoun
I	my	mine
you	your	yours
he	his	his
she	her	hers
it	its	its
we	our	ours
they	their	theirs

Let's look at some examples that show the different usages of the two possessive forms.

Adjectives	Pronouns
My car is brand new.	**Mine** is brand new.
Is **your** essay ready yet?	Is **yours** ready yet?
Our dog is a pedigreed poodle.	**Ours** is a pedigreed poodle.

Oral Practice

Read each sentence out loud.

Is your grandmother still in the hospital?

My sister had to go to the emergency room.

She broke her right arm.

I never broke a limb, but my nose was broken when I was younger.

Our late uncle was in the hospital for ten days before he died.

His family must be very sad right now.

Yes, our aunt and our cousins are in mourning.

Even the family dog seems upset. Its sad eyes tell the story.

Written Practice 2-6

Complete the sentence with the possessive adjective that makes the most sense: **my, your, his, her, its, our,** or **their.**

1. I think I've lost _____ keys.

2. Why did the women leave _____ husbands at home?

3. Tom and I took _____ girlfriends out to dinner last night.

4. A mouse lives in our kitchen and has _____ hiding place under the stove.

5. How do you like _____ new apartment?

6. Ms. Patel invited us over to _____ house for brunch.

7. Bill said he injured _____ left foot.

8. We should spend _____ money more wisely.

9. When will they score _____ first goal?

10. One of the boys did _____ homework on my laptop.

Quantifiers

The *quantifiers* are so named, because they tell *what quantity* of people or things is in question. Once again, it is important to distinguish between quantifiers that act as adjectives and the same words that can act as pronouns.

Numbers can function as quantifiers: **one man, two schools, ten levels, 200 people,** and so on. Let's look at some examples that show the difference between numbers as adjectives and as pronouns.

Adjectives	Pronouns
One bottle of soda is too much for me.	**One** is too much for me.
Sara needs **three** coat hangers.	Sara needs **three**.
There are **nine** players in baseball.	There are **nine** in baseball.

Another category of quantifiers consists of words that describe general quantities, such as **many**, **much**, **few**, **several**, **a lot**, and **a couple**. Let's compare their use as adjectives and as pronouns.

Adjectives	Pronouns
Many Americans travel to Europe.	**Many** travel to Europe.
Few students pass that test.	**Few** pass that test.
A couple soldiers relaxed in the shade.	**A couple** relaxed in the shade.

Few

There are two other quantifiers made from the word **few**: **a few** and **the few**. Let's compare their use and meaning, which are distinct from each other.

Few warriors returned from battle.
(*This is a negative statement. Many warriors went, but not many returned.*)
A few warriors returned from battle.
(*This is a more positive statement. People had worried that none would return, but some did.*)
The few warriors that returned from battle were severely wounded.
(*This sentence emphasizes the condition of the warriors, not their numbers.*
  A relative clause is always attached to the statement containing the word few.)

Analyze the meaning of the following three sentences.

Few people understood his theory.
A few people understood his theory.
The few people that understood his theory were scientists.

Written Practice 2-7

Give an appropriate completion for each sentence.

1. Few _____.
2. A few _____.
3. The few _____.

Quantifiers Used with Both Singular and Plural Nouns

Some quantifiers are used with singular nouns and others with plural nouns. Only a few are used with both singular and plural nouns. For example:

Singular Nouns	**Plural Nouns**
I don't have **much** time.	She has **many** problems.
We need **more** energy.	We need **more** towels.
My father has **little** patience with you.	He has **few** real friends.
Jim did **less** work than Susan.	**Fewer** people read his third novel.
She needed **some** rest.	**Some** boys were teasing her.
He has **a lot of** money.	Tina took **a lot of** pictures.

Ordinal Numbers

A third category of quantifiers consists of the *ordinal numbers*. Ordinal numbers are derived from numbers and describe the order of people or things: **the second movement, their fourth child, the eleventh hour**, and so on. Most ordinal numbers are formed by adding the suffix **-th** to the number: **seventh, tenth, twentieth, hundredth**. A few are irregular:

Number	Ordinal
one	first
two	second
three	third
five	fifth

Numbers that end in **-ty** change the **y** to **i** then add the suffix **-th: twenty** through **twentieth, fifty** through **fiftieth**. If the number being converted to an ordinal is composed of two numbers **(39, 42)**, the rule is to place a hyphen after the first spelled-out word and attach the ordinal suffix to the second: **thirty-ninth, forty-second**.

Ordinal numbers are used for giving dates. Dates can be stated with the ordinal preceding the month **(the tenth of May)** or following the month **(May tenth)**. For example:

Today is the fifth of September.
Her birthday was on the twenty-fifth of June.
They got married on March third.
Ms. Keller gets back from Europe on July seventh.

Oral Practice

Read each sentence out loud.

Children enter the first grade at age six.
May I have a second piece of pie?
Mary is his third wife.
What is the Fifth Amendment to the Constitution about?
I think their anniversary is November twentieth.
Some buildings don't have a thirteenth floor.
Sara's birthday is on the twenty-first of May.
Congratulations! As our millionth customer, you win a prize!

Written Practice 2-8

Complete the sentence with the ordinal form of the number provided. For example:

(6) I'm the _sixth_ person in line for tickets.

1. (1) This is the _____ time Bill has been to the opera.

2. (3) Let's sit in the _____ row near the stage.

3. (100) On the _____ day, they gave the baby panda a name.

4. (5) Their wedding day will be June _____.

5. (12) Shakespeare wrote _____ _Night_ around 1601.

6. (31) Halloween is on the _____ of October.

7. (50) My grandparents are celebrating their _____ year of marriage.

8. (2) Little Susie just got her _____ tooth.

9. (8) He took the driver's test for the _____ time.

10. (19) The _____ question on the exam made no sense.

IDIOMS DEMYSTIFIED

The ordinal **fifth** is used in an idiomatic expression that says that someone *feels out of place* or *feels that he or she doesn't belong.*

Sometimes I just feel like a fifth wheel.

Since most passenger vehicles have four wheels, a fifth one would be out of place or of no use.

QUIZ

Choose the letter of the word or phrase that best completes each sentence.

1. Ms. _____ is taking classes at the university.
   A. Professor Adams   C. Jimmy
   B. Garcia   D. Mary

2. I seem to be spending _____ time studying.
   A. less   C. few
   B. many   D. a few

3. Books can often be powerful _____.
   A. instrument   C. the facts
   B. the tool   D. weapons

4. Close your eyes. I have _____ surprise for you.
   A. the   C. a
   B. an   D. any

5. As she got older, she wrote _____ poems.
   A. fewer   C. the few
   B. much   D. less

6. Their next concert will be February _____.
   A. seven   C. tenth
   B. thirty-one   D. Tuesday

7. _____ girls are on the soccer team.

    A. Those   C. This

    B. A   D. That

8. That _____ belongs to my brother.

    A. one   C. second

    B. five   D. fifth

9. Let me hold _____ door for you.

    A. the   C. some

    B. a   D. first

10. My aunt seems to have lost _____ keys.

    A. this   C. mine

    B. her   D. much

chapter 3

Present and Past Tense Usage

In this chapter you will encounter the conjugational forms that verbs take in the present and past tenses. Each of these two tenses has three varieties, which are used in specific ways.

CHAPTER OBJECTIVES

In this chapter you will learn about:

- Present and past tense sentences that indicate a habitual action
- Present and past tense sentences that indicate an incomplete or ongoing action
- Present and past tense sentences that are an emphatic reply
- Present and past tense irregular verbs

The Present Tense

A present tense verb conjugation contains the verb forms that are used with the various persons: **first person singular and plural, second person singular and plural,** and **third person singular and plural.**

47

The first person pronouns are **I** and **we**, which are singular and plural, respectively. Very frequently a noun is combined with the first person singular pronoun, I, which is a replacement for the first person plural pronoun, we:

John and I = **we**
the children and I = **we**
the whole team and I = **we**

The second person singular pronouns are **thou** and **you**. Today, it is rare to hear anyone use the older form **thou** except in a religious context. Although **you** is technically a plural pronoun, it is used in place of the singular **thou** in modern English. Verbs used with **you** are plural in form, but the pronoun can be used to address just one person. For example:

Allison, **are you** going to the dance tomorrow?
Hi, Bill. **Do you** have a ticket for tomorrow's game?
Honey, **you look** beautiful in that dress!

The same pronoun, once again used with a plural verb, has also a plural meaning. It is used to address more than one person.

I'm talking to the whole team. **You** only **have** one minute left to win this
    game.
Mr. and Mrs. Kelly, how **are you?**
Karen and Jack, **you need** to help unpack those boxes.

The third person singular pronouns are **he**, **she**, **it**, and **one**. There is only one third person plural pronoun: **they**.

He is my only brother.
She lives about two miles from here.
It will take about three hours to drive there.
One has to walk carefully on a slippery sidewalk.

TAKE NOTE *The pronoun **one** is used just like **you** in making a general statement. But use **one** to be more formal, and use **you** in casual speech. In North America, **you** is used far more frequently than **one**.*

Formal: **One** needs to exercise to stay healthy.
Casual: **You** need to exercise to stay healthy.

*Note that **one** requires a singular verb, while **you** requires a plural verb.*

Present Tense Conjugation

The present tense conjugation of verbs is quite simple for the most part. It is only in the third person singular that an ending change is required. The infinitive minus the particle word **to** (for example, **to see, to go, to run**) is used for all other persons. For example:

	To Help	To Find	To Try
I	help	find	try
you	help	find	try
he	helps	finds	tries
she	helps	finds	tries
it	helps	finds	tries
one	helps	finds	tries
we	help	find	try
you *pl.*	help	find	try
they	help	find	try

If the letter **y** ends a verb and follows a consonant, **y** is changed to **i**. Then the ending **-es** is added: **cry → cries, hurry → hurries**. If a verb ends with the sounds, **s, z, sh,** or **ch,** the third person singular ending is **-es: kiss → kisses, wish → wishes**. The verbs **to go** and **to do** also add an **-es** in the third person singular: **go → goes, do → does**.

There are two verbs that have an irregularity in the present tense: **to be** and **to have**. Of the two verbs, **to be** has the more complicated conjugation.

	To Be	To Have
I	am	have
you	are	have
he	is	has
she	is	has
it	is	has
one	is	has
we	are	have
you *pl.*	are	have
they	are	have

Oral Practice

Read each sentence aloud, paying attention to the verb used with the pronoun in the sentence.

I like to spend my weekends in the country.
Do you want to go for a stroll?
He seems to like you.
Does she work in that factory?
It is hard to understand why you always want to argue.
One must get enough sleep every night.
We come here every spring.
Allison and I have a date on Saturday.
Joe and Bill, you need to get here on time tomorrow.
They speak three languages.

? Still Struggling

The conjugational form used with nouns is the same as that used with third person pronouns. If the noun is singular, use the singular ending -(e)s on the verb. If the noun is plural, use a plural verb. For example:

That boy **sings** quite well.
Those boys **sing** quite well.
Every woman **is** prepared to help out with the rescue.
All the women **are** prepared to help out with the rescue.

Oral Practice

Read each sentence aloud, paying attention to the verb used with the pronoun or noun in the sentence.

She plays tennis twice a week.
Carmen and I have dinner plans for tonight.
He goes to a college in the East.
Do those three men work together?

You can stay with us for a few days.
One works only as hard as one must.
Do I know you, sir?
Have we already met, ma'am?

Written Practice 3-1

Reword each infinitive phrase with the subjects provided. For example:

to like pizza.

(I) _I like pizza._

to have a lot of fun.

1. (we) _____

2. (he) _____

3. (my friends and I) _____

to learn a new language.

4. (I) _____

5. (you) _____

6. (they) _____

to be in an unpleasant situation.

7. (she) _____

8. (they) _____

9. (I) _____

to want to order another glass of soda.

10. (you) _____

11. (he) _____

12. (the little girl) _____

to hide out of fear.

13. (it) _____

14. (Maria and I) _____

15. (one) _____

Singular and Plural Determiners

In Chapter 2, you encountered the determiners that can be used as adjectives. It was also pointed out that the determiners can be used as pronouns. Some of the determiners are always singular, some are always plural, and a few can be either singular or plural. Here are some examples.

Singular	Plural	Either
much money	many friends	more money/more friends
little time	few people	some cake/some boys
this house	these houses	a lot of work/a lot of books
that girl	those girls	no proof/no letters
each day	a couple days	which car/which cars
one month	several months	whose son/whose sons

When these determiners are used as pronouns, they take a singular or plural verb, depending on the kind of noun they can modify: **singular or plural.**

Oral Practice

🔘 Track 11

Read each sentence aloud, paying attention to the verbs used with the pronouns.

Much has to be done to repair this house.
Little is needed to make me happy.
I have three gifts. Each is for you.
Look at those hikers. Many look very tired.
There are many students here, but few are studying.
About ten citizens are gathering near our office. Several look very angry.
I have already received fifty letters, and more are sure to arrive tomorrow.
The moviegoers come out of the theater, and a lot are still laughing.
I see two black coats, but which is mine?

TAKE NOTE *The interrogative pronoun* **who** *can be singular or plural. If it refers to one person, it is a singular pronoun; if it refers to more than one person, it is a plural pronoun. For example:*

Who is this strange person? (*singular = one person*)
Who are the two women running for mayor? (*plural = two women*)

Written Practice 3-2

Reword each sentence by changing the word in bold to the words that are needed to make a sentence incorporating the word provided in parentheses in the numbered item. Make any other necessary changes. For example:

I have a lot of candy bars. **One** is yours.

(two) <u>Two are yours.</u>

There are a lot of toys on the floor. **Several** are yours.

1. (some) _____

2. (these) _____

3. (this) _____

I see the men. **A few** look hungry.

4. (each) _____

5. (many) _____

6. (a couple) _____

I found a lot of old hats. Are **these** yours?

7. (a few) _____

8. (this) _____

9. (some) _____

10. (one) _____

Habitual or Incomplete Actions

Most of the verbs encountered in this chapter so far have been in the present tense, which indicates a *habitual action*. Consider the following example sentences that tell what someone does on a regular basis or as an occupation.

John **goes** to the University of Illinois.
Mom **works** in a research laboratory.
A butcher **carves** meat and **slices** sausage.
A doctor **heals** sick people.

Sometimes an adverb that suggests that *an action takes place more than once* can be added to the sentence.

We **often** read out in the backyard.
Tom **seldom** gets home before dusk.
My aunt **always** writes to her son in the army.

Many adverbs precede the verb they modify. If an adverb is a phrase, it follows the verb and other prepositional phrases.

We read out in the backyard **every day**.
Tom gets home before dusk **after work**.
I get up **early in the morning**.

Oral Practice

Track 12

Read each line in the dialogues aloud.

Mark: I like to sit by the fireplace and roast marshmallows.
Allison: Me too. But I eat too many of them.
Mark: You don't have to worry. You work out every day.
Allison: Not every day. Remember, I have a job and go to night school.
Mark: You look great! I try to stay fit, too. That's why I bike on the weekends.
Allison: I should go with you, but you always ride so far.
Mark: Just fifteen miles. My brother sometimes rides over fifty miles.
Allison: He's a lot younger. And he has a lot of free time and doesn't work.
Mark: My father frequently gives him spending money.
Allison: Your brother is very spoiled.

Written Practice 3-3

Reword each sentence with the adverbs provided.

My friend works for his girlfriend's father.

1. (sometimes) _____

2. (often) _____

3. (during summer vacation) _____

Mother brings me hot soup.

   4. (when I'm ill) _____

   5. (usually) _____

   6. (on a cool afternoon) _____

Do you play the piano?

   7. (once a day) _____

   8. (always) _____

John runs a couple laps around the track.

   9. (before his first class) _____

   10. (regularly) _____

Present Progressive Tense

Another present tense conjugational structure is called the *progressive tense*. It is formed from the conjugation of **be** plus a **present participle**. A present participle is the infinitive minus the particle word **to** plus the suffix **-ing**. For example:

I **am** learn**ing**.   She **is** work**ing**.
You **are** sing**ing**.   They **are** talk**ing**.

If a verb has a short vowel that is followed by a consonant, the consonant changes to a double consonant and is added to the verb when **-ing** is attached. For example:

fit	fitting	fan	fanning
jog	jogging	wed	wedding

If the verb has a long vowel and a consonant that are followed by **e**, the **e** is dropped then **-ing** is attached.

ride	riding	blame	blaming
note	noting	sneeze	sneezing

Oral Practice

Read each sentence aloud, paying particular attention to the progressive tense verbs.

Are you joking with me?
Is your sister dancing in the school play?
Am I running too fast for you?

The lawyer is whispering to the judge.
The teachers are leading their students into the auditorium.
Someone upstairs is crying.
I am coming to your house for a visit.

Written Practice 3-4

Convert each verb into a present participle.

1. drop _____

2. hold _____

3. send _____

4. approve _____

5. follow _____

6. make _____

7. say _____

8. drink _____

9. hit _____

10. get _____

Comparing Habitual and Incomplete Actions

The progressive tense is used to show that *an action is in progress or incomplete*. Consider the following examples, which indicate what is happening at this moment—an action in progress.

Bill is walking to the library.
Several men are digging up the street.
The man who was injured is bleeding.
Why is that dog barking?

Besides saying that the action is in progress, the verbs used in the foregoing examples also say that the action is incomplete: Bill is *still on his way* to the library; he has not yet arrived. Several men *continue to dig up* the street; the job is not done. The man *continues to bleed*; the bleeding does not stop. That dog *continues barking*; the barking does not stop.

Now compare the *habitual* present tense sentences, which show a habitual action, with those in the right-hand column, which show one *in progress or incomplete*.

Habitual	In Progress/Incomplete
John goes to school. *He is a student.*	John is going to school. *He is on his way.*
We play soccer. *We are soccer players.*	We are playing soccer. *We are in the middle of a game.*
She bakes cakes. *She owns a bakery.*	She is baking a cake. *She is in the process of making a cake.*

Oral Practice

🔘 Track 13

Read each sentence aloud, paying attention to the kind of verb used.

I always visit my grandmother on the weekend.
They are visiting our city for just a few days.
The elephant is scratching his side on a tree.
My uncle walks to work every day.
The athletes are hiking to the top of that big hill.
She comes home from work at 6 p.m.
I am hoping to win a scholarship.
My girlfriend dances professionally; she's with the Joffrey Ballet.
Who is making all that noise?

TAKE NOTE *The progressive tense is used when it is in a clause accompanied by another clause that describes an interruption of the action. For example:*

He is brushing his teeth when the phone rings.
When the children run into my room, I am still getting dressed.

Written Practice 3-5

For each sentence, indicate the correct form of the verb given in parentheses. For example:

(talk) We <u>are talking</u> on the phone when Tom arrives.

1. (help) Dr. Patel works in a hospital and _____ patients.

2. (drink) My father always _____ a cup of coffee after supper.

3. (run) I _____ around the track when Mary calls to me.

4. (do) We _____ our homework when we suddenly crave a pizza.

5. (walk) She _____ to school today, because the weather is so nice.

Emphatic Response

A third use of the present tense is the *emphatic response*. If a statement is positive, the emphatic response is the negative contradiction. If a statement is negative, the emphatic response is the positive contradiction. The emphatic response uses the auxiliary **do** to achieve this. For example:

Statement	Emphatic Response
You speak English well.	I **do not** speak English well.
They drink too much.	They **do not** drink too much.
You do not have a gift for her.	I **do** have a gift for her.
Mary does not live in Dallas.	Mary **does** live in Dallas.

If the verb in the statement is a form of **be**, the auxiliary **do** is not used.

You **are** the best musician.	I **am not** the best musician.
Bill **is** not going to college.	Bill **is** going to college.

When the emphatic response is spoken, the verb is *intoned strongly*. If the sentence is negated, the adverb **not** is intoned strongly.

We dó work very hard.
They do nót have enough money.
I ám learning a new language.
Ms. Garcia is nót in Spain right now.

Auxiliaries

When auxiliaries are used in the present tense, they accompany other verbs. There is a tendency to use an infinitive with auxiliaries and to a lesser degree the progressive tense, which can sound awkward. Some commonly used auxiliaries are:

be able to	can	may	must	should
be supposed to	have to	might	need to	want to

IDIOMS DEMYSTIFIED

Even in idiomatic phrases, the form of the present tense conjugation plays a role in the meaning of the idiom. Consider the phrase **to brush up on** (*to study something again*).

> I **brush** up on the formulas before a physics test. *I always study the formulas before a physics test.*
> Laura **is brushing** up on her spelling. *She is in the process of studying spelling again but has not yet finished.*
> I **do brush** up on the rules before an exam. *This is an emphatic response to the statement: "You do not brush up on the rules before an exam."*

Now look at another idiom and see how the present tense changes the meaning of the sentence: **to keep an eye on** (*to guard something or to watch carefully*). Consider the difference in meaning of each of the following examples.

> The security guard **keeps** an eye on the people entering the bank.
> Mr. Phillips **is keeping** an eye on the boys in the gymnasium.
> I **do keep** an eye on the roast in the oven.

Let's look at some example sentences with verbs in both the habitual form and the progressive form. Although the progressive form is a grammatical possibility, it is often avoided if it would sound awkward.

Habitual Present	Progressive
I **am able to** help you today.	I **am able to** be working with you once again.
We **are supposed to** fly to Europe.	We **are supposed to** be cooperating with you.
He **can** understand everything.	He **can** be saving more money.
You **have to** read more.	You **have to** be putting in more overtime.
She **may** come to my party.	She **may** be getting a cold.
The girl **must** rest more.	The girl **must** be trying too hard.
I **need to** go home.	I **need to** be studying for the exam.
Someone **should** help her.	Someone **should** be watching the children.
Bill **wants to** star in a movie.	Bill **wants to** be starring in a movie.

The Auxiliary May

When the auxiliary **may** is used with a progressive infinitive (for example, **be coming**), it has one meaning. When the accompanying verb is not a progressive infinitive (for example, **come**), the auxiliary has two meanings.

She may be coming to my party. *There is the possibility that she will come to my party.*

She may come to my party. *She is allowed to come to my party.* Or, *There is the possibility that she will come to my party.*

When the auxiliary **must** is used with a progressive infinitive form (for example, **be going**), it has two meanings. When the accompanying verb is not a progressive infinitive (for example, **go**), the auxiliary has one meaning.

She must be going home. *She has to be going home.* Or, *The speaker suspects that she is going home.*

She must go home. *She has to go home.*

Oral Practice

Read each sentence aloud, paying attention to the auxiliary used and the intended meaning of the sentence.

Jim can run a lot faster than me.

How can you be running a business like this with no experience?

No one wants to play chess against Allison.

I have to get home before dark.

You don't have to be worrying all the time.

Mr. Gomez needs to find a better way to get to work.

Ali may not play soccer this year.

He may be working in his father's store.

Written Practice 3-6

Reword each sentence with the auxiliaries provided in parentheses. For example:

John takes a job in London.

(must) _John must take a job in London_.

These boys look for the misplaced wallet.

1. (can) _____

2. (want to) _____

You join a health club downtown.

3. (should) _____

4. (need to) _____

Martin is building something in the garage right now.

5. (be supposed to) _____

6. (may) _____

We live on food we grow ourselves.

7. (must) _____

8. (be able to) _____

I get my car fixed as soon as possible.

9. (need to) _____

10. (can) _____

The Past Tense

Like the present tense, the past tense has three conjugational forms: **habitual**, **progressive**, and **emphatic**. But the fact that the English past tense has numerous irregularities adds another element to the use of these three forms.

Past Tense Conjugation

First, let's look at conjugations in the past tense. Regular verbs end in **-ed** or **-ied**. If a verb ends in **-y**, the **-y** is changed to **-i-** and then the ending **-ed** is added (try = tried). All persons (first, second, and third) have the same past tense conjugation if a verb is regular. For example:

	Hope	Carry	Talk	Cry
I	hoped	carried	talked	cried
you	hoped	carried	talked	cried
he, she	hoped	carried	talked	cried
we	hoped	carried	talked	cried

you	hoped	carried	talked	cried
they	hoped	carried	talked	cried
one	hoped	carried	talked	cried

It is the irregular verbs that have a variety of past tense formations. Once the past tense conjugation is known, it is used with all the persons. The only exception to this rule is the verb be. Let's look at some example verbs. Note the variety of the past tense conjugations.

	Be	Say	Keep	Have	Go
I	was	said	kept	had	went
you	were	said	kept	had	went
he, she, it	was	said	kept	had	went
we	were	said	kept	had	went
you	were	said	kept	had	went
they	were	said	kept	had	went
one	was	said	kept	had	went

TAKE NOTE *A few verbs are identical in the present and the past tense. For example:*

Present Tense	Past Tense
I cut	I cut
you put	you put
he beats	he beat
she sets	she set
we burst	we burst
they cast	they cast
it costs	it cost

Habitual or Complete Actions

In the past tense, verbs that describe habitual or complete actions function in the same way as in the present tense. The difference is that the action was completed in the past. For example:

My father worked as a tailor. *This was his occupation.*
Aunt Mary spoke German. *German was her native language.*
Bill borrowed a lot of money. *He had a habit of borrowing.*

An adverb that suggests that *an action takes place more than once* can be added to the sentence, such as: **often, frequently, every day, twice a year**.

Oral Practice

Read each sentence aloud, paying attention to the verb tense and its meaning.

Helen brought a cake to the party.
She sometimes has smothered her cakes in too much frosting.
Everyone liked everything she baked.
I was rather jealous of her.
My husband always knew that I made better cookies than Helen.
I believed that Helen borrowed her mother's recipes.
She provided three cakes for the PTA meetings every month.

Past Progressive Tense

Incomplete actions and interrupted actions are expressed by the progressive past tense. Conjugations in this tense are composed of the verb **be** in the past tense (**was** or **were**) plus a present participle. For example: **was singing, was talking, were helping, were sleeping**.

Sentences in the progressive past tense are often accompanied by a clause that describes an interruption. Let's look at some progressive past tense sentences. Take note of those that have an interruption.

I was studying when the lights suddenly went out.
My sisters were dancing in the living room.
No one was watching the boring TV show.
When Jane came into my room, I was playing my guitar.

Oral Practice

Read each sentence aloud, paying attention to the verb tense and its meaning.

My father was asking me about the accident.
Were you driving too fast when the accident happened?
No, I was going the speed limit.
I was turning the corner at Main Street when a dog ran into the road.
You weren't paying enough attention.
I was looking straight ahead and hoping to avoid hitting the dog.

Emphatic Response

The past tense can be used to give an emphatic response. The only difference from its use in the present tense is that the action took place and is described in the past tense. With most verbs, the auxiliary **do** is conjugated in the past tense (**did**) and intoned strongly in the spoken language. With other auxiliaries, the auxiliary is emphasized and intoned strongly in the spoken language. If the adverb **not** is used for negation, it is intoned. For example:

Past Tense Statement	Past Tense Emphatic Response
You didn't write your brother.	I **did** write my brother.
Steve spent over ten dollars.	Steve **did not** spend over ten dollars.
She was working at the mall.	She **was not** working at the mall.
We weren't kissing.	You **were** kissing.

Oral Practice

Read each sentence aloud, paying attention to the verb tense and its meaning. The accented word is strongly intoned.

President Obama gave a speech on Monday.
President Obama did not give a speech on Monday.
We didn't have enough time.
You díd have enough time.
Ms. Marino was dancing with Jim.
Ms. Marino was nót dancing with Jim.
The children were not playing in the attic.
The children wére playing in the attic.

Written Practice 3-7

Reword each sentence in the missing past tense form. For example:

Habitual: Bill wrote some postcards.

Progressive: _Bill was writing some postcards_.

Emphatic: _Bill did write some postcards_.

1. Habitual: Ms. Delgado spoke with Dr. Keller.

   Progressive: _____

   Emphatic: _____

2. Habitual: _____

   Progressive: The girls were cooperating.

   Emphatic: _____

3. Habitual: _____

   Progressive: _____

   Emphatic: I did practice the piano.

4. Habitual: The lawyer signed the contract.

   Progressive: _____

   Emphatic: _____

5. Habitual: _____

   Progressive: Some boys were relaxing in the shade of a tree.

   Emphatic: _____

Oral Practice

Track 14

Read each sentence aloud, paying attention to the kind of verb used.

The girls were playing tennis in the park.
You were wrong about her. I was not wrong about her.
I really enjoyed that movie.
Was he out jogging when the storm began?
The salesman wasn't helpful. No, he was very helpful.
Mark took the rowboat and went fishing.

Questions

Whether a question is stated in the present or past tense, the same structure is used. If a question inquires into the information of an entire sentence, the question begins with a verb, the tense of which is determined by the tense of the sentence that is questioned. If the verb is a form of **be**, that verb begins the question. With other verbs, the question begins with **do/does** in the present tense and **did** in the past tense. For example:

Statement	Question
Bill is at home.	**Is** Bill at home?
The girls were shopping at the mall.	**Were** the girls shopping at the mall?
My boyfriend works as a Realtor.	**Does** your boyfriend work as a Realtor?
John spoke like a gentleman.	**Did** John speak like a gentleman?

When a specific element in a sentence is questioned, the question begins with the appropriate interrogative word (**who, whom, whose, which, what, when, where, why**, and **how**). For example:

Statement	Question
<u>Mr. Jones</u> needs some help.	**Who** needs some help?
The <u>blue</u> dress looks better on her.	**Which** dress looks better on her.
His son came home <u>today</u>.	**When** did his son come home?
My aunt lives <u>in Florida</u>.	**Where** does your aunt live?
Jean found <u>a ring</u> at the beach.	**What** did Jean find at the beach?

Oral Practice

Read each question aloud, noting the difference between general questions and questions begun with an interrogative.

Are you coming to my party tomorrow?
What did you buy at the big sale at Macy's?
Were the foreign students surprised by the mayor's visit?
Whose dog was digging holes in our yard?
Do you take your children to the movies every weekend?
Where did you put my cell phone?
Was this car involved in a fender bender?
How well did you know that woman?

Auxiliary verbs can occur in any kind of question. In a general question, some of the auxiliaries begin the question. Others are introduced by **do/does/did**. For example:

Auxiliary Begins the Question
be able to/Are you able to stand up?
be supposed to/Were the boys supposed to clean their rooms?

can/Can you take care of the baby for a while?

may/May I have the next dance?

might/Might I take a seat next to you?

must/Must the children argue about everything?

should/Should your mother be lifting that heavy chair?

Do/Does/Did Begins the Question

have to/Do I have to do the dishes tonight?

need to/Did she really need to take the day off from work?

want to/Does your brother want to join the army?

The auxiliary verbs function in the same way in questions that are begun with an interrogative word: **Where** can I buy shoes like those? **What** did you want to get at the store?

IDIOMS DEMYSTIFIED

There is a short phrase that can be applied to any statement or question in either the present or past tense: **by the way**. The speaker uses this phrase *to add information about a previous topic* or *to tell the listener that he or she just remembered something pertinent*. It is sometimes used as a synonym for **don't forget**. For example:

Mary: I think that Mark is a wonderful man.
Lucy: **By the way**, did you know that Mark has been divorced three times?
Tom: I went out with Jean last night.
Steve: **By the way**, I need to borrow your car for my date tomorrow.
John: My first payday at my new job is tomorrow.
Sara: **By the way**, you still owe me twenty dollars.

Written Practice 3-8

Reword each sentence as a general question. For example:

Mary poured him a glass of milk. *Did Mary pour him a glass of milk?*

1. The little boy made his bed for the first time.

_____

2. Jack was supposed to help me pick apples.

_____

3. The soldiers were getting tired and hungry.

_____

4. Mr. Patel wanted to rent the apartment again.

_____

5. A strange man came up to my desk.

_____

Reword each sentence with the interrogative word that is appropriate for the underlined word or phrase. For example:

I saw <u>Bill</u> at the store. _Whom did you see at the store?_

6. <u>Grandfather</u> slipped on the ice and fell.

_____

7. The girls' soccer team won <u>another championship</u>.

_____

8. Tom found his wallet <u>under the dining room table</u>.

_____

9. The boy was crying <u>because he skinned his knee</u>.

_____

10. She glared <u>angrily</u> at the rude man.

_____

QUIZ

Choose the word or phrase that best completes each sentence.

1. _____ did you buy at the hardware store?
   A. Was
   B. What
   C. Who
   D. What time

2. A pair of geese _____ waddling across the road.
   A. do
   B. did
   C. was
   D. were

3. _____ you have any idea how to solve this problem?

   A. Do   C. Was

   B. Does   D. Were

4. Someone was supposed _____ keeping an eye on the children.

   A. being   C. to be

   B. were   D. to have

5. _____ the new student speak English well?

   A. Is able to   C. Wants

   B. Do   D. Can

6. I _____ to phone my parents before ten o'clock.

   A. have   C. should

   B. must   D. be able

7. _____ many books did you read last month?

   A. Which   C. Whom

   B. How   D. Might

8. The leaves of the trees _____ in the autumn.

   A. are being   C. falling

   B. turn red   D. does die

9. You're wrong. Maria _____ the grocery shopping yesterday.

   A. does   C. did

   B. must   D. was able

10. My neighbors _____ spend any time on their beautiful patio.

    A. seldom   C. are doing

    B. how often   D. were

chapter 4

Present Perfect, Past Perfect, and Future Tenses

In this chapter you will encounter the conjugational forms that verbs take in the present and past perfect tenses, as well as in the future tense forms. Like the present and past tenses, these tenses each have three varieties that are used in specific ways.

CHAPTER OBJECTIVES

In this chapter you will learn about:

- Present and past perfect and future tense sentences that indicate a habitual action
- Present and past perfect and future tense sentences that indicate an incomplete or ongoing action
- Present and past perfect and future tense sentences that are an emphatic reply
- Irregular verbs in these tenses

The Perfect Tenses

When a present tense conjugational form of the verb **have** is accompanied by a past participle, the tense is called the present perfect tense. For example: **I have walked, you have lived, she has invited, we have learned, they have fixed.** The past participle of regular verbs is identical to the past tense of regular verbs.

Infinitive	Past Tense	Past Participle
cook	cooked	(have) cooked
hope	hoped	(have) hoped
look	looked	(have) looked
name	named	(have) named

TAKE NOTE *Keep in mind that the verb **have** has three specific meanings:*

Transitive verb/shows ownership = I have a new car.
Auxiliary/synonym of must = I have to study tonight.
Perfect tense auxiliary = I have learned the poem by heart.

When a past tense conjugational form of the verb **have** is accompanied by a past participle, the tense is called the past perfect tense. For example: **I had walked, you had lived, she had invited, we had learned, they had fixed.**

There is a difference, of course, between the present perfect tense and the past perfect tense. The present perfect describes an action that was begun in the past and that ended in the present. For example:

I **have worked** here for ten years. *I began working here ten years ago. I still work here.*

She **has played** the piano for two months. *She began playing the piano two months ago. She still plays the piano.*

My neighbors **have raised** two nice children. *My neighbors have two children, whom they have raised since birth. They still are in the process of raising their children, or the children are adults now.*

The past perfect tense describes an action that was begun in the past and that ended in the past. For example:

She **had worked** in Los Angeles for two years. *She had worked in Los Angeles for two years before she was promoted to her present position.*

Tom **had played** tennis in college. *Several years ago in college, Tom was a tennis player. After graduation, he found he no longer had time to practice and dropped tennis altogether.*

My friends **had raised** ducks on their farm. *Several years ago, my friends began raising ducks on their farm. A few years later they stopped raising ducks.*

Oral Practice

Read each line in the dialogue aloud.

Bob: Have you lived in New Orleans for a long time?
Sara: No, I had lived in Boston before I came here.
Bob: I have studied geology for a long time, but I hope to find a job soon.
Sara: Have you always been interested in geology?
Bob: Yes. But before studying geology, I had assisted a professor of botany.
Sara: I envy you. I have never liked the sciences.

When asking questions with perfect tense verbs, the auxiliary **do/does/did** is not required. A general question begins with the auxiliary **have**.

Have you learned your lesson?
Has she always helped you?
Had he never visited a museum?
Had your father walked to work in the past?

Written Practice 4-1

Reword each present or past tense sentence in the present perfect and the past perfect tenses. For example:

Jack works in a large factory.

Jack has worked in a large factory.

Jack had worked in a large factory.

1. My parents dined at a very nice restaurant.

_____

_____

2. Someone wants to dance with you.

_____

_____

3. We never travel by rail.

_____

_____

4. A friendly dog followed me home.

_____

_____

5. My wife always brushes her hair before bed.

_____

_____

6. Do you talk to your neighbors?

_____

_____

7. Did Sara close all the windows?

_____

_____

8. Does the rain damage the fragile plants?

_____

_____

9. That boy sometimes copies my homework.

_____

_____

10. Bill joined a fitness club.

_____

_____

Irregular Past Participles

Many verbs form an irregular past participle. They are introduced by the auxiliary **have** and form the present and past perfect tenses. Many irregular past participles end in **-en**, but still others make a stem change or end in a consonant. For example:

I have **driven**   we had **kept**
you had **said**   they have **read**
she has **spoken**

Some past participles are identical to the present tense.

Present Tense	Present and Past Perfect Tenses
I cut	I have **cut**
you put	you had **put**
he beats	he has **beat**
she sets	she had **set**
we burst	we have **burst**
they cast	they had **cast**
it costs	it has **cost**

Refer to the downloading instructions on the copyright page to see a complete list of irregular past participles.

Habitual or Complete Actions

The form of the present and past perfect tenses (**have** plus **past participle**) previously illustrated is used to describe a *habitual or complete action* in the past. Let's look at some sentences that tell what a person did habitually. Sometimes an adverb that suggests that *an action takes place more than once* can be added to the sentence.

My son has spoken French all his life.
We had written her letters every day.
I have sent her roses ever since the first day we met.
Bill had often heard her singing.

TAKE NOTE *The adverb **never** belongs to the category of adverbs that describe an action that takes place more than once. It is the negative of **ever** or **forever**. Compare the meaning of the following pairs of sentences.*

It seems like I have lived in Buffalo **forever**.
I have **never** lived in Buffalo.
Have you **ever** worked for the social media?
Have you **never** worked for the social media?

Written Practice 4-2

Give the past participle for each infinitive provided. Refer to the downloading instructions on the copyright page for additional material if necessary.

1. sing _____

2. understand _____

3. come _____

4. go _____

5. eat _____

6. drink _____

7. kneel _____

8. send _____

9. say _____

10. teach _____

11. grow _____

12. hold _____

13. bring _____

14. let _____

15. draw _____

Oral Practice

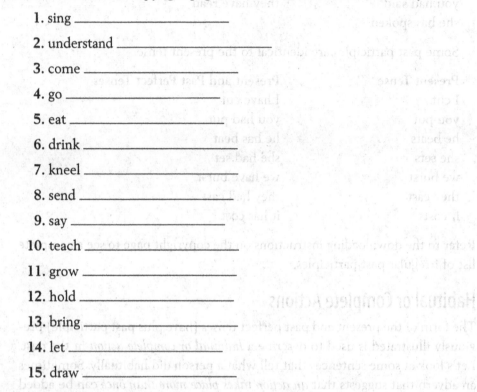 Track 15

Read each line in the dialogue aloud.

Mr. Winters: Have you found a place to live yet?

Phillip: No. A few months ago I had visited some rental apartments, but I didn't like them.

Mr. Winters: My aunt has lived in a nice condo on the East Side for several years.

Phillip: I had forgotten about how nice the East Side is.

Mr. Winters: She has spent her retirement years there and likes it a lot.

Phillip: I'll look into it. Have you already rented an apartment for yourself?

Mr. Winters: Two months ago. And I have bought some new furniture for the place.

Progressive Perfect Tenses

Just like the present and past tenses, the present perfect and past perfect tenses have a *progressive* conjugational form. And like the present and the past, the perfect tenses indicate *an action in progress or incomplete*. A progressive conjugation in the present perfect or the past perfect consists of a form of **have** plus **been** plus **a present participle**. For example:

We **have been living** in Vermont. *We began living in Vermont some time ago and still do.*
Had you **been dining** out a lot? *Did you do a lot of dining out back in the early 2000s? (You no longer do a lot of dining out.)*
The secretary of state **has been** traveling throughout Asia. *The secretary of state began traveling in Asia early in the current administration and continues to do so.*
I **had been standing** in the rain for an hour. *A few hours ago I stood in the rain for an hour, but eventually I got home and was able to dry off.*

Notice that there are not problems when dealing with the differences of regular and irregular verbs. It is the past participle **been** that always occurs in this structure, and the accompanying verb is always a present participle. This means that irregularities are not a concern. For example:

Infinitive	Past Participle	Progressive Perfect Tense
learn	learned	have been **learning**
drink	drunk	have been **drinking**
find	found	have been **finding**
go	gone	have been **going**
keep	kept	have been **keeping**
speak	spoken	have been **speaking**

This conjugational form is used to describe an action that was in progress when an interruption occurred. The clause that describes the interruption can begin the sentence or follow the main clause. The preferred progressive tense is the past perfect.

Interruption	Main Clause
When Jack came into the room	I **had** been taking a nap.
When the taxi hit my car	Bill **had** been texting with his girlfriend.

Main Clause	Interruption
My husband **had** been fixing the roof	**when lightning struck a nearby tree**.
The woman **had** been chatting in the garden	**when the storm came up**.

Oral Practice

Read each line in the dialogue aloud.

Dora: Have you been working at this job long?
Nick: No, I had been selling magazines door-to-door before this.
Tom: Has your brother been taking flying lessons?
Jane: No, he had been serving in the air force and was trained in California.
Luis: Have you been sitting here a while?
Dale: Yes, I have been thinking about home and paying my parents a visit.
Michael: You looked so embarrassed. What had you been doing?
Laura: When my aunt came into the living room, Carlos and I had been kissing.

Written Practice 4-3

Reword each present or past tense sentence in the present perfect tense and the past perfect tense. Careful! Some sentences describe a habitual action, others describe an action in progress. For example:

They were talking about work.

They have been talking about work.

They had been talking about work.

1. Tom is taking the dog for a walk.

_____

_____

2. Maria bought an expensive sweater.

_____

_____

3. My grandparents always drink only tea.

_____

_____

4. Phillip was speaking with Mr. Jackson.

_____

5. Did you see a lunar eclipse?

_____

_____

6. Is the team traveling out of state? (for example, from New York to Pennsylvania)

_____

7. The children were very naughty.

_____

_____

8. Why are those men following us?

_____

9. Dr. Schwartz was giving lectures on smoking.

_____

_____

10. I am finally spending less money.

_____

Oral Practice

🔘 Track 16

Read each sentence aloud, paying attention to the tense and meaning of the verbs.

We have been walking for over an hour. Where is that hotel?
Ms. Olson has never developed a relationship with her neighbors.
Have your parents driven to Canada every summer?

When the door slammed, I had been napping on the sofa.
Allison had been window-shopping at the mall when she saw her
  boyfriend coming.
Had he been drinking when the accident happened?
I have participated in the marathon for years.
The twins had never known their grandparents.

Emphatic Responses

Emphatic responses function in the perfect tenses as they do in the present and past tenses. However, the auxiliary **do/does/did** is not used in the response. Instead, the auxiliary **have** is intoned strongly. If the emphatic response is in the negative, the adverb **not** is intoned strongly. When the response contains an adverb that contradicts the negative statement, the contradictory adverb can be intoned strongly instead of the auxiliary **have**. For example (words with accents are strongly intoned):

Statement	Emphatic Response
You have never understood me.	I háve always understood you.
	(I have álways understood you.)
Martin has been eating too much.	Martin has nót been eating too much.
I had not heard from my son.	You hád heard from your son.
John had been driving too fast.	John had nót been driving too fast.
You had seldom visited me there.	I hád frequently visited you there.
	(I had fréquently visited you there.)

Oral Practice

Read each line aloud. Intone the emphasized word in the emphatic response.

My boss has not paid me yet. Your boss has already paid you.
Doris has been complaining a lot. Doris has not been complaining a lot.
Someone had taken my lunch. Someone had not taken your lunch.
  (No one had taken your lunch.)
Mr. Roberts had been gambling again. Mr. Roberts had not been
  gambling again.
The French girl has often spoken of Bill. The French girl has not spoken of
  Bill. (The French girl has seldom spoken of Bill.)
I had been skiing when the blizzard began. You had not been skiing when
  the blizzard began.

Written Practice 4-4

Give an appropriate emphatic response to each statement. Take note that the statements are in various tenses.

1. I have been writing a novel.

   _____

2. Jack speaks only of his former girlfriend.

   _____

3. Your daughter had not yet received my gift.

   _____

4. The temperature is very high today.

   _____

5. Jean has not been receiving her magazines.

   _____

6. You have never trusted me.

   _____

7. Carla has no idea what that word means.

   _____

8. Jim has been dating someone from Africa.

   _____

9. A large tree had fallen near the garage.

   _____

10. Someone has been slamming the door.

   _____

IDIOMS DEMYSTIFIED

The idioms **to paint the town red** (*go out to several clubs and party*) and **to put on airs** (*to act haughty or superior*) can be used in the perfect tenses. When using these idioms in those tenses, you must be aware of the nuance of meaning they provide.

To Paint the Town Red

Tim and John have been painting the town red since graduation. (*An ongoing period of partying began in the past [since graduation] and continues now.*)

He had been painting the town red when he suddenly came to his senses. (*His ongoing partying was interrupted when he realized that he was headed for trouble.*)

The wedding party has painted the town red. (*The wedding party's partying continued until the present but is now complete.*)

You hád painted the town red with your brother. (*An emphatic response to the statement "I had not painted the town red with my brother."*)

To Put on Airs

Mark has been putting on airs since he won the Mr. Muscle contest. (*Mark began acting superior and continues to do so since he won the Mr. Muscle contest.*)

Until her father scolded her, Maria had been putting on airs. (*Maria's haughty behavior was interrupted by her father's scolding.*)

My cousin had never put on airs. (*In the past, my cousin never acted haughty.*)

That pretty girl has néver put on airs. (*An emphatic response to the statement: "That pretty girl has always put on airs."*)

The Future Tenses

A future meaning is given in two forms: the *simple future tense* and the *future perfect tense*. These two tense forms tell what happens in the future but in distinct ways.

Simple Future Tense

The simple future tense can be formed in three ways.

Simple Future with the Present Tense

The simplest of these is the use of *a present tense sentence that implies a future tense meaning*. This is not a rare form of the future tense; it is used throughout the

English-speaking world. Be aware that a verb in its habitual or progressive form can be used in the future tense in this way. The difference of meaning between the habitual and progressive conjugations also applies in this tense. For example:

Tomorrow I **fly** to London.
Next week, we **are planning** a surprise party for Mary.
On Monday, someone **has to** wash that filthy car.
The football game **starts** in ten minutes.

Simple Future with Will and Shall

A second version of the future tense is composed of the auxiliary **will** or **shall** and an infinitive. **Shall** is typically used with the first person singular and plural (**I, we**). **Will** is used with the other persons, but there is a tendency to use **will** for all persons. For example:

I **shall/will** spend time in South America.
You **will** find your gloves in that drawer.
Will he recognize me after all these years?
We **shall/will** help you all we can.
They **will** send a spacecraft to Mars.

If a progressive verb is used with **shall** or **will**, a progressive infinitive (**be going, be singing, be learning**) accompanies the auxiliary. For example:

I **shall/will be correcting** your essays.
The usher will **be taking** your tickets at the door.
They will **be staying** overnight in the dormitory.

When the future auxiliaries **shall** or **will** are used, negative adverbs stand between the auxiliary and the infinitive. For example:

I shall/will **not** be going to your anniversary party.
We shall/will **never** be in favor of such a law.
You will **not** be taking part in the play this year.
He will **never** learn to play the flute.

There are times when the first person pronouns should be used with **shall**, and **will** should be avoided. When asking someone to make a decision or a choice, **shall** begins the question. For example:

Shall I help you get down from the ladder? (*What is your decision?*)
Shall we go to a concert or a movie tonight? (*Which do you choose?*)
Shall I order a pizza or a couple hamburgers? (*Which do you prefer?*)

When questions like these are negated, the negative adverb stands between the subject and the infinitive: **Shall we *never* get to meet your fiancé? Shall I *not* worry about your behavior?**

There is also a tendency to use **shall** in the first person in a statement that is a response to a "yes" or "no" reply to a posed question. The use of **shall** is for emphasis. For example:

Posed question: Is this the dress you want me to wear to your wedding?
Reply: Yes, it's perfect for you.
Response: Then I **shall** not be coming to your wedding!

and

Posed question: Can this project be done cheaply?
Reply: No, it will cost double what we first thought.
Response: Then we **shall** have to find more funds somehow.

Oral Practice

Read each sentence aloud, paying attention to the form of the future tense.

Mr. Garcia goes to Havana on Friday.
I shall never understand why you put on airs.
Is someone having a birthday party for Tom next week?
You will have to be prepared for an exam in the near future.
We will be depending upon your support of our idea.
When do you travel to Russia? Next month?
My uncle's collie will have pups soon.

Written Practice 4-5

Reword each past tense sentence in the two forms of the future tense. Add an appropriate adverb to each future tense sentence. For example:

John was going to the library.

John is going to the library tomorrow.

John will be going to the library tomorrow.

1. My professor was speaking about evolution.

_____

_____

2. My wife drove to Connecticut.

_____

_____

3. Were you leaving on vacation?

_____

_____

4. My son was spending the summer at a camp in Michigan.

_____

_____

5. The foreign tourists arrived around 4 p.m.

_____

_____

Simple Future with to Be Going

A third future tense structure is comprised of the phrase **be going to** with an infinitive. There is a slight difference in meaning with this phrase. It implies that the action is something the speaker or writer _intends_ to do in the future. Compare the following pairs of future tense sentences and notice how they differ in meaning.

Future action: I will buy a new car next week.
Intended action: I **am going to** buy a new car next week.
Future action: Bill will solve his money problems.
Intended action: Bill **is going to** solve his money problems.
Future action: The young men will enroll in college.
Intended action: The young men **are going to** enroll in college.
Future action: Will you repair that old car?
Intended action: Are you **going to** repair that old car?

Because **be going to** is not a true future tense auxiliary, it can be used in other tenses, the most common of which is the past tense. The use of other tenses can sound awkward and should be avoided. The meaning is still an intended action. For example:

I **was** going to buy a new car next week.
Bill **was** going to solve his money problems.

The young men **were** going to enroll in college.
Were you going to repair that old car?

Note that a future tense sentence with **be going to** can be used with a progressive tense verb: **I am going to *be working* in the garage. My wife is going to *be singing* in the choir. Are they going to *be learning* German?** The meaning, of course, implies an ongoing or incomplete action.

Written Practice 4-6

Reword each past tense sentence in the future tense with **shall/will** and **be going to**. For example:

Richard went to the movies.

Richard will go to the movies.

Richard is going to go to the movies.

1. Who was riding in the convertible?

_____

2. My in-laws [*my spouse's parents*] were traveling in Guatemala.

_____

3. Did I borrow more money from him?

_____

4. Bob sent her an important e-mail.

_____

5. The ambassador spoke with the other diplomats.

_____

Future Perfect Tense

The future perfect tense differs from the future tense in that the auxiliary **shall/will** is accompanied by a *participial infinitive* rather than an infinitive. A participial infinitive is composed of the auxiliary **have** and a past participle—either regular or irregular. For example:

> I shall have spoken.
> You will have discovered.
> She will have written.
> We shall have worked.
> They will have driven.

This conjugational form is used to show a habitual or completed action. But the present perfect tense can use a participial infinitive in the progressive form. In that case, it is composed of the auxiliary **shall/will** plus **have been** followed by a present participle. For example:

> I shall have been learning.
> You will have been making.
> She will have been sleeping.
> We shall have been reading.
> They will have been dancing.

As in other tenses, this verb structure indicates an ongoing or incomplete action.

The future perfect tense is used most often to describe an action that occurs in the present or future and ends in the future. Such sentences are usually accompanied by a clause or phrase that tells when the action will end. For example:

> Anne will have arrived in Denver **by 10 p.m.**
> **By the time the sun sets,** the hikers will have been going down the trail for six hours.
> I will have taken eight tests **before the semester ends.**

In casual speech, it is common to substitute the future tense for the future perfect tense. This avoids the awkwardness of working complex combinations of verbs into informal conversation.

> Anne will arrive in Denver **by 10 p.m.**
> **When the sun sets**, the hikers will have been going down the trail for six hours.
> I will take eight tests **before the semester ends.**

Oral Practice

🔘 Track 17

Read each sentence aloud, paying attention to the verbs and their meaning.

Will John have earned his first paycheck by the end of the week?

We will have been living in San Francisco for two years next month.

I doubt that anyone will have noticed the problem before the automatic system corrects it.

When morning comes, they will finally have arrived in Paris.

Will the fields have been sown by the end of spring?

Next week, Ms. Singh will have been teaching our class for two months.

My cousin will have earned enough for his vacation by May.

Written Practice 4-7

Reword each present tense sentence in the future and future perfect tenses. Add a clause or phrase that tells when the action will end in the future perfect sentence. For example:

Laura makes a chocolate cake.

Laura will make a chocolate cake.

Laura will have made a chocolate cake by the end of the afternoon.

1. Bob is walking for two hours.

_____

_____

2. Mr. James pays off the loan.

_____

_____

3. That girl dances with every boy.

_____

_____

4. Do you write a lot of poems?

_____

_____

5. I perfect my English.

_____

_____

6. Sophia is living with her grandmother for a month.

_____

_____

7. He gets a bad cold.

_____

_____

8. My brother finds a job in the city.

_____

_____

9. The dolphins chase the shark away.

_____

_____

10. The young chemist develops a new formula.

_____

_____

Auxiliaries

Auxiliaries can be added to sentences in the various tenses to change the *shade of their meaning*. You encountered this function of auxiliaries in Chapter 4. For example:

Jack Stands Up.
Jack **is able to** stand up. (*Ability.*)
Jack **must** stand up. (*Obligation.*)
Jack **wants to** stand up. (*Desire.*)

We Learn Spanish.
We **should** learn Spanish. (*Mild obligation.*)
We **need to** learn Spanish. (*Necessity.*)
We **might** learn Spanish. (*Possibility.*)

Speakers of English use auxiliaries in the perfect and future tenses. It is wise to avoid this tense, however, because the future perfect becomes awkward when auxiliaries are added. For example:

My Aunt Has to Visit a Neighbor. (*Obligation*)
My aunt has **had to** visit a neighbor.
My aunt had **had to** visit a neighbor.
My aunt will **have to** visit a neighbor.

Bill Needs to Earn More Money. (*Necessity*)
Bill has **needed to** earn more money.
Bill had **needed to** earn more money.
Bill will **need to** earn more money.

Take note that the auxiliaries **have to, need to, want to, be able to,** and **be supposed to** are the only ones that can be used in the perfect and future tenses. Although **be supposed to** can technically be used in these tenses, it is avoided because it sounds awkward.

When **can** is in the past tense, it changes to **could.** But when it is used in the perfect and future tenses, **be able to** is substituted for **can. Must** is only used in the present tense. In all other tenses, it changes to **have to.** For example:

I Can Run Fast.	**We Must Hurry.**
I have **been able** to run fast.	We have **had to** hurry.
I had **been able** to run fast.	We had **had to** hurry.
I will **be able** to run fast.	We will **have to** hurry.

Written Practice 4-8

Complete each sentence twice with any appropriate phrases.

1. I have been able to _____

    I have been able to _____

2. Mary will have to _____

    Mary will have to _____

3. No one had wanted to _____

    No one had wanted to _____

4. Will you need to _____?

   Will you need to _____?

5. The tourists had wanted to _____

   The tourists had wanted to _____

QUIZ

Choose the letter of the word or phrase that best completes each sentence.

1. I _____ never wanted to travel to Seattle.
   - A. do
   - B. have
   - C. did
   - D. am having

2. The vacationers had _____ camping along the lake.
   - A. been
   - B. had
   - C. being
   - D. having

3. _____ we take a little stroll around the park?
   - A. Are supposed to
   - B. Were able
   - C. Had
   - D. Shall

4. Has _____ found the keys to my desk?
   - A. you
   - B. the children or you
   - C. one of you
   - D. him

5. Tom will have been napping for an hour _____.
   - A. yesterday
   - B. by the time supper is ready
   - C. where
   - D. wanted to

6. Marie had _____ when someone knocked on the door.
   - A. been reading.
   - B. noticed
   - C. found the remote
   - D. sitting and waiting

7. Have you always _____ wear glasses?
   - A. wanted
   - B. be able to
   - C. needing to
   - D. had to

8. **Will our team** _____ **again today?**
   A. being   C. lost
   B. win   D. been trying harder

9. **Mark will** _____ **before the end of the day.**
   A. been leaving   C. being punished
   B. have arrived   D. had been helped

10. **Have you** _____ **here long?**
    A. it   C. been waiting
    B. be waiting   D. have to wait

chapter 5

Adjectives and Adverbs

In this chapter you will encounter adjectives and adverbs and discover how they are used differently. The comparatives and superlatives will also be addressed.

CHAPTER OBJECTIVES

In this chapter you will learn about:

- The forms that adjectives take
- The forms that adverbs take
- Irregularities in the formation of the comparative and superlative
- How intensifiers shade the meaning of adjectives and adverbs

Adjectives

Adjectives are a variety of words that modify pronouns and nouns. They describe pronouns and nouns and provide information about the quality and number of those pronouns and nouns. For example:

How Many	What Kind	What Size
three books	funny books	large books
several women	smart women	slim women

How Often	Belonging to Whom	Limiting
frequent visitor	our visitor	this visitor
occasional errors	whose errors	no errors

Location	Color	Quality
nearby tents	brown tents	shabby tents
domestic beer	dark beer	spoiled beer

When an adjective follows a linking verb, it is located in the predicate and is called a *predicate adjective*. The pronoun or noun modified is the subject of the sentence.

Subject	Predicate Adjective
You	seemed **jealous**.
She	is being **stubborn**.
Mr. Danner	was **rich**.
Ashley	became **dizzy**.

When an adjective stands in front of a noun, it is modifying that noun directly.

The **jealous man** became angry.   Ms. Hartman is a **rich widow**.
The **stubborn mule** did not budge.   I suddenly felt a **dizzy spell** coming on.

Oral Practice

Track 18

Read each sentence aloud, paying attention to the adjectives.

When the judge entered the courtroom, the room grew quiet.
A long list of accusations was read before the eager spectators.
A woman in a black dress took the witness stand.
She was attractive but had an arrogant look.
Our young lawyer approached the attractive woman with a kind smile.
He posed several questions and received appropriate answers.
But when he asked about her deceased husband, she was silent.
The impatient judge insisted upon hearing the witness's answers in her
   own words.

Written Practice 5-1

Provide an adjective that fits the description given in parentheses. For example:

(color) My girlfriend bought a _blue_ skirt.

1. (quality) That old bread is _____!

2. (color) She was angry, and her face turned _____.

3. (limiting) _____ bus will take you to the downtown area.

4. (belonging to whom) I think you picked up _____ coat by mistake.

5. (how many) Go to the store and buy _____ eggs.

6. (how often) I have to attend a _____ meeting with him.

7. (location) I bought my iPad at a _____ store.

8. (what size) Those sweaters won't fit into that _____ box.

9. (what kind) His new novel is not _____.

10. (quality) You can't wear that _____ shirt.

Suffixes

Many adjectives can be identified by their suffix. Suffixes are added to other parts of speech, which change those words into adjectives. For example: **manage** (verb) = **manageable**, **fool** (noun/verb) = **foolish**. Let's look at some adjectives that have been formed with suffixes.

-able/-ible: adorable, curable, accessible, possible
-al: magical, rhetorical, historical, logical
-en: oaken, wooden, sullen, barren
-ful: careful, thoughtful, youthful, doubtful
-ish: stylish, garish, bluish, English
-ive: positive, subjective, furtive, lucrative
-less: careless, hopeless, windowless, jobless
-some: lonesome, fearsome, loathsome, handsome
-y: gory, sunny, crazy, furry

Other suffixes that identify adjectives are: **-ary** (sedentary), **-esque** (picturesque), **-ic** (stoic), **-like** (childlike), **-ly** (lonely), and **-ous** (serious).

Many other words that are used as adjectives do not have identifying suffixes. It is their meaning that tells you that they are modifiers. For example:

The **eager** boy ran to the movie theater.   We came upon a **quaint** village.
A **gentle** rain began to fall.   The redwood trees are **tall**.

Oral Practice

Read each sentence aloud, paying attention to the formation of the adjectives.

The old woman on the corner was selling white carnations.
His diplomatic skills were put to the test when he saw her tasteless
   paintings.
The youthful athlete was known for his wholesome appearance and
   helpful nature.
Our children love Halloween candy and spooky stories.
She is a capable doctor and a gifted communicator.
The little airplane made a rapid descent to the airport and landed with
   a gentle bump.
She gave me a hopeful look and a subtle smile and walked in front of
   the audience.

Written Practice 5-2

Create an original sentence with the adjective provided in parentheses.

1. (thoughtful) _____
2. (generous) _____
3. (painless) _____
4. (dirty) _____
5. (deep) _____
6. (collectible) _____
7. (mechanical) _____
8. (gruesome) _____
9. (childish) _____
10. (negative) _____

Articles as Adjectives

As described in Chapter 2, the definite and indefinite articles are adjectives and describe the specific meaning of a noun or its general meaning. For example:

the man (*specific man*)   a man (*any man in general*)
the boys (*specific boys*)   boys (*any boys in general*)

Plural nouns that are not modified by an article are indefinite: **boys** = *any boys in general.*

But sometimes a plural noun or a collective or mass noun is not preceded by a *visible* article. These *invisible articles* are sometimes called *zero articles.* Perhaps a better name for this function is *invisible definite article*, because the meaning of the noun is not indefinite but definite and specific. Let's look at an example.

I have one small basket and two large baskets. Let's put the apples in *large baskets.*

The baskets have been identified. They are known and specific. Although a definite article is not present, the implied meaning is definite and specific. If you add the definite article to the sentence, the same meaning is given.

I have one small basket and two large baskets. Let's put the apples in *the large baskets.*

Now consider the following examples with the implied definite article.

What should we do with the coins? Let's put *pennies* in a jar and *dimes* in a piggy bank. Or, let's put *the pennies* in a jar and *the dimes* in a piggy bank.
Is she not feeling well? No, she has *high blood pressure.*

Although the definite article would sound awkward here (**the** high blood pressure), this phrase is still modified by a zero article. Now compare the following sentences, which have a zero article modifying plural and singular nouns.

You make **strange choices**.
She was cured of **cancer**.
I chose **short poems** for my essay on Whitman.
Mom put **cheese** and **salami** in my sandwich again.

Oral Practice

Read each sentence aloud, paying attention to the implied zero articles.

There's butter on the table for your toast and cold milk in the refrigerator.

You have so many flowers. You should put roses in the crystal vase and carnations in the white one.

I store these things like this: blouses go on the top shelf of the closet. Shirts go in the lower drawer of the dresser, and underwear belongs in the middle drawer.

I have plenty of paper in the printer and new templates for making the brochures.

Nouns as Adjectives

It has been demonstrated how a suffix can change nouns to adjectives (**fool** = **foolish, child** = **childlike**). But nouns alone can act as modifiers. They can function like any other adjective. For example:

You need a new **kitchen** faucet.
Slow down. This is a **school** zone.
You have quite a large **CD** collection.
Is there a **butcher** shop nearby?
The children are starting a new **class** project.

Written Practice 5-3

Use the noun in parentheses as an adjective that modifies another noun of your choosing. Use that phrase to complete the provided sentence. Add a determiner if needed. For example:

(school) <u>The school building</u> is in need of repairs.

1. (traffic) _____ is not working right now.

2. (sports) There is _____ not far from where you live.

3. (morning) I like to read _____ before I leave for work.

4. (e-mail) _____ is not working right.

5. (television) You do not need _____. We have cable.

6. (soccer) _____ was flooded during the storm.

7. (credit) You have to show your ID when you use

_____.

8. (airline) Check _____ to see when our flight leaves.

9. (ice cream) On a hot day we always go to _____.

10. (light) Where is _____? It's dark in here.

Adjectives Used as Nouns

Some adjectives can be used as nouns. The most common of these are adjectives that refer to nationality, such as the following:

Adjective	Adjective Used as Noun
A German man lives here.	He is a **German**.
An Italian woman lives here.	She is an **Italian**.
An American family lives here.	They are **Americans**.
Mexican men live here.	They are **Mexicans**.

Many other adjectives can also be used as nouns. They tend to be those that modify an *elliptical plural noun* (a noun that is understood but not written or spoken). For example:

The **old** were rescued first. *(the old people)*
She admired the **artistic** greatly. *(the artistic people)*
The **intelligent** often got scholarships. *(the intelligent students)*
The **young** are often too confident. *(the children and adolescents)*

Other adjectives that can act as nouns are: **careless, collectible, elderly, favorite, foolish, ideal, meek, poor,** and **rich.**

TAKE NOTE *Not all adjectives can stand alone and act as nouns. Some must continue to be modifiers and are followed by* **one** *for singulars and* **ones** *for plurals. For example:*

A **funny one** *(funny writer)* is Dr. Seuss.
A **common one** *(common error)* is to misspell receive.
Ms. Garcia grows the **prettiest ones** *(prettiest flowers)*.
The **single ones** *(unmarried women)* are looking for husbands.

This use of **one** *and* **ones** *with adjectives also applies to the adjectives previously illustrated, such as* **the old one, the young ones, a rich one, poor ones.**

Oral Practice

🔘 Track 19

Read each sentence aloud, paying attention to the usage of the nouns and adjectives.

> The garage door was held open by the garage attendant.
> We are proud of the brave and the hardworking, and we honor them.
> The Russians are asking whether the passport office is open today.
> The elders were in charge of the family reunion and event schedule.
> Has the prom queen met the Africans, who came to observe the
>   graduation dance?
> The religious say that the meek shall inherit the earth.
> A carpentry team has to repair the aluminum siding on an apartment house.
> It was the envious who gave the wealthy woman the silent treatment.
> The wise walk the nighttime streets with care.

IDIOMS DEMYSTIFIED

The idiom **a breath of fresh air** uses the adjective **fresh** to describe **air**. But the meaning of this phrase refers to something else. It says that *a welcome change* has taken place or that *something pleasant has replaced something unpleasant*. For example:

> He saw her frowning, but her eventual smile came as **a breath of fresh air**.
> When the handsome man entered the room, it was like **a breath of fresh air**
>   for the ladies.

Another idiomatic phrase that is used exclusively as an adjective is **cut-and-dried**. Those words do not tell the story of this phrase. It means that there is **no questioning** a particular fact or circumstance or that the fact or circumstance is **perfectly clear** to everyone.

> Everyone knew that he had given a **cut-and-dried** answer.
> There was a **cut-and-dried** solution: the merger of the companies had to
>   be avoided.

Participles as Adjectives

Present and past participles are used in the formation of certain tenses: **She is writing a book. They were falling down. John had broken his watch. I have injured my leg.**

The same present and past participles can be used as adjectives. Let's look at sentences that have present participles functioning as adjectives.

Her **writing** table needed some repairs.
The **falling** leaves meant that winter was around the corner.
Did you take a **sailing** class?
No one could calm the **sobbing** boy.
The sound of a **dripping** faucet drives me crazy.

This use of a present participle is often a *shorter version* of a relative clause, a clause that accompanies the noun that is modified by the participial adjective. For example:

The leaves **that were falling** meant that winter was around the corner.
No one could calm the boy **who was sobbing**.
The sound of a faucet **that is dripping** drives me crazy.

Now let's look at sentences that have past participles functioning as adjectives.

Your **broken** arm will take a long time to heal.
The **injured** man stood up with a wince.
Don't cry over a little **spilled** milk.
A **bullied** child can become very frightened.
You are quite **drunk**!

This use of a past participle is often a *shorter version* of a relative clause that contains a passive voice verb. For example:

The arm [of yours] **that was broken** will take a long time to heal.
The man **who was injured** stood up with a wince.
Don't cry over a little milk **that has been spilled**.
A child **that is bullied** can become very frightened.

Oral Practice

Read each sentence aloud, paying attention to the use of the present and past participles.

The two competing teams were energized by the cheering crowd.
We have a limited number of hats on sale.
A torn sail and a damaged rudder lost the race for the disappointed sailor.

I was soothed by the sound of rippling water and chirping birds.

When I finally woke up, I was aware that I had some cracked ribs and a
throbbing head.

Missed birthdays and forgotten anniversaries led to their final breakup.

Speeding cars and aging pavement kept my aunt off the freeway.

Adverbs

Adverbs are used to modify verbs, adjectives, and other adverbs. For example:

Verb Modifier

I know **exactly** what to do.

The boy ran **carelessly** into the street.

Adjective Modifier

The **happily** shouting boy had just won the chess game.

That is a **rather** silly thing to say.

Adverb Modifier

This is a **very** slowly recovering economy.

He smiled at his wife **quite** lovingly.

A large number of adverbs are adjectives that have the suffix **-ly** attached.
Such as:

Adjective	Adverb
abrupt	abruptly
cheerful	cheerfully
quick	quickly
ready	readily
timid	timidly

A few adverbs do not require the suffix **-ly**, such as: **fast**, **hard**, **home**, and
yesterday. You can *test* a word to determine whether it is used as an adverb by
asking **how**, **where**, and **when** of it. For example:

I can't understand her when she talks **fast**. *How does she talk?* (**fast** = adverb)

Tom finally went **home**. *Where did he go?* (**home** = adverb)

We are going to the city **tomorrow**. *When are we going to the city?*
   (**tomorrow** = adverb)

The adverb **hard** has another form—**hardly**. But in this form it has a different meaning (*scarcely*). Compare the following pair of sentences.

You work **hard** every day. *You work with great energy.*
You **hardly** work at all. *You put little effort into your work.*

Prepositional phrases that tell **how**, **where**, or **when** are also adverbial.

We're going to Chicago **by bus**. (*how*)
I'll be in town **next week**. (*when*)
I keep my wallet **in a drawer**. (*where*)

TAKE NOTE *Careful! Several adjectives have the ending -ly, but they are not always adverbs. Some examples:*

daily	homely	monthly	yearly
early	lovely	silly	

Adjectives such as these can be used as adverbs. Compare the following pairs of sentences. Take note of how the second sentence in each pair uses the adjective as an adverb.

He is an **early** riser. (*adjective*)
I always arrive at work **early**. (*adverb/when*)
Granddad receives a **monthly** pension check. (*adjective*)
We receive this magazine **monthly**. (*adverb/when*)

*Test such words with **how**, **where**, and **when** to determine whether the words are adjectives or adverbs.*

Written Practice 5-4

Indicate whether the word in bold in each sentence is an **adjective** or **adverb**.

1. _____ The fox **slyly** crept toward the rabbit's burrow.

2. _____ The weatherman gives the airport an **hourly** report on the storm.

3. _____ That is a very **homely** dog!

4. _____ John has an **early** meeting with Ms. Hall.

5. _____ I think you spelled that word **incorrectly**.

6. _____ I leave for work **every** morning around six.

7. _____ You have to be a **fast** thinker on this job.

8. _____ Laura thought it was an **easy** test.

9. _____ The puppy was napping under the **shady** tree.

10. _____ A package arrived for you **yesterday**.

Intensifiers

Some adverbs *qualify the degree of intensity* of the meaning of an adjective or adverb they modify. These adverbs are called *intensifiers*. Some of the most commonly used are: **extremely, quite, rather, somewhat, utterly, very,** and **too.** Other intensifiers are *degree adverbs*, such as **barely, moderately,** and **slightly.** Let's look at some intensifiers and how they modify adjectives and adverbs.

Adjective Modifier	Adverb Modifier
Maria is a **rather** attractive woman.	This is a **very** slowly moving freight train.
You are **too** young to go alone.	She danced the tango **quite** skillfully.
I have a **slightly** off-color joke.	I think you dressed **too** quickly.
Bob is an **extremely** gifted poet.	The woman spoke **barely** audibly.

Oral Practice

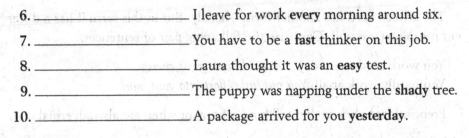 Track 20

Read each sentence aloud, paying attention to the use and meaning of the adverbs.

Jim rudely interrupted the speaker and hastily grabbed the microphone.

You are still too sick to play a very rough sport like rugby.

A rapidly forming storm gradually approached land and boldly threatened the city.

A rather shy boy came slowly up to Sara and quietly asked for the next dance.

Spot is an extremely smart dog; he can effortlessly climb a ladder and easily jump to the ground.

Tonight the girls want to visit a newly opened club in a somewhat shady part of town.

I am moderately sure that Tina will arrive today and bring some sorely needed good news.

She is fairly intelligent and can easily understand problems. But can she type fast?

ANOTHER USE FOR *QUITE*

There is a special phrase that combines an adverb and a definite article in a unique way: **quite the**. This phrase can be used adjectivally to modify nouns. Its meaning is *very special* or *very unique*. For example:

You have **quite the** throwing arm. *Your arm is uniquely strong and accurate when you throw something.*

That was **quite the** accident yesterday. *The accident was especially serious.*

Written Practice 5-5

To complete each sentence, give an adverb or adjective that is modified by an intensifier. For example:

He looked <u>quite hopelessly</u> for the ring.

1. Two boys ran _____ around the track.

2. The old woman read _____ to the first-graders.

3. I'm afraid your story is _____.

4. The stranger moved _____ around the room.

5. The parents asked _____ about their injured son.

6. The accident victim looked _____.

7. Jack took Mary _____ in his arms and embraced her warmly.

8. A bewildered man stared, _____, at his former home.

9. Your _____ appearance at my party made me so happy.

10. The knight stepped _____ into the courtyard and brandished his sword.

TAKE NOTE *The words **good** and **well** need special mentioning. **Good** and **well** have two meanings:*

1. **Adjective:** a good teacher = *a teacher who has talent / the opposite of **bad***
   Adverb: she plays **well** = *she plays with talent / the opposite of **badly***

2. **Adjective:** a **good** person = *a kind person / the opposite of* **unkind**
   Adverb: he speaks **kindly** of me = *he speaks goodheartedly / opposite of* **unkindly**

Although **well** *is the adverbial form of* **good**, *it has another meaning:*

Adjective: he is **well** again = *he is healthy / the opposite of* **sick**

Comparatives

The basic form of an adjective or adverb is called the *positive* form: **good**, **bad**, **tall**, **rapidly**, **slowly**, **kindly**. The comparative of adjectives and adverbs is used to compare two persons or things. Most adjectives add the suffix **-er** to form the comparative. For example:

Positive	Comparative
tall	taller
big	bigger
funny	funnier
rich	richer

When adjectives are long or come from a foreign source such as Latin, the comparative is formed by the introductory word **more** and the positive form of the adjective.

Positive	Comparative
interesting	more interesting
superficial	more superficial
antagonistic	more antagonistic
hysterical	more hysterical

One-syllable adverbs that do not have the suffix **-ly** form their comparative like adjectives: the suffix **-er** is added. The few adjectives that end in **-ly** can be used as adverbs; the comparative is formed by adding **-er**. For example:

Positive	Comparative
soon	sooner
hard	harder
fast	faster
early	earlier

Other adverbs form the comparative with the introductory word **more**.

Positive	Comparative
slowly	more slowly
eagerly	more eagerly
energetically	more energetically
poorly	more poorly

Be aware that in colloquial and casual speech, the simpler comparative form is often used to form adverbs: **He walked slower. She yelled louder. I spoke up quicker.**

Oral Practice

Read each sentence aloud, paying attention to the comparative adjectives and adverbs.

The man seemed calmer today and reached out more sincerely to shake my hand.

Tina worked more intensely and hoped to finish this project more quickly than the last.

Mr. Yates was an older gentleman with sideburns that were bushier than normal and a face just as long to match.

Is there an earlier plane to Dallas, or do I have to wait longer and take the later flight?

She married him for richer or poorer but had no idea just how poor he was.

I find that Mexican writers are more emotional and write more passionately than other authors.

Written Practice 5-6

Provide the comparative adjectives and adverbs for the positive adjective given. For example:

loud   _louder_   _more loudly_

Positive	Comparative Adjective	Comparative Adverb
1. soon	_____	_____
2. bright	_____	_____

3. dark   _____   _____

4. frightful   _____   _____

5. special   _____   _____

6. lovely   _____   _____

7. boring   _____   _____

8. envious   _____   _____

9. shallow   _____   _____

10. logical   _____   _____

Irregular Comparatives

A few comparatives have an irregular form. Note that in all cases, the irregular comparatives are the same for the adjectives and the adverb. They are:

Positive	Comparative Adjective and Adverb
bad	worse
far	farther/further
good	better
little (*an amount*)	less
many	more
much	more
well (*healthy*)	better

Let's look at some example sentences that illustrate how the same comparative can be used as an adjective or an adverb.

Adjective: This is a **better** novel.
Adverb: I feel that Twain wrote **better** than Poe.
Adjective: We need **more** time and money.
Adverb: He talks **more** but says less.
Adjective: This problem is **worse** than I thought.
Adverb: I did **worse** on this exam than on the previous one.

The conjunction **than** is used to introduce the person or thing that is compared with another person or thing. For example:

John is taller **than** Mike.
Mary sings more sweetly **than** her sister.
I have a smarter dog **than** yours.
Their lawyer speaks more eloquently **than** ours.

It is common to omit understood information in phrases following **than**.

> She runs more slowly **than Bill runs**. = She runs more slowly **than Bill**.
> Our house is bigger **than your house is**. = Our house is bigger **than yours**.

The word **than** is often considered a preposition. In that instance, a pronoun in the objective case can follow **than**.

> He is taller than **me**.
> She earns more money than **us**.
> I work harder than **her**.

If the subjective case is used following **than**, it is not used as a preposition but as a conjunction.

Preposition	Conjunction
He is taller than me.	He is taller than I (am tall).

Written Practice 5-7

Give appropriate completions with **than** and a comparative for each sentence. For example:

> These two men eat _more than five other men_.

1. My two sisters work _____.
2. Is Mr. Taylor _____?
3. I sometimes drive _____.
4. We painted the house _____.
5. Yesterday's storm was _____.

Superlatives

The superlative form of an adjective or adverb describes the *ultimate degree* of the meaning of the adjective or adverb. Many adjectives add the suffix **-est** to form the superlative, and the article **the** can accompany this form. For example:

Positive	Superlative
tall	(the) tallest
big	(the) biggest

funny	(the) funniest
cheap	(the) cheapest

Long words or words of a foreign origin, especially Latin, form the superlative differently. A suffix is not used. Instead, the positive form of the adjective is preceded by **most**. The definite article can accompany this form. For example:

Positive	Superlative
boring	(the) most boring
selective	(the) most selective
dangerous	(the) most dangerous
efficient	(the) most efficient

Superlative adverbs are very similar. If a word is short and does not require an **-ly** suffix to be an adverb, the superlative form is identical to the superlative of adjectives. The few adjectives that end in **-ly** can be used as adverbs; the superlative is formed by adding **-est**.

Positive	Superlative
soon	(the) soonest
long	(the) longest
hard	(the) hardest
early	(the) earliest

Most adverbs form the superlative with **most** followed by the positive form of the adverb. For example:

quickly	(the) most quickly
slowly	(the) most slowly
rapidly	(the) most rapidly
awkwardly	(the) most awkwardly

There are a few irregular superlative adjectives and adverbs. Both adjectives and adverbs use the identical form.

Positive	Superlative Adjective and Adverb
bad	(the) worst
far	(the) farthest/furthest
good	(the) best
little (*an amount*)	(the) least
many	(the) most
much	(the) most
well (*healthy*)	(the) best

Oral Practice

Track 21

Read each sentence aloud, paying attention to the superlative forms and the optional use of the definite article.

Jane: Tim is the most likable man in the office but has some of the worst habits.

Richard: He sometimes stays longest on his coffee break and speaks most rudely about our boss.

Jane: He wears the freshest white shirts. They smell most appealing. I like Tim best of everyone.

Jane: Dora is wisest among the oldest girls in our group. She types the fastest and helps others the most.

Richard: She works most comfortably with the youngest girls but is shyest among the men.

Jane: Her sister does the least of any of the managers. Honestly, she's the laziest.

Richard: I'm probably the most experienced in management but have been here the shortest amount of time.

Jane: I find the work most interesting, and I enjoy dealing with the customers.

Richard: Mr. Barnes is the biggest exception. He has the worst manners, and he bellows loudest when something isn't to his liking.

QUIZ

Choose the letter of the word or phrase that best completes each sentence.

1. The _____ mule refused to move.
   A. any   C. lively
   B. stubborn   D. rather lazily

2. That student is _____ than I thought.
   A. a lot smarter   C. somewhat
   B. very quickly   D. seventeen years old

3. I want to buy _____ pair of shoes you have.

   A. the cheapest   C. several

   B. newer   D. a nicer

4. Everyone was watching the _____ lion.

   A. angrily   C. first one

   B. early   D. roaring

5. I suddenly felt _____ dizzy.

   A. some   C. quite

   B. much   D. making

6. Can you fix the _____ leg on that chair?

   A. bend   C. weaken

   B. broken   D. this oldest

7. Laura works _____ with her colleagues.

   A. most cooperatively   C. very bad

   B. more lonely   D. good

8. The freight train began to move even _____ than before.

   A. now   C. yesterday

   B. more slowly   D. least

9. Are _____ old jeans yours?

   A. a lot   C. these

   B. not much   D. probably

10. Of all the guests, Charles always arrives _____.

   A. lately   C. more punctual

   B. the end of the party   D. the earliest

PART ONE TEST

Choose the letter of the word that contains the sound of the IPA symbol.

1. (dʒ)
   A. broke   C. fudge
   B. spin   D. cart

2. (ð)
   A. this   C. with
   B. rose   D. yes

3. (ʊ)
   A. stone   C. fight
   B. look   D. show

Choose the letter of the word or phrase that best completes each sentence.

4. I seem to be spending _____ time studying.
   A. less   C. few
   B. many   D. a few

5. Words can often be powerful _____.
   A. instrument   C. the facts
   B. the tool   D. weapons

6. Wait in the hallway. I have _____ gift for you.
   A. the   C. a
   B. an   D. any

7. As John got weaker, he did _____ exercising.
   A. less   C. the few
   B. many   D. fewer

8. That _____ has been in the family for years.
   A. one   C. second
   B. seven   D. fourth

9. May I carry _____ packages for you?

   A. the

   B. a

   C. that

   D. third

10. _____ did you get in the mail?

   A. Was

   B. What

   C. Who

   D. What time

11. _____ she have any idea how long I've waited?

   A. Do

   B. Does

   C. Was

   D. Were

12. Michael was supposed _____ cleaning his room.

   A. being

   B. were

   C. to be

   D. to have

13. _____ your brother help me carry this trunk?

   A. Is able to

   B. Do

   C. Wants

   D. Can

14. Someone _____ help her find her wallet.

   A. have

   B. needs

   C. should

   D. be able

15. He is wrong. I _____ pay the rent this month.

   A. does

   B. am

   C. did

   D. was able

16. He _____ never wanted to work in the city.

   A. do

   B. has

   C. did

   D. is having

17. The boy scouts had _____ camping in the park.

   A. been

   B. had

   C. being

   D. having

18. _____ we make some supper together?

   A. Are supposed to

   B. Were able

   C. Had

   D. Shall

19. Mr. Patel had _____ when the phone suddenly rang.

   A. been sleeping   C. took a book

   B. noticed   D. sitting and waiting

20. The doctor will _____ by noon.

   A. been leaving   C. being called

   B. have arrived   D. had been helped

21. That little girl is _____ than I thought.

   A. smart   C. a lot older

   B. very quickly   D. six years old

22. She would like to buy _____ dishes you have.

   A. the nicest   C. several

   B. newer   D. a nicer

23. _____ boy stood up and ran home.

   A. Angry   C. First one

   B. An early   D. The sobbing

24. The elderly woman began to feel _____ faint.

   A. some   C. quite

   B. much   D. making

25. I'm not sure I can repair _____ clock.

   A. oldest   C. weaker

   B. that broken   D. these foreign

Part Two

Using Pronouns and Verbs

chapter **6**

Pronouns and Possessives

In this chapter you will find explanations of the various types of pronouns and how they function. In addition, you will encounter the possessive case.

CHAPTER OBJECTIVES

In this chapter you will learn about:

- Personal pronouns
- Relative pronouns
- Possessive nouns
- Possessive adjectives and pronouns

Personal Pronouns

The personal pronouns are categorized as first person pronouns, second person pronouns, and third person pronouns. In each category, there are singular and plural forms. In the subjective case, the personal pronouns are:

	First Person	Second Person	Third Person
Singular	I		you, he, she, it, one, who, what
Plural	we		you, they, who, what

The conjugational forms used with the personal pronouns were discussed in Chapter 3. Refer to that chapter to review the conjugations.

The pronoun **one** is always singular and is the replacement of *a person, every person*, or *people in general*. For example:

One should not text and drive. *A person should not text and drive.*
One needs to stay alert. *Every person needs to stay alert.*
One has to have enough rest. *People in general have to have enough rest.*

In more casual speech, **you** is used in place of **one**.

You should not text and drive.
You need to stay alert.
You have to have enough rest.

The pronouns **who** and **what** ask questions and are the replacements of nouns referring to people and nouns referring to objects, respectively. If the nouns are singular, the pronouns **who** and **what** are considered singular. If they replace plural nouns *that are in the predicate of the verb be*, they remain singular pronouns but are used to represent plurals. For example:

The man has no time. = **Who** has no time?
The men have no time. = **Who** has no time?
The men are strangers. = **Who** are the men?
This book looks interesting. = **What** looks interesting?
These books look interesting. = **What** looks interesting?
These books are textbooks. = **What** are these books?

TAKE NOTE *Who and what can be used to represent plural pronouns when they are in the predicate following a linking verb like **be**. Because they are interrogative words, they begin questions. However, they are not the subjects of sentences, but rather* predicate nominatives *and the pronoun replacements for nouns that are predicate nominatives. For example:*

These men are **strangers**. (*Strangers is in the predicate nominative.*)
These men are **who**. (*Who replaces the predicate nominative noun.*)
Who are these men? (*The interrogative who begins the question.*)
These books are **textbooks**. (*Textbooks is in the predicate nominative.*)
These books are **what**. (*What replaces the predicate nominative noun.*)
What are these books? (*The interrogative what begins the question.*)

Oral Practice

🔘 Track 22

Read each line of the dialogue aloud.

> Mark: I like to go swimming on a hot day. Do you enjoy swimming as much as I do?
>
> Tina: My neighbor does. He swims for thirty minutes nearly every day.
>
> Mark: I hear that his wife prefers golf. They say she plays at the local golf club on weekends.
>
> Tina: I know that club. It has more than 2,000 members.
>
> Mark: We used to play there when our children were younger.
>
> Tina: I believe you have three children.
>
> Mark: Yes, and they all still live at home.
>
> Tina: One should not complain. I think it is nice that you still have them with you.
>
> Mark: Who is that man? Do you know him?
>
> Tina: He is Professor Keller. He teaches at the college.
>
> Mark: Is the woman his wife? She is quite pretty.
>
> Tina: Yes, she is Dr. Marie Keller. She is on the surgical staff at the hospital.
>
> Mark: What is she carrying? Is it an animal?
>
> Tina: Yes, it's her dog. It goes everywhere with her.

Third Person Pronouns

The third person pronouns are replacements for nouns. If a noun is masculine, the pronoun replacement is **he**. If a noun is feminine, the pronoun replacement is **she**. If a noun is neuter, the pronoun replacement is **it**. All plural nouns are replaced by **they**. For example:

Masculine Noun	Masculine Pronoun
His brother helped him.	He helped him.
The actor forgot his lines.	He forgot his lines.

Feminine Noun	Feminine Pronoun
His aunt lives in Hawaii.	She lives in Hawaii.
The actress took a bow.	She took a bow.

Neuter Noun	Neuter Pronoun
The bed was uncomfortable.	It was uncomfortable.
His tent collapsed.	It collapsed.

Plural Noun
Several boys played soccer.
The windows are dirty.

Plural Pronoun
They played soccer.
They are dirty.

Written Practice 6-1

Create an original sentence with each of the pronouns provided.

1. (I) _____
2. (you) _____
3. (he) _____
4. (she) _____
5. (it) _____
6. (we) _____
7. (they) _____
8. (one) _____
9. (who) _____
10. (what) _____

The Objective Case

The personal pronouns have another form: *the objective case*. This pronominal form is used when the pronoun is used as a direct object (D.O.), indirect object (I.O.), or object of a preposition. The objective personal pronouns are:

First Person	Second Person	Third Person
Singular	me	you, him, her, it, one, whom, what
Plural	us	you, them, whom, what

The direct object in a sentence is the object of a transitive verb. The direct object is identified by asking **whom** or **what** of the verb. For example:

I met **the man** in Russia. *Whom did I meet in Russia? the man* = D.O.
I met **him** in Russia. *Whom did I meet in Russia? him* = D.O.
Mary saw **a bird** in the attic. *What did Mary see in the attic? a bird* = D.O.
Mary saw **it** in the attic. *What did Mary see in the attic? it* = D.O.

The indirect object describes *to whom* something is given or made available. The indirect object is identified by asking **to whom** or **for whom**. For example:

He sent **the boys** a gift. *To whom did he send a gift? the boys = I.O.*
He sent **them** a gift. *To whom did he send a gift? them = I.O.*
Tom buys **Ashley** a ring. *For whom does Tom buy a ring? Ashley = I.O.*
Tom buys **her** a ring. *For whom does Tom buy a ring? her = I.O.*

The object of a preposition is the noun or pronoun introduced by a preposition. For example:

I walked **with Alice**. <u>Alice</u> *is introduced by with. = O.P.*
I walked **with her**. <u>Her</u> *is introduced by with. = O.P.*
Everyone sat **on benches**. <u>Benches</u> *is introduced by on. = O.P.*
Everyone sat **on them**. <u>Them</u> *is introduced by on. = O.P.*

Oral Practice

Read each sentence aloud, paying attention to the use of the objective case pronouns.

Martin gave me tickets to the play.
I have often seen you at the art museum.
The next time you speak with him, say hello from me.
When the exhausted woman stumbled, I helped her into a chair.
I'll take the bus to New Orleans, but I know I won't be comfortable on it.
The sailor threw us a line and pulled us safely out of the lake.
I hope both of you have finally learned your lesson.
The girls were brave, and each of them received a reward.
Whom did they visit in Washington, D.C.?
Ms. Johnson found a box. What did she find in it?

Written Practice 6-2

Complete the sentence with the correct form of the pronoun provided in parentheses. For example:

(you)

Thomas met <u>you</u> last year in Chicago.

That young man wants to dance with <u>you</u>.

(I)

1. May _____ have another glass of water, please?

2. My uncle drove _____ to school this morning.

(he)

3. You should not borrow so much money from _____.

4. Mary hopes to visit _____ when she is in Europe.

(she)

5. When will _____ come home from the hospital?

6. Someone sent _____ a large bouquet of red roses.

(it)

7. _____ is impossible to read your handwriting.

8. Why are they hiding in _____?

(we)

9. The reporter interviewed _____ for a TV news
broadcast.

10. I think John can lend _____ his car for the evening.

(they)

11. When _____ come into the room, we will turn on
the lights and scare _____.

12. Mr. Garcia found a wonderful apartment for _____.

(one)

13. How can _____ know what to do in a situation
like this?

(who)

14. For _____ did you vote?

(what)

15. _____ did your wife get you for your birthday?

? **Still Struggling**

The pronoun **who** becomes **whom** in the objective case. However, it is quite common to use **who** in both the subjective and objective cases, especially in casual speech. For example:

Correct: Whom did they visit in Colorado?
Casual: Who did they visit in Colorado?

Although the correct form is to place an accompanying preposition before **whom/who**, the preposition is frequently placed at the end of a clause in casual speech. For example:

Correct: With whom did you speak?
Casual: Who(m) did you speak with?

The same convention applies with **what**.

Correct: In what were the letters hidden?
Casual: What were the letters hidden in?

Word Order with Pronouns

When a sentence contains both a direct object and an indirect object noun, the indirect object precedes the direct object. For example:

I.O.	D.O.
I sent	**the man** **a letter**.

When the indirect object is changed to a pronoun, the word order does not change.

I.O.	D.O.
I sent	**him** **a letter**.

Whenever the direct object changes to a pronoun, the indirect object (noun or pronoun) changes position in the sentence and *becomes a prepositional phrase* introduced by **to** or **for**.

D.O.

I sent **it**   **to the man.**

I sent **it**   **to him.**

Let's look at another example sentence. Take note of how the position of the words changes when the direct object becomes a pronoun.

John bought **Mary flowers.**

John bought **her flowers.** (*no change in word order*)

John bought **them for Mary.** (*direct object pronoun precedes prepositional phrase*)

John bought **them for her.** (*direct object pronoun precedes prepositional phrase*)

Oral Practice

🔘 Track 23

Read each sentence aloud, paying attention to the use of the pronouns.

My mother gave me a long list of chores to do.
I gave it to my brother, and I took Spot, our dog, for a walk.
Spot saw a rabbit and immediately ran after it.
I chased him and held up a treat to coax him back to me.
When I finally caught him and gave the treat to him, he gobbled it down.
When Spot tried to run away again, I found the leash and put it on him.
When I got home, my mother was waiting to hand me a broom.
She gave it to me with an angry look.
And I gave Spot an angrier one.

Written Practice 6-3

Reword each sentence by changing the indirect object noun to a pronoun. Then reword it changing the direct object noun to a pronoun. For example:

We sent our aunt a telegram.

We sent her a telegram.

We sent it to her.

My sister lends her friend a jacket.

1. _____

2. _____

Will you give Mr. Keller these tools?

3. _____

4. _____

Bill finally found Maria the perfect gift.

5. _____

6. _____

The governor assigned the woman a difficult task.

7. _____

8. _____

Mr. Patel often sends his relatives postcards from America.

9. _____

10. _____

Grandmother always tells the children interesting stories.

11. _____

12. _____

We were writing the soldiers long letters.

13. _____

14. _____

I will sell my neighbors my old car.

15. _____

16. _____

Relative Pronouns

The English relative pronouns are **that, who/whom/whose,** and **which.** The relative pronoun **that** is used to introduce a *restrictive relative clause.* Such a clause contains information that is essential to the meaning of the sentence. It usually adds information or a description about the *antecedent* of the relative pronoun. The antecedent is the word to which the relative pronoun is *related* and to which it refers.

When two sentences contain the same noun or pronoun element, one of them can be changed to a relative pronoun. The other becomes the antecedent of that relative pronoun. For example:

John has **the book**. **The book** belongs to his sister.
John has **the book that** belongs to his sister.

The relative clause "**that** belongs to his sister" gives additional information about the book. The topic is a *specific book*, and the important information is about the ownership of the book. Let's look at a few more examples.

We took **a vacation**. **The vacation** was wonderful.
We took **a vacation that** was wonderful.

This vacation was unlike other vacations. It was wonderful.

I met **the fireman**. **The fireman** saved my life.
I met **the fireman that** saved my life.

I didn't meet just any fireman. This one saved my life.

We want to congratulate **the man**. **The man** won the lottery.
We want to congratulate **the man that** won the lottery.

We don't want to congratulate just any man. It has to be the lottery winner.

When the antecedent to a restrictive relative clause is a person, the relative pronoun **who** can be used in place of **that**. As with a relative clause introduced by **that**, a comma does not separate the two clauses. For example:

I met **the fireman who** saved my life.
We want to meet **the man who** won the lottery.

Nonrestrictive relative clauses are separated from the main clause by commas. **Who** is used with persons, and **which** is used with objects. The nonrestrictive clause contains unessential, parenthetic information. For example:

The mayor, who is in Spain right now, wants to raise taxes.

Where the mayor is right now is not essential to the meaning of the sentence.

Two houses, which were built in the nineteenth century, burned to the ground.

When the houses were built is not essential to the meaning of the sentence.

Now compare the following pairs of sentences and observe how they differ in meaning.

My friend **that/who lives in Montreal** is a teacher. *This friend lives in Montreal. I have other friends who live in other cities.*

My friend, **who lives in Montreal**, is a teacher. *I have one friend. He happens to live in Montreal.*

The lamp **that was repaired** is quite old. *This lamp is now repaired. I have other lamps that are still broken.*

The lamp, **which was repaired**, is quite old. *The lamp is old, and at some time it had been repaired.*

Oral Practice

Read each sentence aloud, paying attention to the type of relative clause used in each.

The house that they built for my grandmother is quite small.

The Washington Monument, which was built between 1848 and 1884, is a tribute to George Washington.

That's the man who stole my wallet!

That pretty girl, with whom I was dancing earlier, is a student at Harvard.

Is this the stovepipe hat that Lincoln once wore?

The Dreamliner jet aircraft, which is manufactured by Boeing, is highly fuel-efficient.

I need a medication that will relieve my sore throat.

Possessive Nouns and Pronouns

The preposition **of** can be used to form possessives. Although there are exceptions, such prepositional phrases usually use an inanimate noun as the object of the preposition **of**. For example:

Inanimate	Animate
the color **of** her dress	the father **of** the bride
the sweet smell **of** success	the roar **of** the lion

Other possessives require the use of an **apostrophe** and an **-s**. Most singular nouns just add **'s**: **John's** book, **the woman's** purse, **our leader's** speech. Plural nouns that end in **s** add an **apostrophe**: the dogs' runway, **his parents'** house, **the teachers'** lunchroom. These descriptions of the possessive are helpful generalities. Chapter 15 presents a full description of possessive nouns.

Personal pronouns also have a possessive form. The possessives are listed here in their singular and plural forms.

	First Person	Second Person	Third Person
Singular		my, mine	your, yours, his, his/her, hers/its, its
Plural		our, ours	your, yours, their, theirs

The two forms of the pronouns (**my, mine**) are the possessive adjective and the possessive pronoun. Only **his** and **its** are used as both. Let's look at how they are used differently.

Modifying a Noun	Replacing a Noun
My book is new.	**Mine** is new.
Her son is two now.	**Hers** is two now.
Our car was in an accident.	**Ours** was in an accident.

The third person pronoun **one** forms a possessive with an **apostrophe** and an **-s**:

One's privacy should be respected.

When a possessive adjective is used as a relative pronoun, it uses **whose** for animates and **whose** or **of which** for inanimates. For example:

The man is still in London. **His** father is quite ill.
The man, whose father is quite ill, is still in London.
I saw **that zombie movie** you mentioned, but I'd forgotten **its** title.
I saw **that zombie movie, whose** title/the title **of which** I forgot.

If a possessive noun becomes a relative pronoun, **whose** and **of which** are used in the same way.

The senator comes from Virginia. **The senator's** wife is a physician.
The senator, whose wife is a physician, comes from Virginia.
John bought them **roses**. **The roses'** scent is beautiful.
John bought them **roses, whose** scent/the scent **of which** is beautiful.

Written Practice 6-4

Combine each pair of sentences as one sentence. Make the word or phrase in bold the relative pronoun in a nonrestrictive clause. For example:

Jane and I met in the city. She works **in the city**.

Jane and I met in the city, which is where she works.

1. The children were playing with the dogs. **The dogs'** kennel is in the barn.

   _____

2. My husband still works at the mill. **My husband** is out of town.

   _____

3. I sat through an opera. **The opera** lasted nearly four hours.

   _____

4. This is Mr. Hughes. You met **Mr. Hughes** in St. Louis.

   _____

5. The actress will star in a play. I wrote **about the actress** in an essay.

   _____

6. This is the woman I mentioned. I have worked **for her** for several years.

   _____

7. That's a rather good restaurant. **The restaurant's** menu is extensive.

   _____

8. I was born in a village. **The village** was severely damaged during the war.

   _____

9. We're going to visit our uncle. We bought this fruit basket **for our uncle**.

   _____

10. This is a letter from my cousin. I recently sent **my cousin** tickets for the ballet.

    _____

When a relative pronoun is the object of a preposition, the preposition usually precedes the relative pronoun, especially in writing and formal style. In more casual style, it can stand at the end of the clause. For example:

This is the man **for whom** I plan to work.
This is the man **who(m)** I plan to work **for**.

If the relative clause is restrictive, the preposition must stand at the end of the clause.

We want to help the lady **that** we give some food **to**.
I'd like to meet the general **who** you wrote **about**.

In restrictive clauses that have a relative pronoun used as a direct object, indirect object, or object of a preposition, the subject of the relative clause can be *elliptical*. That is, the subject is understood but neither spoken nor written. For example:

Direct object:	I have a picture of the girl **that** I met in Rome.
	I have a picture of the girl I met in Rome.
Indirect object:	She likes the teacher **who** she gave a book **to**.
	She likes the teacher she gave a book **to**.
Object of preposition:	We saw the film **that** you talked **about**.
	We saw the film you talked **about**.

Oral Practice

Track 24

Read each sentence aloud, paying attention to the kind and use of relative pronouns.

I spent a lot of time at a camp that is located in Michigan.
Our neighbors, who are from Mexico, have large garden parties.
The armchair, which is now upholstered in raw silk, belonged to a duchess.
I know an elderly gentleman who goes by the name of Abraham Lincoln.
You should try a piece of the cake that my sister baked.
The vacation you told me about sounded so interesting.

These old documents, the print of which is fading, must be preserved.
He once lived in a country in which many people were poor.
Where is the dress I bought you yesterday?

Written Practice 6-5

Complete each sentence with any appropriate relative clause. The use of commas and the type of relative pronoun provided are the clues as to whether the clause should be restrictive or nonrestrictive. For example:

She bought an old car that _used far too much gas_. (restrictive)

1. At the end of the street is a large old house, which _____.

2. Our professor, who _____, wrote a book on ethics.

3. Is this the view that _____?

4. I brought them several gifts that _____.

5. That desk, in which _____, belonged to my grandmother.

6. I sent an e-mail to the boss, from whom _____.

7. The people that _____ came from Thailand.

8. The actress who _____ has been in more than ten films.

9. The subject that _____ is my low credit score.

10. The tourists, whom _____, returned to their hotel.

The antecedent of a relative pronoun can be an entire clause. No element in that clause is the specific noun or pronoun to which the relative pronoun refers. Instead, the antecedent refers to the meaning of the whole clause. For example:

Maria graduated with high honors, which made her parents proud.

It is not Maria, nor her graduation, nor the high honors, to which the relative pronoun **which** refers. It is the entire clause: **Maria graduated with high honors.**
Let's look at a couple more examples.

The baby finally slept the night through, which gave the parents some rest.
I finally got over the flu, which allowed me to return to work.
Juan got first prize at the science fair, which means a scholarship for him.

Written Practice 6-6

Provide an introductory clause that is the antecedent to the relative pronoun in the relative clause. For example:

<u>I got a big raise</u>, which made my wife happy.

1. _____, which helped me pay off the loan.

2. _____, which brought tears to my mother's eyes.

3. _____, which means two more days of vacation.

4. _____, which took her breath away.

5. _____, which changed Marco's life forever.

Whoever and *Whatever*

There is a special type of relative clause that has no concrete antecedent. Instead, the antecedent is a *theoretical person*. There is an expression familiar to most English speakers that illustrates this kind of meaning.

He who laughs last, laughs best.

The combination **he who** sounds old-fashioned or extremely formal and is usually replaced by **whoever**. The previous example would be: **Whoever laughs last, laughs best.** Let's look at a few more examples. Remember that **he who** or **whoever** does not refer to a specific person.

Whoever buys your car will get great transportation.
Whoever can pull the sword from the rock will be king.
Whoever saw the accident has to talk to the police.

The preceding structure is used when **whoever** is the subject of both clauses of the sentence. When the theoretical person is a direct object, the word order can change. First look at **he who** used as an object (**him whom**).

Him whom we all love, you must love.

If **whomever** is used as the object, the phrasing sounds more up-to-date. And a second version can also be formed.

> Whomever we all love, you must love.
> You must love whomever we all love.

Let's look at another example of this use of **whomever.**

> Him whom the men respect, the girls will soon adore.
> Whomever the men respect, the girls will soon adore.
> The girls will soon adore whomever the men respect.

If the pronouns **him whom** are both objects as illustrated above, these two versions of the sentence are possible. But if one of the pronouns is a subject (**he whom/him who**), it is how **who(m)ever** is used in its clause that determines the case: subjective or objective. In the example that follows, **whoever** is the subject of the clause **is hungry.**

> We nourish him who is hungry.
> We nourish whoever is hungry
> Whoever is hungry we nourish.

The object of the verb **nourish** is the clause **Whoever is hungry**—not the pronoun **whoever.**

In the next example, the entire clause **Whomever you have chosen to love** is the object of the verb in the clause **I accept.** But in the relative clause, **Whomever** is the object of the verb **have chosen** and is, therefore, in the objective case—**Whomever.**

> I accept him, whom you have chosen to love.
> I accept whomever you have chosen to love.
> Whomever you have chosen to love, I accept.

The key to using **who(m)ever** correctly is to determine whether it is the object or subject of the verb in the relative clause and whether the entire clause is the object or subject of the accompanying clause. For example:

> I'll speak to whoever answers the phone.

The entire relative clause is the object of the preposition **to,** and **whoever** is the subject of the relative clause.

> Whomever they elect must govern fairly.

The entire relative clause is the subject of the accompanying clause, and **Whomever** is the object of the verb **elect** in the relative clause.

The very same uses occur with the relative pronouns **whichever** and **whatever**. The pronouns **that which** are replaced by **whichever** and **whatever**. Their use as subjects and objects follow the same rules and **who(m)ever**. For example:

> That which you buy, you must keep.
> Whichever you buy you must keep.
> You must keep whichever you buy.

The entire relative clause is the object of **must keep.**

> That which you learn, will serve you well.
> Whatever you learn will serve you well.

Whatever is the object of the verb **learn,** but the entire relative clause is the subject of the clause **will serve you well.**

Since there are no changes that occur with **whichever** and **whatever** resembling those that occur with **who(m)ever,** there are no case changes to be made with those two pronouns.

Oral Practice

Read each sentence aloud, paying attention to the use of the pronouns as subjects and objects.

> I will deal with whomever you introduce into our family.
> Whoever finds the treasure will be very rich.
> Whichever grows fastest will be the healthiest plant.
> Whatever happens in the future I shall handle appropriately.
> Mr. James needs to speak to whoever is in charge here.
> Whomever the police arrested is not the right man.
> John will buy whichever fits him the best.
> Whatever you say has to be said respectfully.

Written Practice 6-7

Complete each sentence with any appropriate phrase. For example:

I will hire whomever *you suggest*.

1. Whoever pays the most _____.

2. Whatever _____ I will not betray our friendship.

3. I will probably vote for whomever _____.

4. The little boy wanted whichever _____.

5. Whomever _____ the others will also follow.

6. Whoever _____ should share the money with his or her family.

7. Whatever the boss says _____.

8. Whichever _____ he will surely get sick.

9. Whomever the students like the most _____.

10. This is a gift for whoever _____.

IDIOMS DEMYSTIFIED

The phrase **hot water** can be used with the verbs **get** or **be**. If someone warns that you are about to **get in hot water**, you may be *finding oneself in trouble*. **Be in hot water** means that *you are in trouble*. For example:

Whoever broke that window is in trouble!
Whatever you say must not get me in trouble.

QUIZ

Choose the letter of the word or phrase that best completes each sentence.

1. I plan to send _____ a little present.

   A. they   C. your

   B. her   D. my

2. From _____ have you been receiving all these flowers?

   A. whom   C. he

   B. whichever   D. she

3. Mr. Grover gave them _____.

   A. you

   B. your

   C. from her

   D. to him

4. _____ was all the money hidden in?

   A. Who

   B. What

   C. How

   D. On which

5. My sister _____ is older than my sister Helen.

   A. who is not any younger

   B. that works in Boise, Idaho,

   C. whichever she needs

   D. I want to meet someday

6. _____ you do I'm sure I will find acceptable.

   A. Whoever

   B. That

   C. He, whom

   D. Whatever

7. The sickly child began to grow stronger, which _____.

   A. is now only four years old

   B. whomever they love

   C. brought tears to her mother's eyes

   D. you received it from

8. Why did you take Mary's car? You're in _____ now!

   A. hot water

   B. whatever happens

   C. basement hiding

   D. very careful

9. I hope to learn something from _____.

   A. who will study with me

   B. they are the officers of the bank

   C. which you tried to explain to me

   D. whomever the governor sent

10. _____, which should make you very happy.

   A. This is an old friend

   B. I'm finally coming home tomorrow

   C. Do you have some candles

   D. The woman on the corner is my cousin

chapter 7

Reflexive and Reciprocal Pronouns and Interrogatives

This chapter continues our discussion of pronouns. In addition to a focus on reflexive and reciprocal pronouns, we describe interrogatives and their function.

CHAPTER OBJECTIVES

In this chapter you will learn about:

- Reflexive pronouns
- Intensive pronouns
- Reciprocal pronouns
- Interrogative words and their function
- Word order with interrogative words

Reflexive Pronouns

The reflexive pronouns are another form of the personal pronouns. They are:

Subjective Case	Objective Case	Reflexive Pronoun
I	me	myself
you	you	yourself
he	him	himself
she	her	herself
it	it	itself
we	us	ourselves
you *pl.*	you	yourselves
they	them	themselves
one	him	oneself

The reflexive pronouns are used in place of objects in order to make the subject of the sentence the object of the verb or a preposition. For example:

Direct object: He burned **me** with a hot pan.
Reflexive object: He burned **himself** with a hot pan.
Indirect object: I bought **you** new gloves.
Reflexive object: I bought **myself** new gloves.

If the second person pronoun (**you**) is used, the reflexive pronoun is either **yourself** or **yourselves**. If **you** refers to one person, the reflexive pronoun is **yourself**. If **you** refers to more than one person, the reflexive pronoun is **yourselves**. Let's look at a couple example sentences.

Jim, **you** have to behave **yourself** in class from now on.
Dora, **you** can't blame **yourself** for that accident.
Children, **you** may help **yourselves** to some fresh fruit.
Ladies and gentlemen, I promise that **you** will enjoy **yourselves** at the party.

When a command is given, the implied pronoun is **you**. In a command, therefore, use **yourself** or **yourselves**, whichever is needed to conform to the singular or plural meaning of **you**.

TAKE NOTE *The use of reflexive pronouns should not be confused with the case of reflexive pronouns used with* true reflexive verbs. *Many languages have numerous reflexive verbs. But in English there are only a few. Among them is the verb* perjure oneself. *This verb does not have meaning unless it is accompanied by a reflexive pronoun. A noun or pronoun that does not refer to the subject cannot be used with a reflexive verb. You cannot say* **I perjured him** *or* **I perjured that woman**. *The appropriate reflexive pronoun must be used and no other.*

I perjured myself.
You perjured yourself.
They perjured themselves.

Reflexive pronouns replace noun or pronoun objects. These can be direct objects, indirect objects, or objects of a preposition. Consider these examples.

Direct Object	**Reflexive Object**
I accidentally cut **my friend** with a knife.	I accidentally cut **myself** with a knife.
She saw **his face** in the mirror.	She saw **herself** in the mirror.
Indirect Object	**Reflexive Object**
He wants to buy **her** some books.	He wants to buy **himself** some books.
Why did she send **the man** a letter?	Why did she send **herself** a letter?
Object of Preposition	**Reflexive Object**
I found a warm jacket **for the child**.	I found a warm jacket **for myself**.
You think only **about them**.	You think only **about yourself/ yourselves**.

The third person reflexive pronouns are used when a noun is the subject of the sentence. For example:

Mr. Gomez hurt **himself** in a fender bender.
That woman only likes to talk **about herself**.
The little rabbit sheltered **itself** under a hedge.
The tired soldiers warmed **themselves** by the fire.

Oral Practice

🔘 Track 25

Read each sentence aloud, paying attention to the use of the reflexive pronouns.

Each man had to protect himself from the heavy downpour.
The little girl proudly dressed herself.
You should stand up straight and carry yourself properly.
We wrapped ourselves in our blankets to keep warm.
I'm very independent and rely only on myself.
Bill and Mary, I hope you have prepared yourselves for the coming storm.
The bird tried to defend itself against the cat.
Why do those people spend so much money on themselves?
One should behave oneself as one might expect others to do.

Written Practice 7-1

Complete each sentence with a pronoun or reflexive pronoun.

1. Tom and Mary, please come here. You should introduce _____ to the others.

2. I think I injured _____ when I fell.

3. Jean doesn't like to talk about _____.

4. _____ seated herself at the desk and began to write.

5. We covered _____ with a large, warm blanket.

6. He occupies _____ with his baseball card collection.

7. _____ lowered themselves into the trench to repair the pipe.

8. The fox hid _____ in the brush and waited silently.

9. Professor Higgins found _____ in an unfamiliar neighborhood.

10. Phillip, you shouldn't always brag about _____.

The Interrogative *Who*

When the subject of the sentence is the interrogative **who**, the choice of a third person reflexive pronoun is not obvious. If it is clear that the question is directed at a male or a group of males, the reflexive pronoun will be **himself**. For example:

Asked of an All-Male Team

Who will volunteer **himself** to pass out the towels?

Who is interested just in **himself** and not the team?

Who flatters **himself** that he's a better player than the others?

If the question is directed at a female or a group of females, the reflexive pronoun is **herself**.

Asked of an All-Female Band

Who bought this new costume for **herself**?

Who considers **herself** our leader?

Who took it upon **herself** to turn down that job?

If the question is directed at a group made up of both genders, the *neutral* form to use is **himself**. But this suggests that the females are excluded. There is a current tendency to use the third person plural reflexive pronoun **themselves** to avoid this exclusion. You will hear many native speakers of English use this form, but it is not correct. This use of **themselves** occurs with other pronouns that are called *indefinite pronouns*. Some of these are **somebody, someone, everybody, everyone, anybody, anyone, nobody,** and **no one**. For example:

Correct but exclusive: Who distinguished **himself** in the army?

Incorrect but commonly used: Who distinguished **themselves** in the army?

Correct but exclusive: Somebody should prepare **himself** for the camping trip.

Incorrect but commonly used: Somebody should prepare **themselves** for the camping trip.

Correct but exclusive: Did everyone enjoy **himself** at the party?

Incorrect but commonly used: Did everyone enjoy **themselves** at the party?

Correct but exclusive: Nobody should blame **himself** for this failure.

Incorrect but commonly used: Nobody should blame **themselves** for this failure.

Some verbs that are commonly used with reflexive pronouns are:

amuse	content	enjoy	hurt	occupy
apply	cut	express	injure	prepare
behave	distance	find	introduce	see
blame	dry	help	kill	teach
busy				

Written Practice 7-2

Using the word or phrase in parentheses as the subject of your sentence, create a sentence that includes a reflexive pronoun. For example:

(I) _I pride myself on my athletic ability._

1. (you *s.*) _____
2. (she) _____
3. (my teammates) _____
4. (Ms. Ling) _____
5. (we) _____
6. (Jack and I) _____
7. (several guests) _____
8. (I) _____
9. (it) _____
10. (you *pl.*) _____
11. (Dr. Ravel) _____
12. (someone) _____
13. (the frog) _____
14. (my grandmother) _____
15. (each of you) _____

Intensifiers

Reflexive pronouns can act as *intensifiers*. They occur only in the subjective case and are the *appositives* of the subject. Appositives usually give additional information about the subject but are not part of the meaning of the basic sentence. For example:

John, **a very lanky boy,** came shyly into the classroom.
Several tall trees, **shaking violently in the storm,** were about to fall to the ground.
Lillian and Fred Thompson, **our neighbors,** won a trip to Hawaii.

Reflexive pronouns used as appositives are not separated by commas. Instead of providing additional information, they *emphasize the subject.* For example:

Jill **herself** couldn't understand the man's speech because of his accent.
The two officers **themselves** found the man's behavior odd.

I **myself** plan on becoming a doctor.

Mr. Patel **himself** once served in the navy.

Oral Practice

Read each sentence aloud, paying attention to how the reflexive pronoun is used.

The little girl helped herself to another piece of cake.

You yourself said that the problem could be solved.

I really like the way you express yourself.

Did the boss himself decide to fire me?

We freed ourselves from our captives and ran as fast as we could to the woods.

Ms. Gomez herself was once a member of Congress.

The ant busied itself, struggling to carry the large crumb.

I myself love reading poetry and even writing it.

No one saw himself as the foreman of the jury.

The judge himself was skeptical of what the man said.

Written Practice 7-3

Using the string of words provided, create a sentence that includes an intensifier. For example:

she/buy/blouse like mine

She herself bought a blouse like mine.

1. Tom/drink/at the party

   _____

2. contestants/dressed in/fashion

   _____

3. I/speak/languages

   _____

4. we/be/Europe/Africa

   _____

5. you/suggest/visit/museum

   _____

6. Anna/graduate/college

   _____

7. you *pl.*/eat/restaurant/regular

_____

8. he/join/Marine Corps

_____

9. lamp/cost/more than

_____

10. they/live/mountainside

_____

Implying *on One's Own*

There is another use and meaning for reflexive pronouns. The pronouns usually are placed at the end of a sentence and imply that the subject has done something without help from others. The reflexive pronouns used in this way may or may not be accompanied by the preposition **by**. If the phrase is preceded by **all** (to emphasize that no one gave assistance), the preposition **by** must be included. For example:

The little boy put his shoes on **(by) himself**.
Did you really build that garage **(by) yourself?**
My daughter rarely walks to school **all by herself**.
It's hard to believe that I knitted that sweater **all by myself**.

A phrase synonymous with this usage of a reflexive pronoun is **on one's own**. Compare the following pairs of sentences. Notice how the possessive adjective conforms to the subject of the sentence.

Our daughter baked the cookies **herself**.
Our daughter baked the cookies **on her own**.
We carried the boat to the river **by ourselves**.
We carried the boat to the river **on our own**.
Did you make that kite **all by yourself?**
Did you make that kite **on your own?**

TAKE NOTE *Some speakers of English use a first person singular reflexive pronoun where a personal pronoun in the objective case is required. No matter how frequently you might hear such usage, it is not correct. For example:*

Incorrect usage: You can phone either my wife or **myself** at this number.
Correct usage: You can phone either my wife or **me** at this number.
Incorrect usage: Please send your catalog to my partner and **myself**.
Correct usage: Please send your catalog to my partner and **me**.

Oral Practice

🔘 Track 26

Read each sentence aloud, paying attention to the use of the reflexive pronouns and intensifiers.

I had to content myself with a lower position in the firm than I'd
  expected.
Do yourself a favor and take a long vacation.
Martha herself knew that her grandmother's divorce was a family secret.
Apply yourself and you will get ahead in this life.
We repaired this old radio all by ourselves.
The snake coiled itself up and prepared to strike.
I myself have never been on an airplane until now.
The gardener himself knows that a bush like this cannot survive in
  our climate.
The arrogant man often speaks of himself in the third person.

IDIOMS DEMYSTIFIED

Many idioms require the use of a reflexive pronoun. Here are two high-frequency idioms that do just that.

Make Oneself at Home
This phrase is used to indicate that someone is free to feel, or does feel, very
  comfortable in a specified place, as comfortable as the visitor would feel in
  his own home. For example:
Your room is on the second floor. Please **make yourself at home** there.
John leaned back in the comfy chair and **made himself at home**.

Pull Oneself Together
This phrase means that someone should, or will, regain control of himself and
  that his previous behavior is changing or should change. For example:

Pull yourself together! You cannot go on crying all day.
The murdered man's children mourned for weeks but finally began **to pull
  themselves together**.

Reciprocal Pronouns

There are only two forms of reciprocal pronouns: **each other** and **one another**. They can be used interchangeably and are useful when saying that two people perform the same action as a subject and an object. In the following examples, notice that each person is the subject and then the object of an action. When that occurs, the two persons become a compound subject, and the reciprocal pronoun becomes the object.

John loves Barbara. Barbara loves John.
John and Barbara love **each other/one another**.
The men sent letters to the women. The women sent letters to the men.
The men and women sent letters to **each other/one another**.

Oral Practice

Read each sentence aloud, paying attention to the use of the reciprocal pronouns.

The dog always hated the cat. The cat always hated the dog.
The dog and the cat always hated one another.
My neighbors helped me. I helped my neighbors.
My neighbors and I helped each other.
Raj likes to study with Susan. Susan likes to study with Raj.
Raj and Susan like to study with one another.
The bear stares menacingly at the moose. The moose stares menacingly at
   the bear.
The bear and the moose stare menacingly at each other.

Written Practice 7-4

Reword each pair of sentences as one sentence that contains a reciprocal pronoun.

1. The lawyer does not trust the judge. The judge does not trust the lawyer.

   _____

2. Jill knits a sweater for Karen. Karen knits a sweater for Jill.

   _____

3. My father bought a camera for my mother. My mother bought a camera
   for my father.

   _____

4. My children love me. I love my children.

   _____

5. Do the boys want to dance with the girls? Do the girls want to dance with the boys?

   _____

6. Jim helps Bill with the cleaning. Bill helps Jim with the cleaning.

   _____

7. The actor is jealous of the singer. The singer is jealous of the actor.

   _____

8. Larry has written poems for Laura. Laura has written poems for Larry.

   _____

9. He never visits her. She never visits him.

   _____

10. The governor supported the senator in the campaign. The senator supported the governor in the campaign.

    _____

Interrogatives

When one is asking a question that can be answered with **yes** or **no**, the verb in the sentence precedes the subject. If the verb is a form of **be**, it begins the question. Other verbs use **do/does/did** as their auxiliary in the question. For example:

Are you a student here?
Were the boys at home when the fire started?
Does Jane enjoy working in the city?
Did someone remember to call Mother?

If other auxiliaries are used in the sentence, those auxiliaries are used to begin the question, and they precede the subject.

Can you understand what I'm saying?
Has your father ever been in Ireland before?
Should he text and drive?
Weren't we supposed to turn at that last corner?

Questions that can be answered with **yes** or **no** are general questions about an entire sentence.

Does your aunt live in the mountains of Colorado?
Yes, my aunt lives in the mountains of Colorado.
No, my aunt lives in the mountains of Washington State.

Interrogative words are used to ask questions specific to an element in a statement. The interrogative words are as follows:

what *asks about objects*
what kind of *asks about quality*
when *asks about time*
where *asks about location*
which *asks about choice*
who/whom/whose *asks about a person*
why *asks for a reason or explanation*
how *asks in what way or manner*

When a question is asked about a specific element in a sentence, the appropriate interrogative word replaces that element and begins the question. Except in the case of **who,** the verb will precede the subject. In the following examples, the underlined word or phrase is the specific element asked about.

Statement: <u>Many pioneers</u> began to move westward.
Question: *Who* began to move westward?
Statement: Many pioneers began to move <u>westward</u>.
Question: *Where* did many pioneers begin to move?
Statement: The nanny was reading <u>a book</u> to the children.
Question: *What* was the nanny reading to the children?
Statement: The nanny was reading a book <u>to the children</u>.
Question: *To whom* was the nanny reading a book?

Oral Practice

🔘 Track 27

Read each sentence aloud, paying attention to the use of the interrogative words.

People stood in a long line to buy tickets to the play.
Who stood in a long line to buy tickets to the play?
Where did people stand to buy tickets to the play?
What did people stand in a long line to buy?

I gave each of my children an antique ring on New Year's Eve.
To whom did I give an antique ring on New Year's Eve?
What did I give each of my children on New Year's Eve?
When did I give each of my children an antique ring?
What kind of ring did I give each of my children on New Year's Eve?

Written Practice 7-5

Using the underlined element in each sentence as your cue, give an appropriate question with an interrogative word. For example:

> Jane plans to move to Florida.
>
> *Who plans to move to Florida?*

1. My relatives from Brazil visited <u>me</u> last week.

   _____

2. I really like the <u>brown leather</u> wallet.

   _____

3. They plan to get to Washington <u>on the train</u>.

   _____

4. Our neighbors have a summer house <u>on Lake Winnebago</u>.

   _____

5. The engaged couple hope to go to Hawaii <u>on their honeymoon</u>.

   _____

6. We will drive to Pittsburgh, <u>because Boston is too far</u>.

   _____

7. He saves a hundred dollars every week <u>in order to buy a car</u>.

   _____

8. Jean received a large bouquet <u>from her fiancé</u>.

   _____

9. <u>His</u> late father left him a large sum of money.

   _____

10. Her daughter wants the <u>brown puppy or the black puppy</u>.

    _____

Interrogatives as Conjunctions

When a sentence answers a **yes** or **no** question, the conjunction **that** or **whether** frequently introduces the clause that contains the information in the question. But there is a change in word order: the subject precedes the verb. Consider the following question and the responses to it.

Did the boy give her his name?
I think that the boy gave her his name.
Bob asked whether the boy gave her his name.
We know that the boy gave her his name.
Did you find out whether the boy gave her his name?

In the last example, the sentence is formed as a question. But it is the phrase **Did you find out** that is the question. The clause **the boy gave her his name** is not stated as a question.

Oral Practice

Read each sentence aloud, paying attention to the answers to the initial question.

Does Mr. Patel play bridge well?
Did you know that Mr. Patel plays bridge well?
I heard that Mr. Patel plays bridge well.
Someone said that Mr. Patel plays bridge well.
Were the Smiths recently in Mexico?
John told me that the Smiths were recently in Mexico.
The article stated that the Smiths were recently in Mexico.
Michael asked whether the Smiths were recently in Mexico.

TAKE NOTE *In casual speech, you will often hear the conjunction **if** used in place of **whether**. You will discover that this is quite common. However, the preferred conjunction is **whether**. For example:*

Casual: Did you ask **if** the store is open till midnight?
Preferred: Did you ask **whether** the store is open till midnight?
Casual: No one knows **if** the trains are arriving on time.
Preferred: No one knows **whether** the trains are arriving on time.

When a question is posed with an interrogative word, that question can also serve in clauses following other phrases. But the conjunctions **that** and **whether** are not used. Instead, *the interrogative word serves as the conjunction*. In such sentences, the subject precedes the verb. For example:

> When did Dora get home from college?
> **I don't know when** Dora got home from college.
> **Uncle Joe asked when** Dora got home from college.
> **From whom was she getting flowers?**
> **No one knew from whom** she was getting flowers.
> **Did Bob find out from whom** she was getting flowers?

As pointed out in Chapter 6, in casual speech and writing, the formal form of **from whom she was getting flowers** can be changed to **who she was getting flowers from.**

Oral Practice

Track 28

Read each sentence aloud, paying attention to the use of the interrogatives as conjunctions.

> Derek cannot decide where to build the new house.
> Did you learn why Mr. Peterson has to travel to Berlin?
> I have to choose which prom dress to buy: the white one or the pink one.
> Martin asked her how she found out about his accident.
> Do you know how many times I texted you last night?
> She had to wonder whose convertible that was in the driveway.
> Can you tell me what time the bus to Omaha leaves?
> Tom has to make up his mind which pizza to order.

How

The interrogative **how** is used together with modifiers to form new interrogatives. The list that follows is just a sampling of the many combinations that can occur.

how expensive	how much
how heavy	how often
how light	how short
how long	how smart
how many	how absurd

Let's look how these interrogatives are used in questions and as conjunctions.

How big is your house?
We have no idea how big our house is.
How much did they pay for that big car?
Someone asked how much they paid for that big car.
How clean is the kitchen?
Mr. Garcia has no idea how clean the kitchen is.

Written Practice 7-6

Using the string of words provided, create a question. Then use the interrogative as a conjunction in a clause that follows the one provided. For example:

when/buy/couch

When can they afford to buy a new couch?

She doesn't know _____.

She doesn't know when they can afford to buy a new couch

1. where/find/treasure

_____

Do you know _____?

_____

2. how many/cars/parking lot

_____

Someone asked me _____.

_____

3. with whom/dance/balcony

_____

Did you see _____?

_____

4. whose/dog/under the porch

_____

I wonder _____.

5. what kind of/books/hide

_____

Jim asked her _____.

6. when/guests/arrive

_____

Can you tell me _____?

_____

7. which/suit/wedding

_____

I don't care _____.

_____

8. how long/tablecloth/party

_____

Help me decide _____.

_____

9. what/send/anniversary

_____

Sara asked _____.

_____

10. why/TV set/broken

_____

Did you tell him _____?

_____

QUIZ

Choose the letter of the word or phrase that best completes each sentence.

1. I think that boy injured _____ with that stick.
   A. her   C. myself
   B. anybody   D. they

2. The twin girls graduated and are proud of _____.

   A. one another   C. herself

   B. ourselves   D. every

3. _____ can protect himself from such intense heat?

   A. Him   C. Whom

   B. He   D. Who

4. _____ was sheltering itself under the broad leaf of a plant.

   A. The frightened girl   C. Several children

   B. A little puppy   D. No one

5. Michael and Tina have known _____ all their lives.

   A. each   C. one another

   B. themselves   D. oneself

6. What _____ tell me about this man?

   A. can you   C. they will

   B. she must   D. have they

7. I don't know _____ he will come to the party tonight.

   A. where   C. which one

   B. whether   D. what

8. Robert finally learned what _____ in her diary.

   A. wrote Maria   C. the women noted

   B. Laura was writing   D. printed the girl

9. _____ do they expect the storm to be over?

   A. Whatever   C. How often

   B. Who   D. When

10. Calm _____. You have to stop crying.

   A. yourself   C. themselves

   B. it   D. whom

chapter 8

Auxiliary Verbs

In this chapter you will encounter a variety of auxiliary verbs and will learn how they are used to alter the tense or meaning of an accompanying verb.

CHAPTER OBJECTIVES

In this chapter you will learn about:

- Auxiliary verbs that change the tense of a verb
- Auxiliary verbs that change the meaning of a verb
- Auxiliary verbs that have more than one form
- The function of auxiliary verbs in statements and questions

Auxiliary verbs accompany other verbs. These verbs have two main purposes: to change the tense of the accompanying verb or to alter the meaning of the accompanying verb. A few auxiliary verbs can stand alone in a sentence and act transitively or as linking verbs. Three such verbs are **be**, **do**, and **have**. When a conjugational form of **be** stands alone in a sentence, it means *exist* or *live*. It can occur in any tense. For example:

Present complete: You are helpful.
Present incomplete: You are being helpful.
Past complete: You were helpful.
Past incomplete: You were being helpful.
Present perfect: You have been helpful.

Past perfect: You had been helpful.
Future: You will be helpful.
Future perfect: You will have been helpful.

As pointed out in Chapter 4, when the future or future perfect contains a string of verbs, such as occurs in the *incomplete future*, that tense is avoided because of the awkwardness of the resulting construction.

As an auxiliary, **be** accompanies present participles. This pairing forms the tenses that imply an incomplete action or one in progress. **Be** is the verb that is conjugated in the various tenses. The present participle does not change. For example:

Present: I am baking a cake.
Past: I was baking a cake.
Present perfect: I have been baking a cake.
Past perfect: I had been baking a cake.
Future: I will be baking a cake.
Future perfect: I will have been baking a cake.

See Chapter 3 for a review of the verb forms that imply an incomplete action or one in progress.

Oral Practice

Read each sentence aloud, paying attention to the meaning and function of the verb **be**.

I was out of the country during the millennium celebration.
Bill said that someone was tampering with this lock.
His two older sisters were both lawyers.
We were painting the garage white, but Mr. Kelly said he wanted yellow.
Maria has been my friend ever since she moved to Dallas.
Jim has been working on that car for two weeks.
My son will be an astronaut someday.
My parents will be staying at a motel on Highway 89.

Written Practice 8-1

Reword each completed sentence, using the three other tenses, as indicated.

1. Present: I am not careless with my tools.

   Past: _____

   Present perfect: _____

   Future: _____

2. Present: _____

   Past: Raj was writing an essay on climate change.

   Present perfect: _____

   Future: _____

3. Present: _____

   Past: _____

   Present perfect: Has she been spending time in Poland?

   Future: _____

4. Present: _____

   Past: _____

   Present perfect: _____

   Future: The lawyers will not be at the meeting.

5. Present: We are roasting a turkey for Thanksgiving dinner.

   Past: _____

   Present perfect: _____

   Future: _____

The Verb *Have*

The verb **have** can stand alone and act as a transitive verb. In that form it means *possess, own,* or *be in control of.* And when **have** is used to indicate that someone is taking part in an event, it has both habitual and incomplete conjugational forms. If it signifies that someone possesses something, it is only conjugated in the habitual form. For example:

An Event	Possession
Present complete: We have a meeting.	We have the car.
Present incomplete: We are having a meeting.	
Past complete: We had a meeting.	We had the car.
Past incomplete: We were having a meeting.	
Present perfect: We have had a meeting.	We have had the car.
Present perfect incomplete: We have been having a meeting.	
Past perfect complete: We had had a meeting.	We had had the car.
Past perfect incomplete: We had been having a meeting.	
Future complete: We will have a meeting.	We will have the car.
Future incomplete: We will be having a meeting.	
Future perfect: You will have been helpful.	We will have had the car.

As an auxiliary, **have** introduces a past participle to form the perfect tenses. For example:

Present perfect complete: She has read a book.
Present perfect incomplete: She has been reading a book.
Past perfect complete: She had read a book.
Past perfect incomplete: She had been reading a book.
Future complete: She will read a book.
Future incomplete: She will be reading a book.
Future perfect: She will have read a book.

Oral Practice

Read each sentence aloud, paying attention to the meaning and function of the verb **have**.

I have enough money to buy us both lunch.
They have been talking about taking a vacation this summer.
My aunt has had a serious operation.
We have finally arrived in Paris, France.
Dora had only a few minutes to catch the next bus.

As a child, Tom had broken his right arm twice.

The Joneses will be having an anniversary party soon.

By noon, I will have finished writing my essay.

Written Practice 8-2

Reword each completed sentence, using the three other tenses, as indicated.

1. Present: The bride has a new wardrobe.

   Past: _____

   Present perfect: _____

   Future: _____

2. Present: _____

   Past: My girlfriend brought soda for the picnic.

   Present perfect: _____

   Future: _____

3. Present: _____

   Past: _____

   Present perfect: I have been having parties all winter.

   Future: _____

4. Present: _____

   Past: _____

   Present perfect: Has he been singing in the opera chorus?

   Future: _____

5. Present: It becomes cold every evening.

   Past: _____

   Present perfect: _____

   Future: _____

The Verb *Do*

The verb **do** can stand alone as a transitive verb. When it does, it means *bring to completion, finish,* or *make.* It can be conjugated in all tenses, and it can imply a complete or habitual action or an incomplete action or one in progress. For example:

Present complete: They do their homework.
Present incomplete: They are doing their homework.
Past complete: They did their homework.
Past incomplete: They were doing their homework.
Present perfect complete: They have done their homework.
Present perfect incomplete: They have been doing their homework.
Past perfect complete: They had done their homework.
Past perfect incomplete: They had been doing their homework.
Future complete: They will do their homework.
Future incomplete: They will be doing their homework.
Future perfect: They will have done their homework.

As an auxiliary, **do** introduces the verb in an emphatic response (see Chapter 3 to review emphatic responses) in the present or past tense, or it introduces a sentence that is a question in the present or past tense. For example:

Statement	Emphatic Response
You drive too fast.	I **do** not drive too fast.
She has no coat on.	She **does** have a coat on.
That boy broke a window.	That boy **did** not break a window.

Statement	Question
He has only ten dollars.	**Does** he have only ten dollars?
I needed to get to the airport fast.	**Did** you need to get to the airport fast?
It gets very hot in summer.	**Does** it get very hot in summer?
The children slept the night through.	**Did** the children sleep the night through?

Use **do** to negate most verbs in the present or past tense. For example:

Positive	Negative
She has too much work.	She **does** not have too much work.
Mark took my best pen.	Mark **did** not take your best pen.
The ladies hurried to the elevator.	The ladies **did** not hurry to the elevator.
The dog shakes the water from his coat.	The dog **does** not shake the water from his coat.

Oral Practice

🔘 Track 29

Read each sentence aloud, paying attention to the use of **be**, **have**, and **do**.

> The children were lining up to go out for recess.
> How long have you had that old dog?
> You do not have the right to speak to me like that.
> Jack has been in the navy for three years.
> I will be having a birthday party for Maria.
> Did you really like the ballet last night?
> They lost their house and have been living in their car.
> Her parents have grown tired of supporting her.
> I usually do my chores as soon as I get home from work.

Written Practice 8-3

Reword each numbered sentence, using the tenses indicated.

1. Present: What do you do most evenings?

    Past: _____

    Present perfect: _____

    Future: _____

2. Present: _____

    Past: Did you take the subway to work?

    Present perfect: _____

    Future: _____

3. Present: _____

    Past: _____

    Present perfect: _____

    Future: I will be doing charity work at the hospital.

4. Present: Tom does not like broccoli.

    Past: _____

    Present perfect: _____

    Future: _____

5. Present: _____

Past: John did a drawing of our cats.

Present perfect: _____

Future: _____

TAKE NOTE *The auxiliary verbs* **be, have,** *and* **do** *can be used in an* **elliptical response** *to a question. An elliptical response is one in which the auxiliary stands alone, and the meaning of the response is understood. For example:*

Are you an American?	Yes, I **am.**
Was that man rude to you?	No, he **was** not.
Have you found your passport?	Yes, I **have.**
Has she been here before?	No, she **has** not.
Does your mother live here?	Yes, she **does.**
Did it rain yesterday?	No, it **did** not.

Modal Auxiliaries

You first encountered the conjugations of the modal auxiliaries in Chapters 3 and 4. In this chapter, you will put those auxiliaries to work in a variety of sentences. Three of the auxiliaries have a partner verb with the same meaning or one that is similar. These partner verbs are used to form tenses other than the present tense because some auxiliaries cannot be used in all the tenses. It was pointed out in Chapter 4 that some tense forms exist with the auxiliaries but are not used because they sound awkward.

The three verbs that have partner verbs are **be able to**, **be supposed to**, and **have to**. Their partner verbs are **can**, **should**, and **must**, respectively. Let's look at their conjugation with the verb **work**.

	Be Able to/Can
Present:	He is able to work./He can work.
Past:	He was able to work./He could work.
Present perfect:	He has been able to work./NA
Future:	He will be able to work./NA

	Be Supposed to/Should
Present:	I am supposed to work./I should work.
Past:	I was supposed to work./NA

| Present perfect: | (*This tense sounds awkward.*/NA) |
| Future: | (*This tense sounds awkward.*/NA) |

Have to/Must

Present:	We have to work./We must work.
Past:	We had to work.
Present perfect:	We have had to work.
Future:	We will have to work.

The auxiliaries **ought to** and **may** are used only in the present tense. The auxiliary **might** is the past tense and subjunctive of **may** but is used as if in the present tense.

The modal auxiliaries alter the meaning of an accompanying verb by describing the degree of *obligation, ability,* or *desire* associated with the subject. For example:

I **have to** leave./I **must** leave. = strong obligation
I **am supposed to** leave./I **should** leave. = some obligation
I **ought to** leave. = some obligation
I **need to** leave. = cause for some obligation
I **may** leave. = a possibility, having permission
I **might** leave. = less of a possibility
I **am able to** leave./I **can** leave. = unrestrained or having ability
I **want** to leave. = desire

Oral Practice

🔘 Track 30

Read each sentence aloud, paying attention to the use of the modal auxiliaries and to the degree of obligation, ability, or desire.

You must finally get to work and finish repairing the car.
Who is supposed to clean the kitchen today?
I have always wanted to travel to the United Kingdom.
In a few days, you will be able to use your left arm again.
Someone ought to show Mr. Jackson how to start the lawn mower.
My father said I may use the car tonight.
That might not be a very good idea.
When you are in Spain, you should visit Barcelona.
Ms. Lee will have to stay in Mexico another few days.
Are you supposed to use that tool like that?

Written Practice 8-4

Reword each sentence with the auxiliary provided in parentheses. Retain the tense of the original sentence.

1. The tour guide spoke about the unusual painting.

   (want to) _____

   (be supposed to) _____

2. We are going home now.

   (have to) _____

   (should) _____

3. Maria will help you tomorrow.

   (be able to) _____

   (need to) _____

4. It rains every day in the spring.

   (might) _____

   (can) _____

5. Does she borrow money from you?

   (may) _____

   (be able to) _____

6. I escort the woman down the street.

   (ought to) _____

   (need to) _____

7. Why do you always argue with me?

   (must) _____

   (want to) _____

8. You will show your passport at immigration.

   (have to) _____

   (need to) _____

9. Daniel has juggled for a long time.

(be able to) _____

(want to) _____

10. No one is here.

(be supposed to) _____

(can) _____

IDIOMS DEMYSTIFIED

Some idioms contain the auxiliaries in this chapter that can stand alone in a sentence (**be, do, have**) and can be used with a variety of idioms. The verb **be**, for example, can introduce this idiom:

Be a chip off the old block = *the son is like the father* (*rarely about a daughter*)
Jack is good-looking. He's a chip off the old block.

The verb **do** is often used in certain idioms as well. For example:

Do without = *endure being without someone or something*
The wealthy woman cannot do without luxuries.

The verb **have** is found in numerous idioms. Two examples involve the blues and a bone.

Have the blues = *feel sadness or be depressed*
Maria has the blues about the fight she had with her husband.

Have a bone to pick with someone = *being upset and needing to talk about what the other person has done*
Jean has a bone to pick with him about the lies he told.

Any variety of auxiliaries can be attached to an idiom to change its meaning slightly.

Cope with = *handle a person or problem with difficulty*
I can't cope with your lies anymore.
Tom doesn't want to cope with another winter in Alaska.

Modal Auxiliaries plus *Have*

Some of the modal auxiliaries form a special tense that is composed of *the auxiliary plus **have** plus **a past participle***. This structure occurs commonly with the auxiliaries **must, may, need to, have to, want to,** and **supposed to**.

First let's look at **must**, which in this form has two meanings. Compare the following pair of sentences that describe the same action but result in a slight difference of meaning.

> You **must wash** the dishes before I get home. = *This action (wash) is an obligation to be discharged "before I get home."*

> You **must have washed** the dishes before I got home. = *This action (have washed) is an obligation that has to have been performed in the past, that is "before I got home."*

Now notice the change in meaning when the final clause is omitted. **Must have** has a new meaning.

> You **must have washed** the dishes. = ***Must** does not mean obligation. Instead, someone assumes that you have washed the dishes.*

Let's look at two more pairs of sentences that have a final clause or prepositional phrase and one that does not. Consider how the meaning of each sentence differs.

> They **must find** their passports before boarding the plane.
> They **must have found** their passports before boarding the plane.
> They **must have found** their passports.
> John **must finish** the project by the end of the day.
> John **must have finished** the project by the end of the day.
> John **must have finished** the project.

Oral Practice

Read each sentence aloud, paying attention to the meaning of the verb phrases.

> Someone must have found my wallet.
> My sister must return to work before noon.
> You must have gotten all the documents signed before the end of the meeting.

Jim must hide the map before the pirates return.

If I want my deposit back, I must have returned the car in good condition.

Mother must have made vegetable soup for lunch.

We must send in a payment before the last day of the month.

I must have sent in a payment already.

The other modal auxiliaries use the same structure (*the auxiliary* plus **have** plus *a past participle*), but do not have three forms and have only one meaning. For example:

He **may have broken** his leg. = *It appears that he broke his leg.*

You **may have found** the treasure. = *It appears that you found the treasure.*

I **need to have spent** less time in Las Vegas. = *It would have been wise to have spent less time in Las Vegas.*

You **need to have developed** more skills before you can get the job. = *It would have been wise to develop more skills before you interviewed for the job.*

She **wants to have visited** Asia before she turns thirty. = *Her goal is to visit Asia before she turns thirty.*

We **want to have found** a nice apartment before we move to New York. = *Our goal is to find a nice apartment before we move to New York.*

The lawyer **has to have shown** proof of bail before the judge can release his client. = *The lawyer is obliged to show proof of bail before the judge can release his client.*

They **have to have paid** off all debts before getting a new loan. = *They are obliged to pay off all debts before getting a new loan.*

You **were supposed to have completed** the project by June. = *It was assumed that you would complete the project by June.*

The man **is supposed to be released** from prison soon. = *It is assumed that the man will be released from prison soon.*

In many cases, a clause is attached to a sentence with auxiliaries in this structure to show the *time limit* that is required to carry out the action of the verb.

An Action to Be Carried Out	Time Limit
You must have made the final payment	before I deliver the refrigerator.
Raj wants to have become a citizen	by the time his parents come to visit.
You need to have shown more maturity	before I give you the keys to the car.

Oral Practice

🔘 Track 31

Read each sentence aloud, paying attention to the modal auxiliaries and the meaning of the verbs.

My son may have broken a window in your garage.
We were supposed to have arrived in London before seven o'clock.
Brian wants to have earned his degree before he gets married.
All visitors have to have checked their bags before entering the museum.
I need to have cleaned the entire house by suppertime.
I think you may have discovered a new species.
You were supposed to have filled out the application by now.
I wanted to have been here for dinner, but I got lost.
You had to have received a flu shot before joining the army.
You must have forgotten about the meeting.

QUIZ

Choose the letter of the word or phrase that best completes each sentence.

1. Why do I _____ to be the one to sweep the basement?
   A. wanted   C. can
   B. must   D. have

2. _____ he supposed to arrive here on the afternoon train?
   A. Is able   C. Does
   B. Was   D. Has

3. They _____ arrived home by this time tomorrow.
   A. will have   C. have
   B. shall   D. had

4. _____ you enjoy living in the country?
   A. Do   C. Are able
   B. Have   D. Was supposed to

5. I _____ time enough to catch only the last train.

   A. had   C. are having

   B. have gone   D. had been

6. Laura _____ writing letters to friends in Mexico when Richard arrived.

   A. will be   C. is

   B. had been   D. can be

7. _____ it snow a lot last year?

   A. Does   C. Did

   B. Was able to   D. Can

8. Someone will _____ fix the car by Saturday.

   A. want   C. need to

   B. able to   D. supposed to

9. Mr. Jackson _____ been unreasonable again.

   A. is   C. may have

   B. having   D. does

10. You _____ cope with the reality of your debts.

   A. want   C. are able

   B. have to   D. are

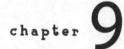

chapter **9**

Contractions and Plurals

This chapter discusses the formation and use of contractions and introduces regular and irregular plural formations.

CHAPTER OBJECTIVES

In this chapter you will learn about:

- How verbs are made into contractions
- How **not** is made into a contraction
- The peculiarities of verbal contractions
- The formation of regular plurals
- The formation of irregular plurals

Contractions

A contraction is a word that is composed of two words by omitting a portion of one of the words and replacing it with an apostrophe. It is always the second word in the combination that is contracted, or shortened.

The Verb *Be*

Many contractions are formed from pronouns combined with a present tense conjugation of **be**. For example:

Present Tense	Contraction
I am	I'm
you are	you're
he is	he's
she is	she's
it is	it's
we are	we're
you *pl.* are	you're
they are	they're
one is	one's
who is	who's
what is	what's

Oral Practice

Read each pair of sentences aloud, paying attention to the use of the contractions.

I am very tired today. I'm tired today.
You are a good friend. You're a good friend.
She is always right. She's always right.
It is hot in here. It's hot in here.
We are finally alone. We're finally alone.
They are not nice. They're not nice.
Who is the man at our front door? Who's the man at our front door?
What is that supposed to mean? What's that supposed to mean?

Using *Be* in Questions

The verb **be** can be contracted with pronouns in statements. In questions, the full verb must be used.

I'm in the right room.	We're still in the city.
Am I in the right room?	**Are** we still in the city?
He's very smart.	
Is he very smart?	

Because **who** and **what** introduce questions, they can be used with contractions of **be** at all times.

Who's on vacation this week?
What's she found in the drawer?

Contractions are not formed from the past tense of **be**. No contracted form exists for any of the following examples.

I **was** very skeptical.	We **were** poorly informed.
Were you skeptical?	**Were** we poorly informed?
She **was** my neighbor.	
Was she your neighbor?	

When the present tense of **be** is the auxiliary of a present participle (*an incomplete action or one in progress*), it can still form a contraction.

I'm working on my car.
You're having a lot of fun.
He's spending too much money.
We're taking a coffee break.
They're learning about American history.
Who's helping with the dishes tonight?

When **be** is part of a modal auxiliary, it can still form a contraction.

Be Supposed to	Be Able to
I'm supposed to	he's able to
you're supposed to	we're able to
she's supposed to	who's able to

Written Practice 9-1

In the following sentences, use the verb **be** as a contraction wherever possible. If a contraction is not possible, leave the sentence as it is.

1. We are driving through a beautiful forest.

   _____

2. I am very pleased with your behavior.

   _____

3. Who is that beautiful woman in the living room?

_____

4. Are you from Mexico or Cuba?

_____

5. What is Mary carrying under her arm?

_____

6. No one is allowed in the laboratory today.

_____

7. Is she an acquaintance of yours?

_____

8. He is supposed to be a great soccer player.

_____

9. They are rather silly questions.

_____

10. Am I strong enough to lift that log?

_____

11. Are you able to get around on your crutches?

_____

12. Someone is watching us from across the street.

_____

13. It is terribly windy today.

_____

14. Is it supposed to snow again tomorrow?

_____

15. They are able to pull down the old fence.

_____

Negating Be

When the adverb **not** negates the verb **be**, the adverb can form a contraction and combine with the verb. For example:

you **aren't**	we **aren't**
he **isn't**	they **aren't**
she **isn't**	who **isn't**
it **isn't**	what **isn't**

TAKE NOTE *The verb **am** no longer forms a contraction with **not**. In older usage, the verb **am** plus **not** was contracted as **ain't**, but this formation is not considered good usage today. **Ain't** is also used as a substitute for other pronouns with the verbs **is**, **are**, and **have**. For example:*

Other Verbs	Ain't
I've got it.	I **ain't** got it.
You aren't alone.	You **ain't** alone.
She hasn't seen him.	She **ain't** seen him.
It isn't fair.	It **ain't** fair.

Because you may hear this word used by native speakers, it is important to know its origin and use.

When using **be** with the adverb **not**, there is a second form of contraction that can be used. It is the contraction of the pronoun and the verb followed by **not**. For example:

I'm **not**	we're **not**
you're **not**	they're **not**
he's **not**	who's **not**

The two formations can be used interchangeably except in the case of the first person singular pronoun **I**.

I'm not/NA	we're not/we aren't
you're not/you aren't	they're not/they aren't
he's not/he isn't	what's not/what isn't

When the verb **be** forms a contraction with **not**, it can be used to introduce a question. Compare that usage with a pronoun in a contraction with **be**.

Statement	Question
I am not at home.	Am I not at home?
I'm not at home.	Am I not at home?
You aren't at home.	**Aren't** you at home?
You're not at home.	Are you not at home?
He isn't at home.	**Isn't** he at home?
He's not at home.	Is he not at home?
We aren't at home.	**Aren't** we at home?
We're not at home.	Are we not at home?

Oral Practice

🔘 Track 32

Read each sentence aloud, paying attention to the formation and usage of the contractions.

We aren't going to the zoo today.
He isn't supposed to use the boss's computer.
I'm not interested in subscribing to more magazines.
Aren't you going to get up and go to work?
Is she not the new teacher that you told me about?
Isn't it strange how often we meet here at the library?
You're absolutely correct about that.
But you're not correct when you spell the words out.
And you aren't correct if you think it's the same thing in other sentences.
He's probably the fittest boy in gym class.
She isn't going out with him anymore.

The Verbs Do and Did

Whether **do** or **did** is used as a transitive verb or as an auxiliary, each one can be formed as a contraction with **not**: **don't, doesn't, didn't**. First, let's look at a few sentences where **do/does/did** is used as a transitive verb.

Positive	Negative
I do my chores.	I **don't** do my chores.
She does the laundry.	She **doesn't** do the laundry.
We did our homework.	We **didn't** do our homework.

In the negative sentences provided above, the transitive verb **do** is introduced by the auxiliary **don't/doesn't/didn't**. Remember that to negate most verbs, you must use a form of **don't**.

Positive	Negative
I like this song.	I **don't** like this song.
He keeps the letter.	He **doesn't** keep the letter.
We prepare lunch.	We **don't** prepare lunch.

The contraction **don't/doesn't/didn't** can be used to introduce questions. For example:

Don't you enjoy opera?
Doesn't it seem chilly in here?
Didn't they play well today?

Written Practice 9-2

Negate each sentence with **don't/doesn't/didn't** and then reword the sentence as a question. For example:

You speak Spanish.

You don't speak Spanish.

Don't you speak Spanish?

1. We developed a new programming language.

_____

_____

2. I know you.

_____

_____

3. Indira forgot her purse again.

_____

_____

4. We spell the words correctly.

_____

_____

5. Someone locked the door.

_____

6. She starts each day with a good breakfast.

_____

7. You danced with the two foreigners.

_____

_____

8. We belong to the same organization.

_____

_____

9. It snowed.

_____

_____

10. They tricked him again.

_____

_____

Singular Nouns with Be

Singular nouns can form contractions with **be**. Since all singular nouns are third person singular, all combine with **is**. Let's look at some examples.

John's a good friend of mine.
The girl's working on an essay.
The garden's looking very good right now.

You will hear plural nouns combined with **are** in a contraction but only in casual speech. In writing, such contractions look strange, and in speech they sound like careless language.

The **boys're** behind the garage.
The **animals're** getting restless.

Plural nouns contracted with **are** should be avoided.

Certain other pronoun types can also form contractions with **be**. For example:

Nothing's going on between us.
Anything's possible.
I'll do **whatever's** necessary.
Somebody's being naughty.
Everybody's helping the elderly couple.
Whoever's involved will certainly be in hot water.

The Auxiliary *Have*

The auxiliary **have** can be used as a transitive verb or as the auxiliary for the perfect tenses. In either case, it can be contracted in both the present and past tenses when combined with pronouns. However, with nouns it tends to contract only with singular nouns. Let's look at some examples.

I've a lot of time on my hands.
You've had a difficult day.
He's/She's been ill for a while.
It's turned out to be a fine day.
We've got a long time to wait yet.
They've lost their passports.
Mary's seen every one of Brad Pitt's movies.
My **sister's** got a cold.

Still Struggling

Because **he's, she's,** and **it's** form the same contraction with **has** and **is**, it is only by context that the difference in meaning can be understood.

He's been in a meeting. (He has been = present perfect tense)
He's no time for this. (He has = transitive verb)
He's working from home. (He is working = action in progress)
He's my best friend. (He is = present tense of **be**)

When **have** is in the past tense (**had**), the contraction is -**'d**, but contractions are not formed with nouns and **had** as a transitive verb is not used. For example:

I'd never been in England before.
We'd already seen that movie.
She'd worked for Dr. Meyer in the past.

When **have** is negated, it can form a contraction with the pronoun or with the adverb **not**, just like the verb **be**. If **have** is used as a transitive verb, the **have** is contracted with the pronoun and is followed by **no** and a direct object noun. Or **have** can be contracted with **not** and is followed by **any** and a direct object noun. For example:

We've not heard a lot about you.
We haven't heard a lot about you.
He's not been in Europe.
He hasn't been in Europe.
I'd no money left.
I hadn't any money left.
She's no right to be in my office.
She hasn't any right to be in my office.

Oral Practice

Read each sentence aloud, paying attention to the kind of contraction that is used.

I don't have any time to go into this problem right now.
Haven't you and your wife visited the new art exhibit yet?
Mr. Lee hasn't found a job in Phoenix.
Their two daughters hadn't been to a ballet until tonight.
We'd have invited you to the party but didn't know you were in town.
Someone's been using my new digital camera.
What's on television tonight?
What's your son been working on in the garage?

Other Auxiliaries

The auxiliaries **shall** and **will** can be contracted with pronouns as **I'll**, **you'll**, **they'll**, and so on. They can be negated as contractions as **shan't** and **won't**. There is a tendency among North American speakers of English to use **won't** over **shan't**. For example:

I'll see you next week at work.
I **won't** bother to phone you until morning.
You'll probably get a letter from her soon.
You **won't** recognize her when you see her.
Hopefully, **it'll** rain soon.
It **won't** rain again until spring.
We **won't** be able to attend the concert.

Can, **could**, **must**, and **should** do not form contractions with pronouns. They can, however, be combined in a contraction with **not**.

I **can't** understand you.
We **couldn't** find our way out of the building.
Joe **mustn't** worry so much.
Shouldn't the girls be home by now?

The auxiliary **would** forms a contraction with pronouns and is also combined in a contraction with **not**.

I'd like to order soup and a sandwich, please.
Wouldn't you like to sit down for a while?

The contracted forms of **would** and **had** are identical. To understand the intent of the speaker or writer, you must consider the context.

He'd like to stay home. (He would = auxiliary plus infinitive)
He'd been ill recently. (He had = auxiliary plus past participle)

Since a verb can begin a question, a verb combined with the contracted form of **not** can introduce a question.

Couldn't you find your glasses?
Won't she be able come to our party?
Mustn't they check their luggage?
Shouldn't someone help that poor man?

Oral Practice

🔘 Track 33

Read each sentence aloud, paying attention to the formation and usage of the contractions.

> Derek: I just can't make up my mind which sweater won't look bad on me.
>
> Anita: You shouldn't worry. You always look good, and you'll look good in the blue one.
>
> Derek: Who's coming to the dance with Laura? Or isn't she going?
>
> Anita: She'll probably go with Steve. She's been seeing him since March.
>
> Derek: I don't know why she wouldn't go out with my brother.
>
> Anita: That's funny. A girl couldn't dance with a man so much shorter than her.
>
> Derek: You mustn't make fun of him. He's very sensitive.
>
> Anita: I'd like him more if he weren't so shy.
>
> Derek: You'll see at the dance that he's not shy at all.
>
> Anita: He'll be there? Wasn't he supposed to fly to Seattle?
>
> Derek: He wouldn't miss that dance for anything.

Written Practice 9-3

Reword each sentence in the negative by combining the verb in a contraction with not.

1. We would prefer to sit outside.

   _____

2. I will drive you to work every day.

   _____

3. He can stay in a hotel.

   _____

4. She has time.

   _____

5. They must stay in the basement.

   _____

6. Laura should dress for a business meeting.

   _____

7. Tom had spent a lot of time in the library.

_____

8. We have been to Pakistan twice.

_____

9. This part of the audience can see the stage.

_____

10. Who has seen that movie?

_____

Plurals

Most English plurals are quite easy to form. They are formed by either the ending **-s** or **-es**. Use **-s** unless the noun ends in a consonant followed by **-y**. Then change the **-y** to an **-i**. For example:

Singular	Plural
book	books
table	tables
boy	boys
day	days
city	cities
factory	factories

If a noun ends in a sibilant sound or similar (**s, ss, z, sh, ch, j, x**), the plural ending becomes **-es**.

Singular	Plural
gas	gases
pass	passes
buzz	buzzes
bush	bushes
watch	watches
fox	foxes

A few nouns are only used in the plural. For example:

Where are my pants?
The scissors were lying on the table.

Tom's trousers are awfully dirty.
The woods look dangerous to me.
The old barracks don't look very comfortable.

Other nouns tend to be used only in the singular. This is particularly notice-able among words that are collective, or noncount, nouns such as: **time, salt, evidence, cowardice,** and **justice.**

Written Practice 9-4

Write each noun in the plural.

1. coat   _____

2. nose   _____

3. worry   _____

4. banker   _____

5. necktie   _____

6. belly   _____

7. kiss   _____

8. march   _____

9. dish   _____

10. cherry   _____

Numbers in the Plural

There is often confusion about writing a number in the plural. The decade that preceded the start of the twentieth century was the **1890s.** This is a plu-ral. No apostrophe is required. However, if a year is clearly a possessive, then an apostrophe plus s should be used: **President Grover Cleveland opened 1893's Columbian Exposition in Chicago.** And if a year or a decade is used in abbreviated form, an apostrophe *precedes* the number: **The '20s were my grandmother's favorite era.**

The plural of other numbers that are an accepted concept is also formed by the ending -s:

I didn't get my W2s.
We're sending out the 1099s today.

TAKE NOTE *There are several* pat phrases *that are composed of a variety of* grammatical elements but that are treated as nouns. When made plural, they end in -s.

dos and don'ts	**thank yous**
ifs, ands, or buts	**yeses and nos**

Nouns That End in *f* and *o*

Some nouns that end in **f** form their plural with the ending **-es** but make an additional change: the letter **f** changes to **v** when the plural ending is added. For example:

Singular	Plural
elf	elves
hoof	hooves
knife	knives
leaf	leaves
life	lives
yourself *s.*	yourselves *pl.*

The nouns **roof** and **dwarf** form the plural by just adding **-s**: **roofs, dwarfs**.

The formation of the plural of nouns that end in **o** is not always clear. Some form the plural with **-s**, others with **-es**, and still others with either **-s** or **-es**. Let's look at some commonly used nouns that end in **o** and their plural formation.

Singular	Plural
auto	autos
cargo	cargoes
echo	echoes
hero	heroes
memo	memos
mosquito	mosquitos/mosquitoes
motto	mottos
oratorio	oratorios
piano	pianos
potato	potatoes
ratio	ratios
solo	solos
tomato	tomatoes
tornado	tornados/tornadoes
torpedo	torpedos/torpedoes
veto	vetoes

TAKE NOTE *An s is used to form the plural of certain nouns that regularly appear as letters. For example:* **URLs, BAs, MAs, PhDs, IQs, SATs.**

Oral Practice

Read each sentence aloud, paying attention to the plural form of nouns.

Where are the leaves to these two tables?
Use good manners and try to learn the dos and don'ts of your workplace.
The quizzes for the next two semesters are in those boxes.
If you control yourselves, you'll get a couple surprises tomorrow.
Before the holidays, Santa's elves help him make toys.
During the 1950s, before they were married, my future parents lived in the suburbs and attended the same schools.
The graduate students receive their PhDs at the start of the ceremonies.
I have few worries and count my blessings and look forward to more happy days.

Foreign Words in the Plural

The noun **solo** is an Italian word, but most speakers of English say **solos**. In Italian, however, many plurals are formed by changing **o** to **i**. For example, the plural of **solo** in Italian is **soli**. Today the Italian plural is used primarily by those in the classical music industry. The Italian word **paparazzi** (from the singular **paparazzo**) is a plural and is used in English as a plural.

The paparazzi have been following the rock star for hours.

However, the plural noun **graffiti** (from the singular **graffito**) is used in English as a singular.

The graffiti on this wall looks awful.

Foreign words that come from Latin or Greek usually retain the plural of the original language. However, a few words that have come to be accepted as part of the culture of the English-speaking world can form their plural with -s. The following examples show plurals of Latin and Greek words formed by means of both rules. There are, however, exceptions in modern usage; some of these are given after this list.

Singular	Plural
datum	data
gymnasium	gymnasiums
medium	media
cactus	cacti/cactuses
crocus	crocuses
fungus	fungi
nucleus	nuclei
syllabus	syllabi/syllabuses
alumnus *m.*	alumni
alumna *f.*	alumnae
appendix	appendixes/appendices
index	indexes/indices
criterion	criteria
phenomenon	phenomena

The plural nouns **data** and **media** are used a great deal in this technological age. Both words are commonly used and accepted as singular nouns, even though in Latin they are the plural forms (of **datum** and **medium**, respectively).

The data from the experiment is not yet available.
Is the American media biased?

The Latin word **opus** (*literary or musical work*) is frequently used in English. Its plural is **opera**, but when English speakers use the plural noun, it is used as if it were a *singular noun* and means a *musical form of drama*.

Beethoven's only opera is called *Fidelio*.

Irregular Plurals

There is a short list of nouns that form their plural in an irregular way. Many of these nouns are in reality the remnant of the standard plural forms of the Anglo-Saxon language brought to England in ancient times.

Singular	Plural
child	children
deer	deer
fish	fish (also fishes)
goose	geese
man	men

mouse	mice
ox	oxen
person	people
tooth	teeth
woman	women

The nouns that end in **-is** form their plural by changing **-is** to **-es**. For example:

crisis	crises
analysis	analyses
basis	bases
thesis	theses

Oral Practice

Track 34

Restate each sentence by changing the singular nouns to the plural form. Make any other appropriate changes. Then listen to the revised sentence, and repeat it.

The man was walking through a field when he noticed a deer in the woods.

The child screamed for his parent and lay bellowing on his bed.

The ox grazed along the edge of the pond and enjoyed the succulent grass.

Please put salt, the potato, and the tomato in the pot and boil the water.

The woman is an alumna of the state university.

A Canadian goose landed near the little lake to feed the goslings hidden nearby.

The angry witch swatted her broom at the mouse that lived in the shoebox.

The girl broke her tooth on the hard, green apple.

Our hero took a knife and cut a hole in the side of the tent.

Written Practice 9-5

Give the plural of each singular noun and the singular of each plural noun.

Noun	Plural or Singular
1. alumnus/alumna	_____
2. cargo	_____
3. crises	_____

4. scissors _____

5. barber _____

6. watches _____

7. sanitarium _____

8. deer _____

9. parenthesis _____

10. foremen _____

11. ID _____

12. foci _____

13. '80s _____

14. scholar _____

15. veto _____

IDIOMS DEMYSTIFIED

A few idioms have plural nouns in them and cannot be used with singular nouns. For example:

1. **be on pins and needles** or **sit on pins and needles** = *be apprehensive about the outcome of something.*
   I was on pins and needles waiting for my test results. We sat on pins and needles before our boss announced who got the promotion.

2. **know the ropes** = *have the proper training* or *be familiar with procedures.*
   Jack got the job because he knew the ropes.
   She needed help. She didn't know the ropes yet.

3. **put on airs** = *pretend to be better than someone is* or *act conceited.*
   Don't put on airs. You're an average man like the rest of us.
   Driving a fancy car is just putting on airs.

TAKE NOTE *A few words that end in -s can be singular or plural. Two examples are **economics** and **politics**. When these words refer to a concept or topic, they are used without an article and are singular.*

Economics is my favorite subject.
Politics sometimes gets in the way of justice.

When modified by a determiner, such words are considered plural nouns. For example:

The economics of the time demand our immediate attention.
His politics are beyond my comprehension.

QUIZ

Choose the letter of the word or phrase that best completes each sentence.

1. **One of the girls _____ feel well today.**
   A. weren't   C. wasn't
   B. don't   D. doesn't

2. **The oxen _____ supposed to graze in this field.**
   A. aren't   C. will not
   B. wasn't   D. won't

3. **I'd _____ enough bread and was stuffed.**
   A. want   C. had
   B. be able to   D. need

4. **I wish the new man knew _____ better.**
   A. could work   C. mustn't
   B. themselves   D. the ropes

5. **Your politics _____ yet become a problem for our party.**
   A. doesn't   C. wasn't
   B. haven't   D. weren't

6. **Each _____ received an invitation to the ceremony.**
   A. alumnus   C. firemen
   B. alumnae   D. freshmen

7. **_____ weren't able to get here in time.**
   A. A family   C. Whose team
   B. Some faculty members D. Anybody

8. I saw frightened _____ near the side of the road.

   A. goose   C. child

   B. ox   D. deer

9. There are _____ at the end of the book.

   A. three appendixes   C. picture of the fish

   B. a long index of names   D. a list

10. You haven't _____ right to criticize me.

    A. no   C. neither

    B. yourselves   D. any

chapter **10**

Infinitives and Gerunds

Two new verb forms are considered in this chapter: infinitives and gerunds. Both forms are *verbals*. The chapter explains how they differ from verbs and illustrates their function in sentences.

CHAPTER OBJECTIVES

In this chapter you will learn about:

- The difference between verbs in conjugations and verbs used as verbals
- How infinitives are used
- How gerunds are used
- How infinitives and gerunds are used in the same way

Infinitives

You have been using infinitives in many ways throughout this book. English infinitives can occur as a single verb form or in combination with the particle word **to**. For example:

be	to be
have	to have
sing	to sing
want	to want

When the infinitive is preceded by certain auxiliaries, the particle word **to** is not used.

I shall **go** by train.
You must **control** yourself better.
Can she **understand** English?
No one should **put** on airs.

With other auxiliaries, the particle word **to** accompanies the infinitive.

We want **to spend** the night in a motel.
Are you supposed **to clean** the kitchen?
Someone needs **to explain** the rules to him.
I'm not able **to join** you for dinner.

It is the infinitive form with the particle word **to** that can act as a verbal. A verbal is a part of speech that is derived from a verb but can act as a noun, an adverb, or an adjective. Let's look at some infinitives that are used as nouns.

Subject of the Sentence
To own a sports car has always been his wish. (*To own* is the subject of *has*.)
To leave early would have been rude. (*To leave* is the subject of *would*.)

Adverb
We dropped by **to say** hello. (Why did we drop by?)
She borrowed some money **to pay** her rent. (Why did she borrow some money?)

Adjective
I think this is the house **to buy**. (*To buy* modifies *house*.)
Ms. Kelly is not a woman **to trust**. (*To trust* modifies *woman*.)

In the case of infinitives used as adjectives, note that the infinitive is a shortened version of a relative clause. The previous examples with relative clauses in place of the infinitive would be:

I think this is the house **that you should buy.**
Robert became a man **that all people should admire.**
Ms. Kelly is not a woman **that you should trust.**

To ensure that you are using an infinitive as an adjective, test the sentence by changing the infinitive to a relative clause. If the change makes sense, the infinitive is an adjective.

When an infinitive is used as a noun, adverb, or adjective, it can be followed by a verb and a predicate. That entire phrase is an *infinitive phrase* and can function like other infinitives.

To leave would be rude.
To leave early with the people I just met would be rude.
Ms. Kelly is not a woman **to trust.**
Ms. Kelly is not a woman **to trust with this kind of secret.**

Oral Practice

Read each sentence aloud, paying attention to the use of the infinitives as nouns, adverbs, or adjectives.

I found a nice gift to give to my boyfriend.
To smoke so much is very hazardous to one's health.
I brought my son along to help carry the dresser out to the van.
It would be wonderful to live abroad.
She bought a pink blouse to go with her black skirt.
Over there are two suspicious-looking men to watch.
To dream of wealth is easy, but to earn it is another thing entirely.
Aunt Laura came for a visit to meet my new wife.

Forming the Infinitive with the Progressive Form

Infinitives that can be used as nouns, adverbs, or adjectives come in more than one form. The simplest form has been illustrated above: the particle word **to** followed by a verb: **to help, to want, to say.**

Another infinitive form is composed of the particle word **to** and the progressive or ongoing form of the verb. Compare the conjugation of a progressive or ongoing verb with its infinitive form.

Progressive	Infinitive
he is speaking	to be speaking
we are talking	to be talking
she is learning	to be learning
it is raining	to be raining

This infinitive form is used just like the simple form. The difference is that the progressive infinitive implies an incomplete or ongoing action. Compare the following sentences.

To run is good exercise.
To be running in a race made Maria nervous.
To sing made her happy.
To be singing in a choir someday was her goal.
To study in Germany was his only wish.
To be studying in Germany made every day exciting.

Written Practice 10-1

Reword each sentence by changing the infinitive to a progressive infinitive. Don't hesitate to make changes to the sentence as shown in the underscored sample, paraphrasing slightly, if necessary.

To sit for so long is uncomfortable.

To be sitting so close to Mary made Jim nervous.

1. To spend time with him is what she needed.

   _____

2. To work from home was more convenient.

   _____

3. To borrow money is a bad idea.

4. To seek fame is so shallow.

_____

5. To travel with Jack makes a journey more fun.

_____

6. To converse with the governor was exciting.

_____

7. To learn English becomes her goal.

_____

8. To watch television can be boring.

_____

9. To sleep late was his worst habit.

_____

10. To shop makes me happy.

_____

Oral Practice

🔘 Track 35

Read each sentence aloud, paying attention to the kind of infinitive phrase used and its function.

To be doing research at the Library of Congress was an honor.
I need you to be on your very best behavior.
John called me to say that he was sorry about what he said.
To mock the man's accent was a horrible thing to do.
Can you stop by tomorrow to help me load the van?
Ms. Patel needs to be spending less time shopping and more time studying.
To be dancing with the famous actress was like a dream to Jim.
These are problems to be solved immediately.
To start to smoke again would be stupid.
This is a good job applicant to interview.
I believe that this nanny is the one who should be taking care of the children.
The purpose of this machine is to record all incoming messages.

Forming the Infinitive with the Perfect Form

Infinitives can be formed from a perfect tense verb. In such an infinitive, the auxiliary **have** is accompanied by the particle word **to**. For example:

Perfect Tense	Infinitive
I have met	to have met
she has taken	to have taken
we have paid	to have paid
they have listened	to have listened

It is possible to change a perfect tense infinitive to its progressive form. But care must be given not to *stuff* too many verbs into a phrase that becomes awkward. Often, the simple perfect tense will suffice. Compare the two forms. The progressive tense, which is needed far less often than the simple perfect tense, usually should be avoided. Its use is merely to emphasize the *duration* of an action.

Perfect Tense	Progressive Perfect Tense
to have smoked	to have been smoking
to have worked	to have been working
to have learned	to have been learning

Consider the following two sentences. The progressive sentence is plausible, but the change is not needed.

To have smoked for thirty years has left its mark on his health.
To have been smoking for thirty years has left its mark on his health.

Written Practice 10-2

Change each infinitive phrase to a present perfect infinitive phrase. Then create an appropriate sentence with the new phrase. For example:

to work in the same company

to *have worked in the same company*

To *have worked in the same company for years gave him great pride.*

1. to learn this difficult language _____

_____

2. to borrow money from him _____

_____

3. to travel in Mexico _____

4. to interview the famous actor _____

_____

5. to clean the floor _____

_____

6. to shovel the driveway _____

_____

7. to rush him to the hospital _____

_____

8. to follow the suspect _____

_____

9. to impress the woman _____

_____

10. to photograph the president _____

_____

Forming the Infinitive with the Passive Voice

The passive voice will be taken up in detail in Chapter 16. But the passive verb form must be mentioned here because it can be formed as an infinitive.

The passive voice consists of the conjugation of the auxiliary **be** plus a past participle. Compare that conjugation with the infinitive.

Passive Voice	Infinitive
he is punished	to be punished
we are found	to be found
she is admired	to be admired
I am rewarded	to be rewarded

The passive voice can be formed as a progressive or ongoing action, but that form sounds awkward when it's made into an infinitive. For example: **he is being punished, I am being rewarded.** The phrases would not read smoothly if changed to their infinitive forms: **to be punished, to be rewarded.**

Written Practice 10-3

Reword each passive phrase as an infinitive phrase. (It isn't necessary to create a complete sentence.) For example:

> They are located on a map.
>
> <u>to be located on a map</u>

1. The money is hidden in the garage.
   _____

2. She is struck by a wonderful idea.
   _____

3. I am surrounded by great friends.
   _____

4. The child is embraced by her mother.
   _____

5. They are being thanked for their military service.
   _____

The Passive Voice in the Perfect Tense

The passive voice can appear in a perfect tense. Just as with active voice verbs, the passive perfect tense can be changed to an infinitive. For example:

Passive Voice	Infinitive
he has been fired	to have been fired
we have been hired	to have been hired
she has been kissed	to have been kissed
it has been written	to have been written

Written Practice 10-4

Reword each perfect tense passive phrase as an infinitive phrase. (It's not necessary to create a complete sentence.) For example:

> They have been located on a map.
>
> <u>to have been located on a map</u>

1. The money has been hidden in the garage.

_____

2. I have been introduced by the host.

_____

3. We have been escorted about the museum.

_____

4. The heroes have been given medals.

_____

5. She has been elected governor.

_____

Oral Practice

Track 36

Read each sentence aloud, paying attention to the kind of infinitive phrase used and its function and meaning.

To have been selected for the committee was a great honor.
You were promoted to improve the services of this department.
Mr. Garcia is a man to be reckoned with.
To be fired for being late just once isn't fair.
To have stolen from his own father was despicable.
This is an important book, to be read by everyone in this class.
That was a mistake to be avoided.
To be living in the United States is something I take for granted.
To be tricked by that thief was the final embarrassment.

Gerunds

Gerunds are verbals that are used as nouns; they are formed like *present participles*: that is, by adding **-ing**. Gerunds tend to be used only in the singular. When used as verbs, present participles are introduced by the auxiliary **be**. Present participles, which are found in all tenses, are used to describe an action in progress or ongoing. Let's review present participles in the various tenses in the following few sentences.

IDIOMS DEMYSTIFIED

Idioms that contain verbs can often express those verbs in their infinitive form and, therefore, the idioms can be used as nouns, adverbs, or adjectives. Let's look at a few examples.

to be afraid = *to fear*
to show off = *to try to attract attention for the sake of making a good impression*
to break the ice = *to be the first to approach another person*
to foot the bill = *to pay the bill*
to see eye to eye = *to agree (with someone)*

Compare these idioms with how they function as verbals.

To be afraid of the dark is rather childish. (subject)
Did you come here just **to show off**? (adverb)
I had to be the first **to break the ice with him**. (adjective)
Jim, I think it's your turn **to foot the bill**. (adjective)
To see eye to eye with my boss is impossible. (subject)

I **am going** to work in ten minutes.
No one **was watching** the game.
Tom **has been studying** all evening.
She **had been ignoring** me.
Mr. Thomas **will be preparing** his taxes.

Present participles can be used as adjectives. For example: **the weeping child, a rushing river, Sleeping Beauty**.

But gerunds can be used only as nouns. Because they are derived from verbs, they can be accompanied by objects and prepositional phrases. Let's look at some example sentences.

Subject of the Sentence
Living in Idaho gave me a new respect for nature.
Working so hard helped me get fit.

Direct Object
I like **spending** time with you.
Jim prefers **skiing**.

Object of a Preposition

We'd like to thank you **for helping** us with the children.

I got this medal **for being** a good citizen.

Oral Practice

Read each sentence aloud, paying attention to the use of each gerund.

Speeding will get you in a lot of trouble.

Have you always liked planting your own garden?

I'm interested in becoming a physician.

John hates being an only child.

Not acting selfish is Bill's new goal for himself.

Sharing my free time with others has always been difficult for me.

Raj prefers reading about historical figures.

Reading and writing are the basics of learning for children.

Thank you for sending your payment in on time.

My wife loves singing in the town chorus.

How do I warn my son about sunbathing without sun block?

TAKE NOTE *Use care to distinguish between present participles and gerunds. You will frequently hear native speakers of English casually use a participle where a gerund is appropriate. When a noun or pronoun is followed by a verb form that looks like a present participle, the word is indeed being used as a present participle. The phrase is adverbial and tells* **when** *or* **where** *or an action is taking place. For example:*

I recorded Maria **singing** in the school play. (**Where** did I record Maria?)

We heard him, **shouting** at the referee. (**When** did we hear him?)

When the noun or pronoun is followed by a gerund, the noun is in the possessive and the pronoun is formed as a possessive adjective. The gerund phrase tells **whose** *action is involved. For example:*

I recorded Maria's **singing** in the school play. (**Whose** singing did I record?)

We heard his **shouting** at the referee. (**Whose** shouting did we hear?)

Written Practice 10-5

Complete each sentence with any two appropriate gerund phrases. For example:

I thanked him for _being a good friend._

I thanked him for _helping me study._

1. _____ is important to me.

   _____ is important to me.

2. My daughter is interested in

   _____

   My daughter is interested in

   _____

3. _____ has changed my
   life.

   _____ has changed my
   life.

4. They really like _____.
   They really like _____.

5. Why does your family prefer

   _____?

   Why does your family prefer

   _____?

6. _____ doesn't always
   make you happy.

   _____ doesn't always
   make you happy.

7. People say that _____
   can harm your health.

   People say that _____
   can harm your health.

8. The boys love _____.

   The boys love _____.

9. _____ reminds me of my

   childhood in Africa.

   _____ reminds me of my

   childhood in Africa.

10. Being allowed to go on the trip depends on

    _____.

    Being allowed to go on the trip depends on

    _____.

Using Gerunds and Nouns Together

In many sentences, either a gerund or a noun can serve the function of a noun.
For example:

> **To fly** to Hawaii is much faster than **to go** by ship.
> **Flying** to Hawaii is much faster than **going** by ship.
> My new goal is **to be** a better husband.
> My new goal is **being** a better husband.
> **To become** a better speaker requires a lot of effort.
> **Becoming** a better speaker requires a lot of effort.

Oral Practice

🔘 Track 37

Read each sentence aloud, paying attention to the difference between the use
of a gerund or an infinitive.

> Learning to ride a horse without a saddle seemed dangerous.
> My sister prefers to stay home with the children.
> Many of the students like to hear Ms. Roberts recite poetry.
> Being able to go on the camping trip depends upon your earning enough
>   money.
> To be or not to be, that is the question.
> His constant complaining is starting to ruin my mood.
> Maria would love to go to a concert to hear the Rolling Stones in person.
> Is being so young difficult for you, competing with the older students?
> The only solution to your money problems was to find a job right away.

Running for office becomes a matter of finding donors to finance your political campaign.

I've come here today to tell you about our new pension plan.

TAKE NOTE *Determiners are often used to modify gerunds, just as they can modify other nouns. Let's look at a few examples:*

The **reading** of the will is tomorrow.

Her **spending** is out of control.

Your **spelling** is terrible.

This **throbbing** in my chest frightens me.

Some **complaining** is often necessary.

Written Practice 10-6

Change the verb provided to a gerund, and create an original sentence with it. Then change the gerund to an infinitive, and give a similar sentence. For example:

make

Making a good salary means hard work.

To make a good salary, you have to work hard.

1. be

_____

_____

2. speak

_____

_____

3. hike

_____

_____

4. swim

_____

_____

5. climb

_____

_____

IDIOMS DEMYSTIFIED

Idioms that contain verbs often use those verbs as gerunds and, therefore, they can be used as nouns. Let's look at a few examples.

having a sweet tooth = *enjoying pastries and candy*
pulling someone's leg = *teasing or joking with someone*
paying a call on someone = *visiting someone*
catching (transportation) = *boarding a bus, train, airplane, or other form of transportation, often at the last minute*
taking after someone = *looking like or being similar to someone*

Compare these idioms with how they function as verbals.

My weight is caused by my **having a sweet tooth.**
Pulling John's leg only makes him angry.
We always enjoyed **paying a call on** my cousins.
Catching a bus after midnight isn't easy in this neighborhood.
Why do you hate me for **taking after my father?**

QUIZ

Choose the letter of the word or phrase that best completes each sentence.

1. **Professor Ling is truly a scholar _____.**

A. being

B. who was being

C. to admire

D. is admiring

2. **To purchase so many gifts _____ a lot of money.**

A. are

B. requires

C. weren't

D. is being

3. Did you come here just _____?

A. to argue with me   C. not to know

B. having so much to do   D. arriving late

4. _____ helps to keep me fit.

A. Working out   C. Readings

B. To have done   D. I am exercising

5. _____ writings make an important impression on people.

A. She   C. You

B. She is   D. Your

6. _____ final running of the marathon will be next year.

A. When   C. Is

B. The   D. Is not

7. To _____ mistaken for a movie star was a compliment.

A. wasn't   C. have been

B. being   D. will be

8. A little _____ is natural in a relationship.

A. to bicker   C. to be angered

B. arguing   D. having been

9. My goal is _____

A. to be a good friend to everyone   C. him, finally winning a race

B. having gone   D. she was dancing with me

10. To _____ of the unknown is common.

A. having gone   C. seeing eye to eye with her

B. liking sweets   D. be afraid

PART TWO TEST

Choose the letter of the word or phrase that best completes each sentence.

1. From _____ has she received this bouquet?
   A. whom
   B. whichever

2. _____ were the books packed in?
   A. Who
   B. What
   C. How
   D. On which

3. _____ you do will help us greatly.
   A. Whatever
   B. That
   C. He, whom
   D. Whomever

4. Michael's German shepherd won first prize, which _____.
   A. is now only four years old
   B. whomever they love
   C. made the whole family quite proud.
   D. you received it from

5. I hope to learn something from _____.
   A. who sent us this distressing letter
   B. they are the officers of the bank
   C. which you tried to explain to me
   D. whomever you hired to tutor me

6. Did that woman injure _____ when she fell?
   A. herself
   B. yourself
   C. myself
   D. they

7. The brothers served in the Marines and are proud of _____.
   A. one another
   B. ourselves
   C. herself
   D. every

8. _____ was cooling itself under the broad leaf of a plant.
   A. The frightened girl
   B. A kitten
   C. Several children
   D. No one

9. **Do you know _____ Ms. Patel will travel here by plane?**
   A. where
   C. which one
   B. whether
   D. what

10. **Calm _____. You boys have to stop crying.**
    A. yourself
    C. themselves
    B. it
    D. yourselves

11. **Why do I _____ to go to bed so early?**
    A. wanted
    C. can
    B. must
    D. have

12. **Uncle Phillip _____ arrived home by this time tomorrow.**
    A. will have
    C. have
    B. shall
    D. had

13. **_____ you regret moving to New York?**
    A. Do
    C. Are able
    B. Have
    D. Was supposed to

14. **Jim _____ studying in his bedroom when Richard arrived.**
    A. will be
    C. is
    B. had been
    D. can be

15. **Mr. Keller _____ cope with the loss of his wife.**
    A. want
    C. are able
    B. has to
    D. are

16. **One of my teammates _____ feel well today.**
    A. weren't
    C. wasn't
    B. don't
    D. doesn't

17. **_____ mice supposed to like cheese?**
    A. Aren't
    C. Will
    B. Wasn't
    D. Won't

18. **I wish I knew _____ better.**
    A. could work
    C. mustn't
    B. themselves
    D. the ropes

19. **Every** _____ **showed up at the ceremony.**
   - A. alumnus
   - B. alumnae
   - C. firemen
   - D. freshmen

20. **You haven't** _____ **time to wait for the boss to return.**
   - A. no
   - B. yourselves
   - C. neither
   - D. any

21. **Your father is a gentleman** _____.
   - A. being
   - B. who was being
   - C. to admire
   - D. is admiring

22. _____ **is supposed to lower my blood pressure.**
   - A. Working out
   - B. To have done
   - C. Readings
   - D. I am exercising

23. _____ **reading of grandfather's will is next Monday.**
   - A. When
   - B. The
   - C. Is
   - D. Is not

24. **To** _____ **called a coward was hurtful.**
   - A. wasn't
   - B. being
   - C. have been
   - D. will be

25. **Her purpose in life is** _____.
   - A. to be a good friend to everyone
   - B. having finally gone
   - C. him, finally being elected
   - D. he was flirting with me

Part Three

Some Fine Points

chapter **11**

Prepositions

This chapter is about prepositions. Although these parts of speech have some uses that are quite familiar to all, they also are used in combination with other words to achieve a meaning different from the usual meaning of the preposition.

CHAPTER OBJECTIVES

In this chapter you will learn about:

- Prepositions and the objective case
- How prepositions accompany verbs
- How prepositions accompany adjectives
- How prepositions accompany nouns
- Hyper forms

Prepositional Phrases

Prepositions are used to introduce phrases called *prepositional phrases*. A prepositional phrase is a combination of a preposition and a noun or pronoun. When a pronoun follows a preposition, it will always be in the *objective case*. For example:

Noun	Third Person Pronoun
with Mr. Garcia	with him
to Ashley	to her
in the drawer	in it
from my relatives	from them
through time	through us

First and second person pronouns can also be introduced by a preposition, but they are not replacements for nouns.

of me	for us
by you *s.*	beside you *pl.*

Many determiners can be introduced by a preposition, which means that they are now being used as pronouns, not as adjectives.

By this I mean that the purchase price will rise.
This is Jane's bed, but don't sleep **in hers**. Sleep **in mine**.
I was asking **about those**.

Many prepositional phrases are used adverbially to show *location*. Let's look at an example phrase, in which the location changes as the preposition changes.

The box is **on** the table.	The box is **near** the table.
The box is **under** the table.	The box is **behind** the table.

Let's look at another example sentence that describes a location. In this case, the entire prepositional phrase changes.

Is the picture **in the drawer**?	Is the picture **beside the mirror**?
Is the picture **over the piano**?	Is the picture **under the bed**?

Some other commonly used prepositions are:

about	down	before	up
until	during	below	without
across	of	between	into
after	out	despite	onto
along	since		

The prepositions **into** and **onto** are often replaced by **in** and **on**. The function of the former prepositions is to describe more precisely a *motion to a place*. For example:

John ran **into** the house.	John ran **in** the house.
I threw a book **onto** my desk.	I threw a book **on** my desk.

In many cases, **in** is preferable to **into**, and **on** is preferable to **onto**.

Many prepositions describe location. But some of them are used adverbially with other meanings. Still other prepositions form prepositional phrases that are used adverbially. For example:

when? = in a week, between August and October
why? = because of the storm, on account of the weather
how? = by steamship, on the train
whose? = of the dancer, (belonging) to my son

Oral Practice

Read each sentence aloud, paying attention to the use and meaning of the prepositions.

It takes grandfather a long time to walk from his living room chair to the kitchen.
For some reason, Jack came to the party without his wife.
During the last election, a number of new candidates won over incumbents.
We strolled hand in hand along the river and leaned close to one another.
The director was arguing with one of the actors behind the scenery.
I hope to be in Chicago on Monday and will be staying at the Drake Hotel.
Until I came to the United States, I knew very little about the Constitution.
With an umbrella in his hand, the boy jumped off the roof and landed next to his father.
A group of laughing girls hurried around the corner and bumped into me.

Compound Prepositions

A compound preposition is composed of a preposition or other part of speech with another preposition. Here are some examples:

alongside   outside
before   within
beside   without
into

Sometimes a word that is written separately from the preposition can function as a new preposition. For example:

according to   instead of
because of   next to
in accordance with   on account of
in place of

Oral Practice

Track 38

Read each sentence aloud, paying attention to the use of the prepositions.

I stood next to Mary's bed and stared into her sleepy eyes.
During the summer, we usually get several letters from our cousins in
   Poland.
Laura doesn't want to go out with you anymore on account of your nasty
   temper.
The girls rested alongside a gentle stream and peered up at the azure sky.
The man in the brown suit has been standing outside the café for more
   than an hour.
According to the encyclopedia, the younger prince became king in place of
   his older brother.
The mayor sat at the head of the table, and two aldermen sat next to him.
The puppy jumped onto the bed and yapped at his young master.
In accordance with the laws of our country, most adult citizens have the
   right to vote.

Written Practice 11-1

Complete each sentence with an appropriate prepositional phrase. For example:

We stretched out on <u>the cool grass</u>.

1. The boys were roughhousing inside

   _____.

2. What do you know about

   _____?

3. This article is concerned with

   _____.

4. According to _____, it
   will probably rain tomorrow.

5. The robber slipped the rings into

   _____.

Complete each sentence with an introductory phrase before each prepositional phrase. For example:

<u>We stretched out</u> on the cool grass.

6. _____ because of a
   terrible cold.

7. _____ without her purse
   and glasses.

8. _____ outside city hall.

9. _____ below the surface
   of the water.

10. _____ between Sunday
    and Wednesday.

The Preposition *Like*

There is often confusion about how to use the preposition **like**. Like other prepositions, **like** is followed by a noun or a pronoun in the objective case. Although many use **like** as a conjunction, in formal style that is incorrect. **As** if and **as** are the appropriate conjunctions to use where so many use **like**. **As if** and **as** are followed by a complete clause. For example:

The baby looks **like me**. (**me** = objective case)
Do you want to be a pilot **like your father**? (**your father** = objective case)
John always studies **as if** the exam were tomorrow. (**as if** + clause)
This woman works as hard **as any man** (works). (**as** + clause)

Notice that when the meaning of a clause introduced by **as** is clear, it's not necessary to write out the full clause. The previous example could be written as follows:

This woman works as hard as **any man works**.

You can test a sentence to see whether **like**, **as if**, or **as** should be used in the sentence. If **like** precedes a noun or pronoun, it is being used correctly. If **as if** or **as** introduces a whole clause with a subject and predicate, it is being used correctly. If the structure is **as + adjective + as** and introduces a whole clause, it is being used correctly. However, the clause that follows **as + as** sometimes omits information that is understood. For example:

It's hot. It's **like** a midsummer day.
Tom dances **as if** his feet hurt.
Nina is **as** pretty **as** a movie star (is).

Written Practice 11-2

Create two original sentences with the prepositions provided in parentheses. For example:

(from)

I received a gift from Aunt Susan today.

Mr. Zhukov comes from Russia.

1. (on account of)

_____

_____

2. (like)

_____

_____

3. (as . . . as)

_____

_____

4. (according to)

_____

_____

5. (in place of)

_____

_____

6. (as)

_____

_____

7. (about)

_____

_____

9. (underneath)

_____

_____

10. (instead of)

_____

_____

Using Specific Prepositions

Adjectives are commonly used with specific prepositions to achieve a desired meaning. For example, when you say, **"I am interested in math,"** the preposition in no longer describes a real location. The preposition **in** accompanies **interested** because that preposition has _traditionally_ been used with the participial adjective **interested**. There are numerous such adjectives. Let's look at a few adjectives and participles (used as adjectives) and the prepositions that accompany them.

accompanied by   identical with/to

anxious about   independent of

based on   oblivious of/to

contemporary with	preferable to
depending on/upon	used to

There is also a long list of verbs that can be accompanied by specific prepositions. Some of the commonly used ones are:

admit to	impose on
ban from	instill in
center on	shiver from
differ from	subscribe to
forbid from	trust in
speak, talk, tell about/of	speak, talk with

In Chapter 10, you discovered that participles can be verbals that function as nouns. Certain present and past participles can also function as prepositions. For example:

assuming	owing to
concerning	provided
considering	regarding
during	respecting

Some verbals that function as prepositions can be followed by clauses. For example:

Assuming that you are of age, you can enter this bar.
Regarding the accident you had, the following form must be filled out.

There are a few nouns that should be accompanied by a specific preposition. Among them are:

belief in	mastery of
contemporary of	patience with
excerpt from	pretext for

Oral Practice

Track 39

Read each sentence aloud, paying attention to the kind of preposition that is used.

Assuming that you're correct, we have to sell these stocks immediately.
Despite all his complaining, Rick went along with the idea and enjoyed himself.
I have no patience with how you speak to me and against my family.

Have you read this excerpt from the article on climate change by Professor Laski?

Your report centers on the events in the Middle East but does not tell about the culture there.

Jack's mastery of the violin is related to his general intelligence.

Because of her belief in her husband, she stood behind him during all their troubles.

I don't want to impose my will on you, but you pay no attention to me otherwise.

Written Practice 11-3

Create two original sentences with the preposition provided in parentheses. For example:

(despite)

Despite all their arguing, the elderly couple loved one another.

Despite the raging storm, I left.

1. (contemporary of)

_____

_____

2. (assuming)

_____

_____

3. (differ from)

_____

_____

4. (provided)

_____

_____

5. (trust in)

_____

_____

6. (during)

_____

_____

7. (depending on)

_____

_____

8. (like)

_____

_____

9. (mastery of)

_____

_____

10. (of)

_____

_____

Colloquialisms and Hyper Forms

Many learners of English practice the rules of English grammar but hear native speakers abuse those rules. This is common in any language. People speak automatically and, when they are comfortable in a casual situation, say things that communicate an idea but may be completely ungrammatical. Take note that the following explanations are not suggestions about how you should speak English. Instead, they are intended to make you aware of some common errors in casual speech and to help you understand what *a native speaker really means*.

One such error is the use of an objective case pronoun where a subjective case pronoun is needed. This often occurs when a sentence contains a compound subject. For example:

Casual Speech	Correct Speech
Me and Bill are working.	Bill and I are working.
Mark and **her** went to town.	Mark and she went to town.

IDIOMS DEMYSTIFIED

Many idioms require the use of a preposition to achieve the desired meaning. A few such idioms follow with example sentences.

cope with = *deal with a problem with difficulty*
I can't cope with your lying anymore.
How do you cope with a difficult job like yours?

do without = *tolerate or bear being without*
In this economy, we have to do without some luxuries.
My aunt just cannot do without air conditioning in summer.

be fed up with = *be completely annoyed or disturbed with*
I'm fed up with this job and am quitting!
She's fed up with our relationship and says that it's over.

get over someone/something = *no longer interested in someone or something*
Mary still can't get over the loss of the hundred-year-old oak.
Jean is married now. You have to get over her.

how about = *ask whether someone is interested in doing something*
I don't want to cook. How about pizza tonight?
How about a stroll in the park?

If an objective case pronoun were used as the subject, a native speaker would spot the error immediately. For example, no one would say:

Me am working.	**I** am working.
Her went downtown.	**She** went downtown.

It is only in sentences that contain a compound subject that the error illustrated in the column on the left takes place.

A similar problem arises when the object of a preposition is a compound made of a noun and a pronoun. In a prepositional phrase, the pronoun should be in the objective case. But some native speakers use the subjective case. The same thing happens when a noun and pronoun are the compound direct object of a sentence. These are *hyper forms*—they represent a tendency to overcorrect what does not need correcting at all. This occurs primarily with the first person singular (**I/me**). For example:

Casual Speech	Correct Speech
The gift is for Jane and I.	The gift is for Jane and **me**.

The doctor chatted with
    Mr. Jones and I.
	The doctor chatted with
	    Mr. Jones and **me**.

The puppies followed Bill and I.	The puppies followed Bill and **me**.

Her children visited my husband
    and I.
	Her children visited my
	    husband and **me**.

If the pronoun were the only object, no one would make this error.

Oral Practice

Read each sentence aloud, paying attention to the case of the pronouns used.

I found an old letter that was addressed to my mother and me.
Poor Mary. She and Tom had a terrible fight after their son's birthday party.
During the game, Carmen and I talked about Tom and her and about the fight.
Except for Ms. Ling and me, no one else from our group was chosen for
    the committee.
Did Juan and I finally get that recipe right?
When you get to Quito, please stop by and say hello to me and my family.
When Daniel and I were in Argentina, we stopped by their house to visit them.
Is that car really for Jean and me to use while we're staying with you?
That's Ms. Cole. She and Mark have been seeing one another for two months.

Colloquial Use of *Like*

How **like** is used as a preposition has been discussed earlier. There is a colloquial use of **like** that is commonly used by younger people and is accepted as a correct form. In traditional grammar, it is incorrect. But since you will hear **like** used in its new form often, it will be discussed here. Being familiar with this nonstandard usage will aid your comprehension of English. But it's preferable to avoid using **like** in this manner, particularly in formal speech and writing.

In some cases, **like** implies a great deal of information, although to the newcomer to this use of the word, those implications are a mystery. It is the continuous use of the word by large groups of people that give it its accepted meaning. The following examples imply a lot.

I'm, **like**, wow! *I am very surprised/amazed/mystified!*
We were, **like**, that's impossible. *We couldn't believe it. It seemed impossible.*
I was, **like**, no way. *I was dismayed by what I heard/saw. I wanted no part of it.*

Like is also commonly used as a synonym for *approximately, nearly,* or *it must be/it seems to me to be.* For example:

It's, **like**, 80 degrees in here. *It's approximately 80 degrees. It seems like 80 degrees to me.*
We were, **like**, almost home when it began to rain. *We were very nearly home.*
She has, **like**, five dollars. *She has approximately five dollars.*

Like is often added to a sentence as *filler* to accentuate the meaning of the sentence.

John was, **like**, so late getting home that Dad was very mad.
Are you going to, **like**, eat that whole pizza yourself?

Use this brief explanation of this colloquial usage of **like** to improve your understanding of what others are saying. For the sake of being precise in your speaking and writing, however, it's wise to avoid this vague expression.

Colloquial Use of *At*

In many parts of the United States, the preposition **at** is added to a question of location where it is absolutely not needed and is incorrect. The most common question is: **Where are you *at* now?** The interrogative word **where** already serves the function of asking for a location, and the preposition **at** has no function at all. It certainly wouldn't be used in the reply to the question. For example, you would never hear people say the following:

I am **at** on the bus.
We are **at** still in class.

There are yet other prepositions that are never used in a **where**-question. **At** in questions is also just wrong. Let's compare a few other prepositions with **at** in this kind of question to make the point clear that the insertion of a preposition in a **where**-question makes no sense.

Where are you at now?
Where are you on now? *I'm on the bus.*
Where are you in now? *I'm still in class.*
Where are you near now? *I'm near the bus stop.*

QUIZ

Choose the letter of the word or phrase that best completes each sentence
(N/A = not applicable).

1. My brothers have worked for this firm _____ August.

   A. like   C. assuming

   B. since   D. cope with

2. I have no idea where my sister is _____.

   A. of   C. at

   B. on   D. N/A

3. Mr. Johnson was telling us _____ his travels in Scandinavia.

   A. of   C. despite

   B. onto   D. on account of

4. We decided to remain at the inn _____.

   A. into the summer   C. during the blizzard

   B. beneath the water   D. fed up with it

5. Ms. Patel said that I speak Spanish as well _____ Juanita.

   A. as   C. as if

   B. like   D. N/A

6. James threw his coat _____ and immediately turned on the TV.

   A. of the hook   C. depending on his wife

   B. onto the bed   D. not concerned with

7. _____ going to dinner in the city tonight?

   A. Should we   C. Are you able to

   B. Does he want   D. How about

8. Do _____ have to do the dishes?

   A. Bill and I   C. he

   B. Mary and me   D. somebody

9. We had our picnic _____ two large oak trees.
   A. below them   C. provided
   B. between   D. about

10. I have a very strong belief _____ democracy and liberty.
   A. of   C. in
   B. from   D. upon

chapter **12**

Imperatives

This chapter is about the imperative form of verbs. Imperative verbs are used to give commands.

CHAPTER OBJECTIVES

In this chapter you will learn about:

- The basic imperative form
- Commands given politely
- Commands that include the speaker
- Commands given through suggestions

Imperative Verbs

An imperative verb gives a *command*. Imperative verbs are in the second person singular or plural (**you**); however, the pronoun **you** is rarely included in the command. A speaker who wishes to point out a particular person, the individual to whom the command is directed, can begin with the pronoun. The use of the pronoun makes the command sound *abrupt*, as if it has come from an authority figure. For example:

You, get in line over there.
You, help carry those boxes into the warehouse.

When the pronoun is plural, nouns such as **men** or **women** can be added for clarity.

> **You men**, drive your trucks to the loading dock.
> **You women**, change into uniforms in the locker room.
> **You kids**, get off that fence!

The imperative of a verb is a simple form. It is the infinitive of a transitive or intransitive verb with the particle word **to** omitted. Imperatives have no tense forms and occur only as the infinitive with the particle word omitted. For example.

Infinitive	Command
to sing	Sing a bit louder.
to write	Write a letter to Uncle Peter.
to be	Be as quiet as possible.
to have	Have a good time on your cruise to Alaska.
to smoke	Smoke only in the designated area.

Modal auxiliaries (**can**, **must**, **have to**, and so on) do not form imperatives. There is an exception, however: **to be able to** can be used in this way because it is the verb **be** that is made imperative in the phrase. For example:

> **Be able to** recite this poem from memory by tomorrow.
> **Be able to** run an eight-minute mile by June.

Negation

When an imperative verb is negated, it is preceded by the auxiliary **do** plus **not**. Naturally, the contracted form **don't** is acceptable. Remember that commands are given in the second person. Therefore, **does not/doesn't** should never be used. Since imperatives have no tense forms, the auxiliary **did not/didn't** is not considered here. Let's look at some commands that are given in the negative.

> **Don't** stand so close to the edge.
> **Do not** touch the objects on display.
> **Don't** feed the animals.
> **Do not** bring your iPhones to class.
> **Don't** run near the edge of the pool.

TAKE NOTE *There is a nonmodern form of negation that is found in older books and is sometimes used today when a writer or speaker wishes to sound* *formal or poetic. In this older form of negation, the adverb **not** follows the imperative verb. For example:*

Older Imperative	**Current Imperative**
Be **not** afraid.	**Don't** be afraid.
Waste **not**, want **not**.	**Don't** waste anything. You won't need anything.
Fear **not** the unknown.	**Don't** fear the unknown.
Love **not** an untrue man.	**Don't** love an untrue man.

These examples illustrate the existence of the older form of negation of imperatives. They should not serve as a template for how you speak or write. Use the current imperative form.

When a sentence with a subject and a conjugated verb is changed to the imperative, the tense of the conjugated verb is changed, as well. The imperative is always formed from the infinitive. If other clauses in the sentence have a verb conjugated in another tense, change the verb to the *present tense* in the imperative sentence. For example:

Conjugated verb: Tom **ran** a mile before the sun **came** up.
Imperative: Run a mile before the sun **comes** up.
Conjugated verb: I **will read** a chapter after Bob **leaves** for work.
Imperative: Read a chapter after Bob **leaves** for work.
Conjugated verb: When it **stopped** raining, we **hurried** back home.
Imperative: When it **stops** raining, **hurry** back home.

Written Practice 12-1

Reword each sentence as a command. Note that the verbs in these sentences are in various tenses. Remember that the subject of an imperative sentence is the unseen/unspoken pronoun **you**. For example:

> We bought ourselves some ice cream.
>
> *Buy yourselves some ice cream.*
>
> She looked for my slippers.
>
> *Look for my slippers.*

1. You learned how to tie your shoes before you started school.

_____

2. We will study very hard to pass our tests.

_____

3. Jack doesn't bring his laptop home.

_____

4. You are careful whenever you use a sharp knife.

_____

5. My wife made a huge chocolate cake for the party.

_____

6. They don't wait for me. They keep walking.

_____

7. I tried not to smile when Mary came through the door.

_____

8. When Daddy sat down at the table, we gave him a kiss.

_____

9. We were as quiet as possible.

_____

10. The men painted the eaves, repaired the shutters, and cleaned out the gutters.

_____

Oral Practice

🔘 Track 40

Read each sentence aloud, paying attention to the formation of the verb in the imperative.

Sign here; then take a seat in the lobby.
You there, keep moving and don't touch anything.
Help those in need, and be happy for those who live with abundance.
Don't forget your umbrella, and put all the documents in your briefcase.
Make a lunch for Susan, turn off the coffeepot, and lock the door before you leave.
Be here in time for supper, and don't bring any guests home.
Come shopping with me, and spend a little money.

Don't be so selfish. Give Jimmy one of your toys to play with.
Wait for me! Don't get on the bus without me!
Be able to lead the class in reciting the Pledge of Allegiance.

TAKE NOTE *Verbs that are in their progressive form (**is running, was making**) must change to the simple tense (**run, make**) to form a comparative. Sentences that contain an emphatic response (**I do understand this word. She doesn't like liver.**) are never used in the imperative. And imperatives are never stated as questions unless they appear in indirect discourse. For example: **Did he say, "Go home right away!"**?*

Polite Commands

The simplest way to make a command polite is to add the word **please**. In many cases, **please** can stand at the beginning of a sentence. For example:

Please carry a few books to the attic for me.
Please don't shout.
Please drive safely and don't text.

If you place **please** at the end of a sentence, it must be preceded by a comma. In speech, a slight pause between the sentence and **please** implies some impatience or exasperation.

Don't smoke in this area, **please**.
Put your dirty dishes and utensils in the dishwasher, **please**.
Don't tease that old dog, **please**.

A command can sound more polite if the speaker begins with the auxiliary **do**. This format is the opposite of beginning a command with **don't**. Unlike another use of this auxiliary, the sentence *does not form a question* with **do** when it is in a command. The structure is simple: place **do** before another command that begins with a verb. The command is now *softened*; it sounds more polite. Also, if the auxiliary is intoned and emphasized, the speaker is being somewhat insistent that the action be carried out.

Ordinary Command	Command with Do
Have a seat.	**Do** have a seat.
Give my regards to John.	**Do** give my regards to John.
Visit us again when you're in town.	**Do** visit us again when you're in town.

Oral Practice

Read each sentence aloud, paying attention to the kind of imperative used and to the element of courtesy.

Please refrain from putting your arms out the window of the bus.
You there, stop where you are and show me your papers, please!
Help Uncle Phillip get the luggage out of the trunk.
Please hurry with our bill. We're late for a concert.
Try to fix the radio and contact the Coast Guard. We're taking on water.
Be careful with that crystal vase, please.
Stop the car immediately, and let me out!
Don't wander so far away from our campsite again, please.
Grandma, please sit next to me and tell me that story again.

Let

Many imperative sentences begin with the verb **let**. It provides a command that says that the person to whom you are speaking should allow someone to do something. **Let** is, therefore, followed by a direct object and an infinitive with the particle word **to** omitted. For example:

Let the other boys have a chance to play the game.
Please **let** her join your club and become your friend.
Let someone else do the mopping and dusting this week.
Let your father get a little extra sleep this morning, please.
Don't **let** that snake get out of its cage!
Let your hair grow a little longer, then dye it blond.

Written Practice 12-2

Reword each sentence in the imperative. Make any necessary changes. Then reword the sentence again, beginning it with **please**. Reword the original sentence one more time, ending it with **please**. For example:

Jane pays the bill.

Pay the bill.

Please pay the bill.

Pay the bill, please.

1. Michael stood up straight and saluted.

_____

_____

2. She is pronouncing this word correctly.

_____

_____

3. Grandmother was growing vegetables and flowers in her garden.

_____

_____

4. He cooks something wonderful for us.

_____

_____

5. The men are being careful.

_____

_____

Let's

Let's is a contraction for **let us.** The pronoun **us** tells you that the speaker making the command is also included in the action of the command. For example: **Let's work in the garage.** = *You will work in the garage. I will also work in the garage.*

Let's is followed by an infinitive with the particle word **to** omitted. Both transitive and intransitive verbs can be used with **let's.** Since the speaker making the command is included in the command, it is a polite imperative. Let's look at some examples.

IDIOMS DEMYSTIFIED

Most idioms that contain verbs can form those verbs in the imperative. Let's look at a few examples of such idioms and how they function as commands.

answer (the door/phone/bell) = *respond to a knock at the door/the ringing of the phone/the ringing of the doorbell*
There's a stranger on the porch. Don't answer the door.
Let John answer the phone, please.

be up to date/out of date = *be modern/old-fashioned*
Be a bit more up to date and wear some lip gloss.
Don't be so out of date. Learn to dance.

take forty winks = *take a nap*
Let her take forty winks. It will make her feel better.
You look exhausted. Take forty winks.

Let's take a walk down to the river.
Let's try to get into the early showing of that new movie.
Let's go to the corner and buy some ice cream.
Let's talk over our problems and see if there's a way to be friends again.
Let's just forget the whole idea!

When **let's** is negated, the adverb **not** follows **let's**.

Let's **not** walk as far as the corner.
Let's **not** tell Jim where we are.

Oral Practice

🔘 Track 41

Read each sentence aloud, paying attention to the difference between **let** and **let's**.

Let the dog run around in the yard for a while.
Let's go up to the attic and find things to take to the rummage sale.
Don't let your new jeans get dirty while you're playing at the park.
Let's not argue about money anymore.
Let me take a look at that awful scratch on your arm.

Let's hurry to Macy's. There's a big sale going on.

Don't let anything stop you from getting to your appointment on time.

Let's not do the dishes until tomorrow morning. I'm dead tired.

Written Practice 12-3

Reword each command with **do**, **let**, and **let's**. When using **let**, add an appropriate direct object. Consider how the meaning changes in each case. For example:

> Sit near the fire.
>
> *Do sit near the fire.*
>
> *Let Bill sit near the fire.*
>
> *Let's sit near the fire.*

1. Spend some time with the children.

_____

_____

_____

2. Write Aunt Sally a thank you note.

_____

_____

_____

3. Help him find the keys.

_____

_____

_____

4. Don't rent that action movie for tonight.

_____

_____

5. Pour some wine into each glass.

6. Use the flashlight in that dark cave.

7. Prepare some lunch for the girls.

8. Plant some tulips near the porch.

9. Coach the wrestling team.

10. Don't sing that old song.

Polite Commands

There are a few phrases that introduce a sentence that is not a true command. The verb in such a sentence is not in the imperative. But these phrases *politely suggest* an action that should be carried out. They are in essence a form of a command.

In two cases, the auxiliary verb **should** is part of the phrase. And two of the phrases are in the form of a question. Let's look at some example sentences.

> **Maybe you should** help Mary with the laundry.
> **Maybe you should** spend more time studying.
> **Maybe you should** take the garbage out.
> **Maybe you should** rent a couple movies for tonight.

> **Don't you think you should** get more sleep at night?
> **Don't you think you should** find a good job soon?
> **Don't you think you should** learn to speak English?
> **Don't you think you should** make your bed?

> **Why don't you** stop by tomorrow for a visit?
> **Why don't you** call me before four o' clock?
> **Why don't you** return those books to the library?
> **Why don't you** hold your voice down a little?

If these phrases are directed at someone other than **you**, a suggested command does not occur.

> Maybe **your brother** should join the army.
> Don't you think **she** should take the dog for a walk?
> Why don't **the women** like this play?

Oral Practice

🔘 Track 42

Read each sentence aloud, paying attention to the type of command that is given.

> Michael: I'm so tired. Let's take forty winks.
> Jane: I'm fine. Why don't you go upstairs and stretch out on the bed?
> Michael: No, let me help you take down the drapes first.
> Jane: I can handle it. Do go upstairs and rest.
> Michael: Maybe you should wait to do the drapes until tomorrow.
> Jane: Why don't you just do as you're told? Now go.
> Michael: All right. But if the phone rings, don't answer it. It might be Joe.
> Jane: Poor Joe. Don't you think you should still be friends with him?

Michael: Don't talk to me about Joe. He's out of my life.
Jane: He was your best friend. Why don't you just give him a call and talk things over?
Michael: Maybe you should call him and make him your friend.
Jane: You can be so stubborn. Go to bed!

QUIZ

Choose the letter of the word or phrase that best completes each question.

1. **Look for the suitcase in the cellar, but _____ careful.**
   A. have
   B. don't go
   C. be
   D. do look

2. **_____ accompany Aunt Susan to the mall this afternoon.**
   A. Please
   B. Does
   C. Don't go
   D. Should

3. **_____. Someone rang the bell.**
   A. Go to the phone
   B. Answer the door
   C. Maybe you should
   D. Have a good time

4. **_____ not go out for dinner this evening.**
   A. Let
   B. Does
   C. Why don't you
   D. Let's

5. **_____ cook those two steaks on the grill.**
   A. Don't
   B. Should
   C. Have
   D. You like

6. **_____ join us for dinner tomorrow.**
   A. Maybe can
   B. Do
   C. Let
   D. Let's

7. **Don't _____ anyone try to talk you out of buying this car.**
   A. speak
   B. be
   C. worry
   D. let

8. Let's _____.
   A. maybe we should help them   C. your sister do it
   B. not discuss it anymore   D. you should go upstairs

9. Try _____, and get a new hairdo.
   A. as they   C. don't you think
   B. to be up to date   D. not today

10. _____ on that white sofa, please!
   A. Don't sit   C. Why don't you
   B. Has fun   D. Let's

13

Conjunctions and Clauses

This chapter is about conjunctions and clauses. The two types of conjunctions are the coordinating and subordinating conjunctions, and the two types of clauses are the independent and dependent clauses.

CHAPTER OBJECTIVES

In this chapter you will learn about:

- How coordinating conjunctions connect grammatical elements
- Subordinating conjunctions and comma usage
- Independent clauses
- Dependent clauses

Coordinating Conjunctions

The list of coordinating conjunctions is quite short. They are **and, but, or, nor, for, so,** and **yet.** The job of these conjunctions is quite simple. They are used to connect two elements that are *grammatical equals.* That is, a noun is combined with a noun; a phrase is combined with a phrase; and an independent clause is combined with an independent clause. Let's look at some examples.

Nouns

I already bought **tea, sugar, cream,** and **milk.**

Young men, old men, but **not mere boys,** were called upon to defend the village.

Phrases

I hope **to work as a gardener, to serve as a forest ranger,** or **to design landscaping.**

The soldiers train **at fitness camps, with weapons,** and **in the classroom.**

Independent Clauses

Jean wants to become an engineer, **so she is studying physics and chemistry.**

My hobby is painting, **yet I find little time to hone my skills.**

And is used to add things together. It is rather like a plus sign (+). For example: Jack **and** Jill.

But introduces a contradiction to something previously introduced. For example: **It's quite hot, but I still love the summer.**

Or provides another possibility to one that has already been introduced. For example: **We can stay home, or we can go to a movie.**

Nor follows a negative statement and provides one that says *also not this.* For example: **He was not wise, nor was he as foolish as many believed.** In an independent clause, **nor** is immediately followed by the verb, not by the subject.

For introduces a reason for the statement that precedes it. This conjunction is not used to combine elements other than clauses. For example: **She remained perfectly still, for her senses perceived the danger.**

So introduces a clause that is the result of the action of the clause that precedes it. This conjunction is not used to combine elements other than clauses. For example: **Bill concentrated on sending a text, so his car ended up in a ditch once again.**

Yet introduces a clause that says *despite* the information in the preceding statement, the implied warning is not or was not heeded. For example: **He heard growling and snorting, yet he moved forward into the dark cave.**

When independent clauses are combined by means of these conjunctions, a comma is generally used to separate the clauses. If the clauses are quite short, it is possible to omit the comma.

Oral Practice

🔘 Track 43

Read each sentence aloud, paying attention to the use of the conjunctions.

Mr. Morgan sent me a list of complaints and demands.

John and Maria fell in love quickly, and they soon ran away to get married.

Give me a dozen cookies but none with frosting, please.

My grandmother makes liver and onions quite often, but I hate liver and onions.

Would you like the white blouse or the pink one?

Should we visit your parents tomorrow, or should we go on a picnic?

I want neither a party for my birthday nor any other kind of celebration.

Ms. Ling won't put up with such language, nor will she tolerate rude frowns.

The sleeping pup soon perked up his ears, for he heard his master's voice.

He wants to play basketball in college, so he chose State University for his studies.

You are so young, yet taller than I expected.

Jim was big and strong, yet I stood my ground and waited for the first punch.

Written Practice 13-1

Complete each sentence with any appropriate clause.

1. My uncle is in the army, and my aunt

_____

2. The summers are very hot here, but in winter

_____

3. Do you know how to swim well, or

_____?

4. My parents don't like to watch television, nor

_____

5. The little boy stayed away from the water, for

_____

6. _____, so I got on my bike and rode away.

7. _____, yet I think she
found me appealing nonetheless.

8. _____, but we saw a
storm brewing across the lake.

9. _____, nor do I like the
way you dance.

10. _____, or I will be forced
to call the police.

Subordinating Conjunctions

Unlike coordinating conjunctions, subordinating conjunctions connect grammatical elements that are *unequal*. The list of subordinating conjunctions is quite long; therefore, they will be illustrated by type: single-word conjunctions and multiword conjunctions.

Single-Word Conjunctions

after	than
as	that
if	though
once	when
since	while

Subordinating conjunctions can follow an independent clause and connect it to another clause. In this format, a comma is not used with the conjunction. For example:

Jack wanted to become an astronaut **after** he saw *Star Wars*.
I'll make waffles for breakfast **if** you get up now.
The man just shook his head and smiled, **since** he didn't understand
    English.

When the subordinating conjunction begins a sentence, a comma precedes the independent clause.

When Bill entered the kitchen, he saw the dog sleeping on the table.
Once the paint dried, the room was clean and attractive again.
While the storm raged, we cuddled together on the couch.

Multiword Conjunctions

although	indeed
because	nevertheless
besides	nonetheless
notwithstanding	therefore
however	unless

The conjunctions **although**, **because**, and **unless** can begin a sentence or follow the independent clause. A comma is used only when the subordinating conjunction precedes the independent clause.

I enjoy golf a lot, **although** I'm still very much an amateur.
Because Carmen loves music so much, her father bought her a guitar.
I won't come to your party **unless** you invite my brother, too.
Although the rain has stopped, it's too damp to paint the fence.

The conjunctions **besides**, **however**, **indeed**, and **therefore** are used to introduce a clause that follows an independent clause. The independent clause is separated from the other clause by a *semicolon*. A comma usually follows the conjunction. For example:

Loud music isn't allowed; **besides** being a nuisance, it destroys one's ability
   to concentrate.
I like writing this essay; **however**, I need another week to finish it.
Mr. Withers is quite old; **indeed**, he turns ninety-eight next week.
I'm too old for you; **therefore**, I can't see you anymore.

Oral Practice

Read each sentence aloud, paying attention to the use and position of the conjunctions.

While seated at the table, Grandfather suddenly dozed off.
Although I don't see anything wrong with looking attractive, wearing too
   much makeup is bad.
Mr. Garcia was a stern father; however, he was loving and caring and a very
   kind man.
Please clean up your room if you find time today.
Sara paid attention in math class, though she often daydreamed about her
   coming vacation.

The happy couple continued dancing even after the music stopped.
The room is shabby and cold, nonetheless I plan to stay another day.
Did you know that it's not wrong to end a sentence with a preposition?
Unless you train that dog better, she won't be allowed in this house.

TAKE NOTE *The conjunction **than** is used to show a comparison between two persons or things. It is a subordinating conjunction that frequently introduces an elliptical clause. That is, some of the information in the clause is understood (as opposed to being spoken or written). For example:*

John is taller than Mike. (. . . than Mike is tall.)
The black horse ran faster than the white one. (. . . than the white one ran fast.)
You speak better German than Dora. (. . . than Dora speaks German.)

Written Practice 13-2

Complete each sentence with any appropriate clause.

1. It is much too cold today; therefore,

_____.

2. While _____, I stayed in
the kitchen and baked a cake.

3. _____ unless the weather
gets better.

4. I had to work late today because

_____.

5. _____; however, she is
very generous with her neighbors.

6. _____ than Phillip and
Jean.

7. After a vigorous tennis match,

_____.

8. I could understand you a lot better if

_____.

9. Although _____, I still didn't have enough money to buy the camera.

10. Once I knew that the children were safe, _____.

Correlative Conjunctions

The correlative conjunctions are pairs of words used to connect individual elements or clauses. Both words in the pair are needed to achieve the meaning of the conjunction. Some of the most commonly used are:

as . . . as
both . . . and
either . . . or
if . . . then
neither . . . nor
not only . . . also
where . . . there

Let's look at some example sentences that illustrate how these conjunctions function.

I am **as** tired **as** I have ever been.
Both the mayor **and** the chief of police endorse the new law.
Your statement indicates that you are **either** very egotistical **or** very ignorant.
If the sun comes out, **then** the snow will melt.
Neither Anne **nor** Laura liked the new manager very much.
John is **not only** handsome, he is **also** charming and witty.
Where there is smoke, **there** is fire.

Phrasal Conjunctions

Phrasal conjunctions are made up of two or more separate words. The words together derive a new meaning, which permits them to function as a conjunction. For example:

as long as   inasmuch as
as though
in the case that   so that
in order that

Let's look at some example sentences.

As long as you stay in the bike lane, you can ride your bike to Uncle Ken's house.

You look **as though** you'd seen a ghost.

In the case that you lose your passport, contact the embassy immediately.

I've written out the instructions **in order that** you might understand them better.

Inasmuch as your son is a minor, he cannot join the army.

Jane can go to the party tonight, **provided** she has finished her homework.

I'll accompany you there **so that** you'll be sure to arrive.

Written Practice 13-3

Basing your sentences on the examples previously provided, create an original sentence with each conjunction. For example:

so that

Here's a flashlight so that you can see your way in the dark.

1. both . . . and

_____

2. neither . . . nor

_____

3. inasmuch as

_____

4. not only . . . also

_____

5. provided

_____

6. either . . . or

_____

7. where . . . there

_____

8. as long as

_____

9. as though

_____

10. in order that

_____

Participles as Conjunctions

In some cases, present and past participles have been used as subordinating conjunctions. In this usage, which has been around for a long time in English, the participles are often called *disguised conjunctions*. This is because they are in reality *verbals used as conjunctions*. Let's look at some of these conjunctions that are in frequent use.

according	judging
assuming	owing to
barring	provided
concerning	regarding
considering	supposing
given	taking into account

These conjunctions introduce a clause that often does not have a subject, and their function is primarily adverbial. For example:

According to the almanac, we should have a very cold winter.
Barring any last minute cancellations, there should be about thirty at the party.
I suggest we cancel the trip to the mountains, **given the conditions of the roads**.

Oral Practice

Track 44

Read each sentence aloud, paying attention to the kind of conjunction used.

Considering what that trip might cost, we had better rethink our vacation plans.
That is either a 747 or some other kind of jumbo jet.
Dora is not only an excellent pianist, she also has a beautiful soprano voice.
You can cross that old bridge safely, as long as you don't look down.

Provided you have the proper visa, you can travel extensively in Russia.
You're welcome to borrow my tools, supposing that you know how to use
   them.
Ms. Carlson draws and paints as though she had been studying art for years.
Where there are little boys, there is often mischief.
Owing to the length of your manuscript, we cannot consider publishing it.
Both Jim and I work out in the fitness center at the university gymnasium.
Regarding your application for a loan, I am happy to tell you that you will
   receive a check in two days.

TAKE NOTE *You have probably noticed that example sentences often begin with a conjunction. There was a time when that practice was considered wrong. Today, however, many good writers use conjunctions as the first element of a sentence. Making the independent clause the first clause in a sentence is, of course, also correct.*

When we arrived in St. Louis, we hurried to see the Mississippi River.
We hurried to see the Mississippi River **when** we arrived in St. Louis.

IDIOMS DEMYSTIFIED

A clause that contains an idiom is frequently introduced by a conjunction. For example:

If you can't **cope with** this climate, you should go back to New York.
I gave up many luxuries, **but** I just can't **do without** my smartphone.

But there is a unique English idiom that is composed of conjunctions alone.

ifs, ands, or buts = *excuses*

When someone asks that something be done, that person can say that there must not be any excuses for not completing the task. For example:

Statement: "You have to finish painting the bedroom today, and I don't want to hear any **ifs, ands, or buts** about it."

The maker of the preceding statement is expecting to hear excuses like the following:

Excuse 1: "I could finish painting <u>if</u> I had much larger brushes."
Excuse 2: "I need a lot of help, <u>and</u> Bill and Maria won't help me."
Excuse 3: "I tried to finish yesterday, <u>but</u> I hurt my wrist."

Clauses

Independent clauses have already been identified. They are sentences that make sense standing alone, without the addition of any other phrases or clauses. For example:

I was surprised that she did not win first prize.
John's work has been lacking in quality for a long time.
Spring is my favorite time of the year.

Dependent Clauses

A dependent clause is one that does not make complete sense when it stands alone. Thus a dependent clause requires the addition of an independent clause to complete its meaning. Dependent clauses can begin with a subordinating conjunction. Compare the following pairs of sentences, and take note of how the addition of an independent clause completes the meaning of the sentence.

Considering how well Jean sang. (*incomplete, makes no sense*)
Considering how well Jean sang, I was surprised that she did not win first prize.
Therefore, we have to let him go. (*incomplete, makes no sense*)
John's work has been lacking in quality for a long time; therefore, we have
  to let him go.
Although autumn is quite beautiful. (*incomplete, makes no sense*)
Although autumn is quite beautiful, spring is my favorite time of the year.

Written Practice 13-4

In the blank provided, give an independent clause that completes each sentence. For example:

Although you're young enough, *you aren't strong enough.*

1. When the storm was finally over,

  _____

2. _____ as though she

  really understood the poem.

3. Considering Barbara's poor health,

  _____

4. _____; however, you all will receive a refund.

5. In order that someone might be able to claim the lost bag, _____.

6. _____, provided you bring along your own sleeping bag.

7. While I set up the tent, _____

8. As long as you help us clean the house, _____

9. After I took a long, hot shower, _____

10. Regarding your poor grades in math, _____

11. _____ if you don't mind sleeping in the attic.

12. _____ inasmuch as you love him so much.

13. According to the weather forecast, _____.

14. _____, nor do I ever eat raw oysters.

15. Supposing that you can complete your degree this semester, _____

Interrogatives

You encountered interrogative words in Chapter 7. They are used to form questions, such as the following:

Why don't you live in Nebraska anymore?
Where is the nearest gas station?
With **whom** did you go to the prom?

Interrogative words can also be used to introduce a dependent clause. For example:

I don't know **why** you don't live in Nebraska anymore.
This woman needs to know **where** the nearest gas station is.
Did grandmother ask with **whom** you went to the prom?

Although interrogatives are used to ask questions, in dependent clauses they are not necessarily in a question. The dependent clause is never a question, but the accompanying clause can be in the form of a question. For example, in the preceding examples, the phrases **I don't know** and **This woman needs to know** are not questions. The sentences end with a period. The phrase **Did grandmother ask** is a question; therefore, the entire sentence ends with a question mark.

If a question does not begin with an interrogative word, the conjunction **whether** is used to form the dependent clause. In colloquial speech, many people replace **whether** with **if**. Let's look at a few examples.

Does Mr. Johnson still live in Connecticut?
I'd like to know **whether (if)** Mr. Johnson still lives in Connecticut.
Could the men lift that heavy piano?
Jane wondered **whether (if)** the men could lift that heavy piano.
Has your cousin often borrowed money from you?
Mike asked me **whether (if)** my cousin has often borrowed money from me.
Will the car be repaired by tomorrow?
Did you ask the mechanic **whether (if)** the car will be repaired by tomorrow?

Remember that an auxiliary or a verb precedes the subject in a question. When the questions become dependent clauses, the subject precedes the verb.

Why **is he** angry?
I don't know why **he is** angry.

Oral Practice

Read each sentence aloud, paying attention to the use of the interrogative words.

When is the next train to Cleveland?
Does anyone here know when the next train to Cleveland is?
How old are Michael and Phillip?
I'll find out from their sister how old Michael and Phillip are.
Which suit did Mr. Hall finally decide to buy?

I don't think anyone knows which suit Mr. Hall decided to buy.
What is the longest river in Europe?
Ashley checked an atlas to find out what the longest river in Europe is.
How deep is Lake Superior?
Did you ask your teacher how deep Lake Superior is?
Where are all those people going?
I wonder where all those people are going.
Will grandmother be well again?
Kristin asked me whether (if) grandmother will be well again.
How often is there an eclipse of the moon?
You can go online to find out how often there is an eclipse of the moon.

Relative Clauses

Although relative clauses were discussed in Chapter 6, they will be discussed again as they relate to dependent clauses. A relative clause provides information that describes its antecedent in an independent clause. Relative clauses are introduced by a relative pronoun. The English relative pronouns are **who** (**whom**, **whose**), **which**, and **that**. These pronouns function like conjunctions that introduce a dependent clause. Relative clauses cannot stand alone. That is, the meaning of a relative clause is complete only when it is attached to an independent clause, in which the antecedent of the relative pronoun is found. For example:

Who works in Boston. (*incomplete, makes no sense*)
This is **the man**, who works in Boston. **the man** = *antecedent to* **who**
Whom I met on vacation. (*incomplete, makes no sense*)
I'd like to introduce **the writer**, whom I met on vacation. **the writer** =
    antecedent to **whom**
Which belongs to my neighbor. (*incomplete, makes no sense*)
This is **the antique shovel**, which used to belong to my neighbor. **the**
    antique shovel = *antecedent to* **which**

The forms of **who** are used with antecedents that are animate. **Which** is used with antecedents that are inanimate. And these two relative pronouns form relative clauses that are *nonrestrictive* or *parenthetical*. That is, they provide additional information about the antecedent that is not pertinent to the main clause. Here's an example:

This man, **who used to work in Fargo**, just won the lottery.

The fact that this man worked in Fargo has nothing to do with the main thought of the sentence, which is the man's good fortune in the lottery. Let's look at another example.

The last train, **which probably needs a good cleaning**, left twenty minutes ago.

The important fact is that the train left twenty minutes ago. The information that the train is probably dirty is not pertinent and does not need to be included.

The relative pronoun **that** is used when a relative clause provides pertinent information that describes the antecedent and is part of the broader meaning of the sentence. For example:

This is the family **that won the lottery**.

Here, the relative clause tells the reader about the family: they are lottery winners! Let's look at another example.

I bought a used car **that has no air-conditioning**.

The used car is described by the relative clause: it has no air-conditioning.

It is important to know how to distinguish the two forms of relative pronouns (nonrestrictive and restrictive) in order to achieve the desired meaning. Note that nonrestrictive clauses are separated from the rest of the sentence by commas. Compare the following sentences.

My son, who is in college, wants to get married.
My son that is in college wants to get married.

In the first example, parenthetical information is given about the person's son: he wants to get married, and, *by the way*, he happens to be in college.
In the second example, the man has more than one son, and one of them is in college and wants to get married. But he has another son that is not in college. It is the *son that is in college* that wants to get married. Not the *other son*.

When the relative pronoun **who** is used in the objective case (direct object, indirect object, object of a preposition), its form is **whom**, and any prepositions that accompany **whom** precede the pronoun in formal style. In informal style, the preposition can be placed at the end of the clause. For example:

Formal: The lawyer, **for whom** I sometimes worked, quit the case.
Informal: The lawyer, **whom** I sometimes worked **for**, quit the case.

Prepositions precede **which** or stand at the end of a relative clause: Here's the book **about which** I had spoken. Here's the book, **which** I had spoken **about**.

The pronoun **whose** is used as a *possessive* relative pronoun. Let's look at a couple examples.

My boss, **whose** daughter goes to college, is leaving town for a week.
Let me introduce my sisters, **whose** husbands recently became firemen.

When **that** is in the objective case, any accompanying preposition has to stand at the end of the clause.

This is the brother of the fellow **that** I introduced you **to** at the gym last week.
That's the barrel **that** the raccoon was hidden **in**.

Oral Practice

🔘 Track 45

Read each sentence aloud, paying attention to the kind of relative clauses that are provided.

Our governor, who recently became a pilot, has a summer home in the mountains.
Did I show you the new laptop that I bought yesterday?
The athlete, whose parents wanted to come to the game, made the point that won the championship.
A car that can go that fast is a menace to pedestrians.
Would you like a piece of the apple pie that Ms. Garcia made?
The neighbors, from whom I received these postcards, are in Switzerland.
I found the watch that my grandfather received upon graduating from college.
The girl that I gave the flowers to won't even talk to me.
The trunk, in which I keep some special mementos, once belonged to a Russian prince.
This map, which is so hard to fold, will help us to get to the border.
The children, whom I led safely out of the woods, seemed completely unafraid.
The man that Laura is pointing to is following us.

? Still Struggling

When the relative pronoun **that** is in the objective case, it can be omitted from the relative clause while retaining the original meaning of the clause. For example:

This is the watch **that** I bought. = This is the watch I bought.
Here's the box **that** she hid it in. = Here's the box she hid it in.
Is this the gift **that** Bob gave you? = Is this the gift Bob gave you?

It is possible for an entire clause to be the antecedent of a relative pronoun. When this occurs, the relative pronoun is always **which** because it refers to an inanimate antecedent—an entire clause. The relative pronoun **which** refers to the meaning of the entire action of the clause. For example:

John broke a neighbor's window, which angered his father greatly.

John did not anger his father. The neighbor did not anger the father. The broken window did not anger the father. The entire situation described in the clause **John broke a neighbor's window** angered the father. Let's look at a few more examples. Consider why the relative pronoun refers to the entire introductory clause.

The mayor took all the tax money and fled the country, which shocked the whole town.
Carmen won a medal at the race, which made her parents quite proud.
Mark's wife ran off with the butcher, which caused quite a scandal in the family.

Written Practice 13-5

Complete each sentence with a nonrestrictive relative clause. For example:

Have you seen her latest movie, which _was based on a novel by Tolstoy?_

1. The ballerina, with whom

_____, speaks little English.

2. An old friend from school, who

_____, came by for a visit.

3. That nest, which _____,
looks like it is ready to fall from the tree.

4. This floorboard, under which

_____, is intentionally
loose.

5. Mr. Marconi, whose

_____, joined a veterans'
organization recently.

6. I'm going to spend some time with my cousin, who

_____.

7. The carpenters, whom

_____, work so slowly.

Complete each sentence with a restrictive relative clause. For example:

The car that *my brother bought* has a lot of problems.

8. I really like the house that

_____ in.

9. My family knows several sailors that

_____.

10. Have you found any books that

_____?

11. Where are the boxes that

_____ from?

12. Words that _____ aren't
necessarily poetry.

13. A friend that _____ may
spend the winter in Puerto Rico.

14. We don't know any of the people that

_____ with.

15. I want a laptop that

_____.

QUIZ

Choose the letter of the word or phrase that best completes each sentence.

1. I'd like to go on the trip with you, _____ I just can't get away from work.

   A. well   C. but

   B. for   D. therefore

2. _____ you have strong writing skills, we plan to offer you an editing job.

   A. Inasmuch as   C. Concerning

   B. Whether   D. As if

3. The cupboard is bare, and _____.

   A. where is everything now   C. someone needs to go shopping

   B. can find nothing to eat   D. is an embarrassment
      anywhere

4. I have no idea _____ the woman understood me.

   A. surely   C. however

   B. presuming   D. whether

5. _____ Mr. Kelly was asleep on the sofa, the dog devoured the steaks on the table.

   A. Although   C. Either

   B. Provided   D. While

6. I like how you think; _____, I want you to begin writing my speeches.

   A because   C. given

   B. therefore   D. neither

7. Is that the man _____ fell into the fountain at city hall?

   A. that   C. from whom you

   B. whom   D. which

8. Can someone tell me _____ to set this old clock?

   A. how   C. that

   B. why   D. on which

9. Where are the documents _____?
    A. that is so important
    C. which was written by them
    B. I sent you yesterday
    D. when the lawyer signed them

10. My neighbors' daughter was injured in an accident, _____ saddened me greatly.
    A. which
    C. whose daughter
    B. that
    D. she

chapter **14**

Negation

This chapter will describe the English forms of negation and their use, as well as the alternative forms of negation.

CHAPTER OBJECTIVES

In this chapter you will learn about:

- The two forms of negation
- How to negate a sentence or elements in a sentence
- Elliptical responses

English is one of the European languages that can negate a sentence, or an element in a sentence, without using what is called a *double negative*: that is, two words expressing negation or denial. The most commonly used form of negation is the adverb **not**.

Negating *Be*

When **not** negates a form of **be** in the present or past tense, it follows the verb. No auxiliary is required. For example:

Present	Past
I **am not** tired.	I **was not** tired.
You **are not** right.	You **were not** right.

Present	Past
He/She/It **is not** here.	He/She/It **was not** here.
We **are not** at home.	We **were not** at home.
They **are not** my friends.	They **were not** my friends.

When negated sentences with **be** are formed as questions, the adverb **not** follows the subject of the sentence.

Present	Past
Am I **not** tired?	Was I **not** tired?
Are you **not** right?	Were you **not** right?
Is he/she/it **not** here?	Was he/she/it **not** here?
Are we **not** at home?	Were we **not** at home?
Are they **not** my friends?	Were they **not** my friends?

In other tenses that call for auxiliaries, **not** stands between the auxiliary and the infinitive or participle. If the sentence is a question, **not** follows the subject.

Perfect Tenses	Future Tense
I **have not seen** him.	We **shall not help** with the cleaning.
She **had not found** it.	You **will not be** well enough.
They **will not have arrived** by then.	

Perfect Tenses	Future Tense
Have I **not** seen him?	Shall we **not** help with the cleaning?
Had she **not** found it?	Will you **not** be well enough?
Will they **not** have arrived by then?	

In informal style, it is common to form a negative contraction with the verb **be** in the present and past tense or with the auxiliary. For example:

I am not	I'm not (ain't = *See Chapter 9*.)
you are not	you aren't
he/she/it is not	he/she/it isn't
we are not	we aren't
they are not	they aren't
you were not	you weren't
he/she/it was not	he/she/it wasn't
I have been	I haven't been

he/she/it has been	he/she/it hasn't been
we had been	we hadn't been
I shall not	I shan't
you will not	you won't

If a question is asked with a negative contraction, the contraction begins the sentence, and the subject of the sentence follows.

Aren't you a friend of hers?
Isn't that a beautiful view?
Wasn't his lecture interesting?
Weren't the children well behaved today?
Haven't we been here before?
Hasn't John been well?
Hadn't they been in Mexico?
Won't you be more careful now?

Oral Practice

🔘 Track 46

Read each sentence aloud, paying attention to the use of the adverb **not**.

Mother: Aren't you out of the shower yet?
Son: I'm not out of bed yet. I didn't get home until midnight.
Mother: You weren't supposed to stay out so late.
Son: Midnight is not late on a Saturday night.
Mother: You won't be staying out late tonight. You have work tomorrow.
Son: No, tomorrow's a holiday. I'm not going to work.
Mother: I forgot. I hope you're not going to sleep late. I need help.
Son: With what? There aren't any more bushes to trim.
Mother: Not outside. The washing machine isn't running and needs to be fixed.
Son: I'm not a mechanic. I might make it worse.
Mother: It's just not draining. I think a hose is clogged.
Son: I'll look at it, but I'm not promising anything.

Negating Other Verbs

When **not** is used to negate verbs other than **be**, the auxiliary **do/does/did** is used to form the negation and the contraction in the present and past tenses. For example:

Positive	Negative	Negative Contraction
I speak	I **do not** speak	I **don't** speak
he learns	he **does not** learn	he **doesn't** learn
you heard	you **did not** hear	you **didn't** hear

In the perfect and future tenses, the auxiliaries are negated.

Positive	Negative	Negative Contraction
I have spoken	I **have not** spoken	I **haven't** spoken
he had learned	he **had not** learned	he **hadn't** learned
you will hear	you **will not** hear	you **won't** hear

When questions are formed, the auxiliary begins the sentence and is followed by the subject and the adverb **not**. If the auxiliary is a negated contraction, it begins the sentence and is followed by the subject of the sentence. For example:

Do I not speak clearly enough?
Don't I speak clearly enough?
Does he not want to pass the final exam?
Doesn't he want to pass the final exam?
Did you not hear that joke?
Didn't you hear that joke?
Have I not spoken with you before?
Haven't I spoken with you before?
Has it not rained yet?
Hasn't it rained yet?
Had Maria not learned her lesson?
Hadn't Maria learned her lesson?
Will you not hear my explanation?
Won't you hear my explanation?

Written Practice 14-1

Reword each sentence by placing the adverb **not** in the correct position. Then reword the sentence with the verb and **not** forming a contraction. For example:

John is in the living room.

John is not in the living room.

John isn't in the living room.

1. We are taking a ride out into the country.

   _____

   _____

2. Is that your new car?

   _____

3. My cousins were in California last week.

   _____

4. Did your grandmother speak English well?

   _____

   _____

5. The little girl was playing in the sandbox.

   _____

   _____

6. Was I friendly enough to them?

   _____

   _____

7. My aunt keeps her jewelry in a safe.

   _____

8. Will Robert get home before supper?

_____

_____

9. We shall lend him money again.

_____

_____

10. Do you like living in the dormitory?

_____

_____

Modal Auxiliaries

The modal auxiliaries that are in a phrase that begins with **be** are negated by placing **not** after the verb form in the present and past tenses. For example:

Be Able To
We are able to stay fit.
We **are not** able to stay fit.
We **aren't** able to stay fit.

Be Supposed To
She is supposed to babysit tonight.
She **is not** supposed to babysit tonight.
She **isn't** supposed to babysit tonight.

The auxiliaries **want to**, **need to**, and **have to** form their negation with **not** like other transitive or intransitive verbs.

She wants to help.
She **does not** want to help.
She **doesn't** want to help.

I needed to get some rest.
I **did not** need to get some rest.
I **didn't** need to get some rest.

Do I have to study more?
Do I **not** have to study more?
Don't I have to study more?

The auxiliaries **can**, **could**, **must**, **might**, **may**, and **should** are negated like the verb **be**. However, **might** and **may** sound awkward when formed as a contraction; therefore, **mightn't** and **mayn't** should be avoided.

I can find the keys.

I **cannot** find the keys.

I **can't** find the keys.

Can you **not** find the keys?

Can't you find the keys?

She **could** wait for us.

She **could not** wait for us.

She **couldn't** wait for us.

Could she **not** wait for us?

Couldn't she wait for us?

We must hurry.

We **must not** hurry.

We **mustn't** hurry.

Must we **not** hurry?

Mustn't we hurry?

You might be wrong.

You **might not** be wrong.

Might you **not** be wrong?

That may be true.

That **may not** be true.

May that **not** be true?

We should go home.

We **should not** go home.

We **shouldn't** go home.

Should we **not** go home?

Shouldn't we go home?

Oral Practice

Read each sentence aloud, paying attention to the form of **not** that is used.

We can't understand anything you say.

I don't like being the only one who enjoys classical music.

This might not be the right road to take us back to the city.

You shouldn't talk about your relatives like that.

Martin didn't buy that expensive laptop after all.

My niece could not find a parking place near the theater.

I mustn't eat so much, and you shouldn't cook so much food for me.

Haven't you ever seen a blimp before?

The adverb **not** is used extensively to modify verbs. When the verb is negated, the general meaning of the sentence is negated. But when other elements are negated, it is only they that are specified for negation, and the rest of the sentence is not. This kind of negation can form a short phrase.

The rest of the sentence is elliptical—*understood but not spoken or written*. For example:

John drives a new BMW.
John does not drive a new BMW. = *The sentence is negated.*
Not John. (Jim drives a new BMW.) = *The subject is negated.*
Not a <u>BMW</u>. (John drives a Cadillac.) = *The direct object is negated.*

It is possible to negate the subject and direct object in a complete sentence, but only in the spoken language can the intoned word be heard. In the written language, the emphasized word may be underlined. For example:

<u>John</u> does not drive a new BMW.
John does not drive a new <u>BMW</u>.

It is only in its elliptical form that the individual element can be isolated and the intent made clear.
Let's look at another example.

My sister comes home every weekend.
My sister does not come home every weekend. = *The sentence is negated.*
Not <u>my</u> sister. (Tom's sister is the one who comes home every weekend.) = *The possessive is negated.*
Not my <u>sister</u>. (My brother is the one who comes home every weekend.) = *The subject is negated.*
Not <u>home</u>. (My sister goes to the lake cottage every weekend.) = *The adverb of location is negated.*
Not <u>every weekend</u>. (My sister comes home just once a month.) = *The adverb of time is negated.*

Here are several more examples of using **not** to negate something other than a verb. Always form a short phrase:

Not during the winter. Not inside the house. Not with Jim. Not here. Not there. Not Michael. Not a birthday party. Not fast. Not louder. Not the biggest one.

Other Forms of Negation

There are numerous other words that are used for negation. Besides being a negative adverbial interjection to a question, **no** can be used as an adjective.

Negative Response
Do you want to go to dinner? **No, thanks.**
Is there anything to eat? **No, the fridge is empty.**

Adjective
There are **no cookies** left in the jar.
There are **no seats** in the balcony.
I found **no way** to get out of this situation.

No way is also used adverbially to mean *not under any circumstances*. It is usually in the prepositional phrase **in no way: In no way will I consent to such an operation.** In colloquial English, **no way** can stand alone, acting as an elliptical response to a statement the speaker either doesn't believe or considers exaggerated. For example:

Statement: I met the president of the United States last night.
Elliptical response: No way! (*I don't believe you.*)
Statement: My brother has dated every pretty girl in town.
Elliptical response: No way! (*This must be an exaggeration.*)

The words **never** and **nowhere** are used adverbially. **Never** can stand before a transitive or intransitive verb that is conjugated in the present or past tense.

I **never** work in the yard when it's hot outdoors.
The women **never** traveled without a guide.

If the conjugated verb is an auxiliary, **never** can stand before or after the verb.

She **never** has cared for Bob.
She has **never** cared for Bob.
I **never** was able to play chess well.
I was **never** able to play chess well.
Tom **never** can leave his diabetic little girl home alone.
Tom can **never** leave his diabetic little girl home alone.

Nowhere tells *where* an action takes place. Some negatives are pronouns, for example: **none**, **no one**, and **nobody**. Like other pronouns, they replace nouns in a sentence.

Those gifts are not for Mr. Patel. = **None** are for Mr. Patel.
I know **every person** at the party. = I know **no one** at the party.
The call is for **the treasurer** in our office. = The call is for **nobody** in our office.

The negative **nothing** is a noun and functions like any other noun in a sentence. The difference is that it carries *a negative meaning*.

Not even a flower makes her happy. = **Nothing** makes her happy.

All our planning had **this disastrous outcome.** = All our planning came to **nothing.**

I don't want even **a smile** from you. = I want **nothing** from you.

Oral Practice

🔘 Track 47

Read each sentence aloud, paying attention to the negative words and their use.

My brother likes to come for a visit a lot but not every weekend.

I'd never seen a gigantic waterfall like Niagara before.

Weren't you supposed to be in yesterday's soccer match?

No one from our factory showed up at the union meeting.

There is really nothing that my wife wants that isn't reasonable.

Will nobody explain this strange formula to me and my colleagues?

I spoke to no one about the surprise party. It was Karen who didn't keep the secret.

I want no excuses and no arguments about how we approach this project.

There is a little cake left, but I'm afraid none is for you.

I have a few letters here, but none are addressed to the manager.

Did you never wish you could see your homeland again?

I didn't invite those men. Not Jim. Not Martin. None of them.

Any

Most negative words have a counterpart that is formed with **not** and **any** or a word derived from **any**. Let's look at some example sentences that use the adjective **no** and how the same sentence is said with **any**.

Negative	Negative with Any
I want **no** help from you.	I **don't** want **any** help from you.
There is **no** bread left.	There **isn't any** bread left.
She has **no** money to spare.	She **hasn't any** money to spare.

If the negative word is **none**, **any** is used again in the alternative form.

I have **none**.	I do **not** have **any**.
Is **none** for me?	**Isn't any** for me?
None of them speak English.	**Not any** of them speak English.

If the negative word is **no one**, **any** becomes **anyone**.

No one greeted me.	**Not anyone** greeted me.
I met **no one** I liked.	I **didn't** meet **anyone** I liked.

If the negative word is **nothing**, **any** becomes **anything**.

There is **nothing** here for us.	There **isn't anything** here for us.
Nothing interests him.	**Not anything** interests him.

If the negative word is **nowhere**, **any** becomes **anywhere**.

He was **nowhere** to be found.	He **wasn't anywhere** to be found.
She is **nowhere** in the house.	She **isn't anywhere** in the house.

The conjunction **nor** introduces a clause that follows one that is introduced by **neither** or another negative. In the **nor**- clause, it is possible to have a form of **any**. For example:

She has neither clothing I want, **nor any** garment I would ever wear.
There is no one here I know, **nor** is there **anyone** I want to meet.
He owns nothing of value, **nor** does he have **anything** of beauty.

TAKE NOTE *Never has an alternative form, but **any** is not used in that form. Instead, **never** becomes **not ever**. For example:*

Negative	**Negative with Ever**
I **never** speak to them.	I **don't ever** speak to them.
Will you **never** pay me a visit?	**Won't** you **ever** pay me a visit?

Oral Practice

Read each sentence aloud, paying attention to the kind of negative form that is being used.

My cousin never calls me on my birthday anymore.
I don't want anything from you, and I don't wish to give anything to you.
Isn't there any milk in the refrigerator?

Nothing makes my mother happier than having her children home for the holidays.

Don't you have anything a little cheaper in sweaters like this?

I haven't danced with anyone from that Mexican dance troupe yet.

Didn't the nurse keep any of the flowers we sent Uncle Michael?

I won't ever go to that restaurant again and won't eat any raw meat or fish again.

Nobody said that turning forty is easy, but it isn't anything to be ashamed of.

IDIOMS DEMYSTIFIED

Many idiomatic phrases can be negated like any other phrase.

put on airs = *act conceited or pretentious*
Don't put on airs. It's so unattractive.

run out of = *exhaust the supply of (something, either tangible, like a product, or intangible, like patience or time)*
We can't run out of milk. The stores are closed.

A few idioms have a negative meaning and are always accompanied by a negative word. For example:

not all there = *unable to think clearly or weak-minded; mentally challenged*
I don't think the poor fellow is all there. He just talks to himself.
This medicine makes me feel like I'm not all there.

wouldn't dream of it = *to be sure that one would never do something*
Enter the triathlon? I'm out of shape. I wouldn't dream of it.
Martin wouldn't dream of arguing with his father.

Elliptical Responses

When a question is posed, the response to the question can include all the elements of the question along with the answer. For example:

Do you want to go to the theater with me tonight?
Yes, I want to go to the theater with you tonight.
No, I don't want to go to the theater with you tonight.

These responses are obviously cumbersome and unnecessarily detailed. English responds to a question with a fragment of the question (usually the auxiliary or verb) with the appropriate subject and omits everything else. For example:

> Do you want to go to the theater with me tonight?
> Yes, I do.
> No, I don't.

With the verb **be** in the present or past tense, that verb is used in the elliptical response. When negated, a contraction can be used in informal style.

> Are they feeling a little better today?
> Yes, they are.
> No, they are not/aren't.
> Was Dora in the mountains during the blizzard?
> Yes, she was.
> No, she was not/wasn't.

With the perfect tense and future tense auxiliaries, those auxiliaries appear in the elliptical response.

> Have you been to see a doctor lately?
> Yes, I have.
> No, I have not/haven't.
> Had Robert finally found a job in the city?
> Yes, he had.
> No, he had not/hadn't.
> Will your husband be able to join us tomorrow?
> Yes, he will.
> No, he will not/won't.

If a question is seeking a response to a verb or an object in the question, that verb or object can appear in the elliptical response, but that is optional. For example:

> Would she like to try a piece of this cake?
> Yes, she would.
> Yes, she would like to.
> No, she would not/wouldn't.
> No, she would not/wouldn't like to.
> Did you buy some candy for the children?

Yes, I did.
Yes, I did buy some.
No, I did not/didn't.
No, I did not/didn't buy any.

Oral Practice

Read each sentence aloud, paying attention to how the elliptical responses are given.

Would you be interested in buying some property in this county?
No, I wouldn't. I plan to live in a warmer climate.
Can your wife join the choir and share her beautiful voice with us?
No, unfortunately, she can't. She already sings with an orchestra in Toledo.
Must you always look for the worst in people?
No, I mustn't. But I can't help it—so many of those I meet are unkind
    and rude.
Does your dog really like to sleep with those little kittens?
No, he doesn't like it. But the kittens love him and always stay near.
Do you want a sandwich or a doughnut or anything else to eat?
No, I don't want anything. Thanks.
Should that little boy ride his bike in the middle of the street?
No, he should not. That's dangerous.

QUIZ

Circle the letter of the word or phrase that best completes each sentence.

1. I don't want _____ that's stored in the attic.

   A. nothing   C. anything

   B. any of you   D. not any

2. "Can you explain this letter?" "Sorry, _____."

   A. I can't   C. not any

   B. no letter   D. nowhere

3. _____ finished making that dress for me?

    A. Has she not   C. Can she not

    B. Won't she   D. Couldn't she

4. They _____ yet memorized the poem by Longfellow.

    A. have   C. can't

    B. won't   D. hadn't

5. Mr. Carlson wants _____ that was left in the apartment by those former tenants.

    A. no   C. not ever

    B. never   D. nothing

6. _____ want to help out with the packing?

    A. Shouldn't   C. Mustn't

    B. Don't you   D. She won't

7. The men really don't need _____ money from you.

    A. any   C. no one

    B. none   D. anybody

8. _____ your answer not be wrong? Why are you so sure?

    A. Might   C. Won't

    B. Does   D. May not

9. _____ we chatted about this once before?

    A. Didn't   C. Had not

    B. Could   D. Haven't

10. You really _____ be in such a hurry.

    A. never   C. anywhere

    B. needn't   D. nowhere

15

Capitalization and Punctuation

This chapter presents the rules for the capitalization of nouns, names, and other grammatical elements. The proper use and function of punctuation marks is also considered.

CHAPTER OBJECTIVES

In this chapter you will learn about:

- When to capitalize a word
- Which words in a sentence do not need to be capitalized
- The function of punctuation marks
- The use of punctuation marks

Capitalization

In part, European languages created their rules for capitalization by imitating what was done in Latin. In addition, these languages followed their own developing traditions, which made their rules of capitalization unique.

English was no different. There was a time when nearly all nouns were always capitalized. Consider the following text taken from the United States Constitution, which was written at a time when European conventions of capitalization were still being observed in English. You will see that every noun is capitalized except the word *defence* (British spelling). The spelling of *defence* with a lowercase *d* seems to have been an oversight on the part of the eighteenth-century copyist.

> We the People of the United States, in Order to form a more perfect Union, establish Justice, insure domestic Tranquility, provide for the common defence, promote the general Welfare, and secure the Blessings of Liberty to ourselves and our Posterity, do ordain and establish this Constitution for the United States of America.

> Article. I.

> Section. 1.

> All legislative Powers herein granted shall be vested in a Congress of the United States, which shall consist of a Senate and House of Representatives.

> Section. 2.

> The House of Representatives shall be composed of Members chosen every second Year by the People of the several States, and the Electors in each State shall have the Qualifications requisite for Electors of the most numerous Branch of the State Legislature.

> No Person shall be a Representative who shall not have attained to the Age of twenty five Years, and been seven Years a Citizen of the United States, and who shall not, when elected, be an Inhabitant of that State in which he shall be chosen.

Modern English is not so generous with the use of capital letters.

The simplest rule of capitalization is to use a capital letter with any word that begins a sentence. It can be any part of speech. For example:

noun: Tools are as important as a worker's skills.
pronoun: They were born in Asia.
adjective: Wealthy people are often quite generous.
adverb: Slowly the man turned and caught sight of his wife.

verb: Run to the corner and mail this letter.
article: A rabbit hid in the shadows.
interrogative: What did you buy at the mall?
conjunction: While I was in Washington, I visited the White House.
preposition: In the autumn, we clean the gutters and rake the leaves.

Pronouns

The first person singular pronoun **I** is always capitalized. All other pronouns are capitalized only when they begin a sentence.

> **I** live in Boston.
> **You** work in the city, don't **you**?
> **He** danced with **her** all night.
> Are **we** acquainted with **them**?
> **Who** is **she**, and **what** is **she** carrying?
> That pup is lost. **It** followed **me** all the way home.

Nouns

Common nouns are words that describe people, objects, qualities, quantities, or ideas in general. For example:

soldier	hundreds
tree	democracy
beauty	

Common nouns are not capitalized unless they are the first word in a sentence or in the title of a work or film.

> **Houses** made of brick require less maintenance.
> Two of the **houses** on this street are more than 200 years old.
> Have you read *Bleak House*?

Proper nouns can be first names, middle names, last names, and titles that accompany names. They are always capitalized. For example:

John	Mr. Stanhope
Maria	Professor Jones
Steinbeck	Ms. Barton
Gandhi	President Barack Hussein Obama

Foreign last names or British titles that have a preceding preposition break the rule about capitalization. The preposition that precedes a foreign name should not be capitalized. For example:

Werner **von** Braun   Charles **de** Gaulle
Leonardo **da** Vinci   Anwar **el**-Sadat

Other proper nouns are those that describe the official name of an organization, business, product, or a language, country, or nationality. Street names and addresses should also be capitalized. If the conjunctions **and**, **but**, **for**, **or**, and **nor** and most prepositions appear in such a name, they are not capitalized. In the case of company names, an ampersand (&) usually replaces **and**. For example:

Western Electric
Johnson & Johnson
United States of America
High German
Russia is part of the Commonwealth of Independent States
3103 North Scott Street
the corner of Main Street and Third Avenue

Capitalize all days of the week, months of the year, and official holidays.

The baby was born on **Monday** of last week.
My son was born last **May**.
We expect the twins to be born before **Thanksgiving**.

School subjects are not capitalized, but the specific title of a course is. For example:

I love **geography**.
Are you studying French **poetry**?
She decided to enroll in **English as a Second Language 102**.

TAKE NOTE *Prepositions and articles are capitalized when they begin a sentence. They should not be capitalized unless they are in the logo or advertising of a business or organization. When they appear, capitalized, in a logo or advertising, it is the company or organization that has chosen to depart from the standard form of capitalization; the usage should not be applied by individuals in their own writing.*

A Tale of Two Cities	**Catering By Jacques Of Beverly Hills**
To Kill a Mockingbird	**Yoga And Spa For Women**

Many nouns are hyphenated. They are a combination of certain prefixes (for example, **anti, pre, non**) or a noun and another noun. If the noun after the hyphen is a proper noun, both the prefix and the noun will be capitalized. If the noun is a common noun, only the prefix will be capitalized when the word begins a sentence or if it is in the title of a work. For example:

> **Anti**-intellectual comments do not help the political climate.
> She is studying **pre**-Columbian civilizations.
> If he had **non**-B hepatitis, his condition would be worse.

It is important to consult a dictionary for accurate use of hyphens with prefixes.

If a preposition or an article (**a, an, the**) is included in a hyphenated word, the preposition or article should not be capitalized. The nouns follow the rules already laid out for common and proper nouns.

> This is Commander-**in**-Chief Jones of our veterans' lodge.
> I bought the children a jack-**o**'-lantern for Halloween.
> She disappeared into the fog like a will-**o**'-**the**-wisp.

Numbers (ordinal and cardinal numbers and fractions alike) are common nouns and can be connected to other numbers by means of a hyphen. If one number is capitalized in the title of a work, all numbers in the combination will be capitalized. But when a hyphenated number begins a sentence and is not in a title, only the first element is capitalized. For example:

> Did you read his book *The **Two-Thirds** Majority Does Not Exist?*
> **Twenty-seven** children will be in this kindergarten class.
> Their candidate received **fifty-one** percent of the votes.

Hyphenated numbers are used to give someone's age and to modify the phrase **days old, months old,** and **years old.**

> The baby is just **twenty-three** days old.
> My great-grandmother is now **ninety-five** years old.

But if the phrase is used as a noun or adjective, all the words in the phrase are hyphenated.

> She is a **ninety-five-year-old**.
> Anne has a **ninety-five-year-old** great-grandmother.

These hyphenated numbers follow the regular rules of capitalization.

Fifty-five isn't really so old.
I wanted to borrow **fifty-five** dollars.
My brother just bought the book *Fifty-Five: The New Forty-Five*.
My husband is a happy **fifty-five-year-old**.

Written Practice 15-1

In each item, change to a capital letter every lowercase letter that's improper as the sentences stand.

1. someone found her purse in the grove street bank and returned it.

   _____

2. do i know you from my days at indiana university or from the army?

   _____

3. no one told me that the essay for my history class was due this
   friday.

   _____

4. jack london not only wrote about nature, he also lived and worked in
   the wild.

   _____

5. we were in paris but got to see very little else of france.

   _____

6. my father worked for the ford motor company in detroit.

   _____

7. colonel james hardy was the commandant of fort sheridan in illinois
   only briefly.

   _____

8. ms. garcia met the governor of our state while in the capital.

   _____

9. our son got a job at the golden gate savings and loan company.

   _____

10. he enjoys most of winter but hates the month of january.

_____

11. for twenty years my aunt has owned a ford fairlane, and it still has low mileage.

_____

12. the honor guard raises the american flag while the marine corps band plays the national anthem.

_____

13. mayor thompson promised to build the town a new elementary school.

_____

14. the president is only a temporary resident of the white house.

_____

15. when anne took latin, she needed a lot of help from mr. smith after school.

_____

16. john miller wanted to borrow thirty-five dollars from her.

_____

17. dr. keller said that some preexisting conditions are not covered by insurance.

_____

18. in the summer of last year, senator rodriguez was in an accident in new orleans.

_____

19. is uncle thomas coming to my twenty-first birthday party?

_____

20. hundred-year-olds seem to thrive in that country.

_____

Punctuation

Punctuation marks are helpful in making clear the intent of a writer. These marks indicate where a thought ends, whether the thought is a statement or question, and what additional information is attached to the thought.

Period

The period is the simplest punctuation mark to use with sentences. It indicates the end of a thought in a declarative or imperative sentence. A complete sentence is composed of a subject and a predicate. If one of these elements is missing, the phrase is not a sentence. Let's look at some complete sentences that end in a period.

The air is fresh and crisp today.
My daughter returned home from college last night.
No one wants to buy my old car.
You can stay overnight in the guest room.
Please remain seated until your name is called.

If a sentence is elliptical, it will look like an incomplete sentence. However, the full information in the sentence *is understood*, and the phrase can end in a period.

"What do you want?"
"**Nothing.**" (*I want nothing.*)

A period is used to punctuate abbreviations. Some abbreviations need only a period at the end of the abbreviation. For example:

doctor	Dr. Ling
mister	Mr. Cole
professor	Prof. Maloney

Other abbreviations are composed of letters representing more than one word, and no periods are used.

master of arts	MA
doctor of philosophy	PhD
International Business Machines	IBM
General Motors	GM
Columbia Broadcasting System	CBS
Public Broadcasting System	PBS
uniform/universal resource locator	URL

When referring to the time of day, the abbreviations **a.m.** (*ante meridiem*) and **p.m.** (*post meridiem*) are used. The former identifies time before noon, and the latter identifies time after noon. These two abbreviations are sometimes capitalized: **A.M.** and **P.M.**

When an abbreviation ends a sentence, a second period *is not used to identify the completion of the sentence.*

The bus finally arrived at 6:30 a.m.

On Saturday, Natasha will receive her PhD.

Question Mark

The question mark ends a sentence that asks a question. There is no difference between a question that is a **yes-no** question and one that begins with an interrogative word. For example:

Are you going to buy a new car?

Does that man know us?

Has Mr. Patel ever been in Hawaii?

Who is knocking at the door?

Where did I put my glasses?

What is that strange fellow hiding under his coat?

A question mark is sometimes used to show surprise or disbelief in a declarative or imperative sentence. In speech, this is done with intonation. In the written language, the question mark makes this implication.

John: I have the feeling that you're the one who took the money.

Tom: This is what you think of me?

Maria: Your children have no manners and fight too much.

Jean: Your children behave perfectly?

Exclamation Point

The exclamation point or exclamation mark ends an interjection or exclamation. It implies great surprise or emotion, particularly anger/irritation or fear.

Wow! You look beautiful in that dress!   Get out of here!

No, I do not want to buy any encyclopedias!   Run for your lives!

A sentence written as a question can sometimes end with an exclamation point to show emotion.

Am I supposed to believe that!

Do you think that I'm such a fool!

Comma

The comma is often misused. Some overuse the comma, and others simply avoid it even when it is necessary.

In its simplest usage, the comma separates elements in a series of more than two words or phrases. Each element is followed by a comma, and the final element is preceded by **and** or **or**. For example:

He bought a tie, a new suit, leather gloves, and a silk shirt.
When you're at the store, get eggs, milk, bread, and a pound of butter.
Do you want to go out with Bill, Alex, or Michael?

The elements in a series can be complete sentences.

My husband put the kids to bed, my mother did the dishes,
and I relaxed on the sofa.

If you use **as well as** following **and**, a comma is still required, and **and** appears with the element that precedes **as well as**. In these cases, however, **as well as** means **additionally** or **including**.

I invited friends, relatives, and my fiancée, **as well as** a few members of the swim team.
He had one bulldog, three poodles, and two huskies, **as well as** an old cat.

Written Practice 15-2

Using the string of phrases provided, create a sentence with the phrases shown in a series. For example:

apples/oranges/any kind of berries

I love to eat apples, oranges, and any kind of berries.

1. Buick/Toyota/Cadillac

   _____

2. in the spring/in the summer/in the fall/in the dead of winter

   _____

3. a case of soda/four pizzas/several bags of potato chips

   _____

4. I washed the car/my daughter made some lunch/my son cleaned the garage

---

5. *To Kill a Mockingbird/Catcher in the Rye/The Great Gatsby*

A comma is also used to separate a parenthetical negative phrase from the rest of the sentence. The phrase gives additional information about an element in the basic sentence.

His wife, **not his lawyer**, stood up to those who accused him.
Their candidate was elected, **not ours**.
John decided to buy the compact car, **not the luxury model**.

In Chapter 13, you encountered dependent clauses, which when written at the beginning of a sentence are followed by a comma.

When he was in Rome, he visited the Vatican.
Although it began raining, the boys continued their run around the track.

The comma is not used when the dependent clause follows the main clause. However, if the dependent clause is not *restrictive* (giving pertinent information about the main clause), a comma can separate the two clauses. For example:

The little girl cried when her puppy died. (*restrictive*)
I wouldn't mind some coffee, if you don't mind. (*not pertinent information*)
Raj was happy because she agreed to go out with him. (*restrictive*)
She offered to help, although the work was already done. (*not pertinent information*)

A comma is used to separate the name of a city from the state in which it is located.

They live in **Philadelphia, Pennsylvania**.
We're spending our vacation in **Reno, Nevada**.
I love visiting **New Orleans, Louisiana**.

When the state is written in its abbreviated form, a comma is still required to separate it from the name of the city.

Chicago, IL
Miami, FL
Columbia, SC

If the name of a person and his or her address are provided with the city and state, commas are used to separate all four elements. For example:

This is a letter for Ms. Helen James, 295 W. Montreal Drive, Gary, Indiana.
I sent the books to Eduardo Arias, 1110 San Pedro Ave., San Diego, CA.
Her business card read: Ashley Brown, 141 Montrose St., Minneapolis, MN.

It is important to differentiate between *restrictive* and *nonrestrictive* phrases and clauses. Restrictive clauses, which provide information essential to the main sentence, should not be separated by commas. Nonrestrictive phrases and clauses, however, should be separated from the main sentence by commas. For example:

Restrictive: The man **with a sword in his hand** was one of the king's knights.
Nonrestrictive: The man, **with a sword in his hand**, charged into the battle.
Restrictive: The woman **that I met in Madrid** owns this boutique.
Nonrestrictive: The woman, **whom I met in Madrid**, was once a famous ballerina.
Restrictive: Several guests **hiding in the closet** were hoping to surprise the birthday boy.
Nonrestrictive: Several guests, **hiding in the closet**, had come from around the country.

Oral Practice

Track 48

Read each sentence aloud, paying attention to the restrictive and nonrestrictive phrases and clauses, as well as comma usage where this punctuation appears.

I met the children that are my son's best friends.
Our new teacher, who comes from Canada, speaks four languages.
The boy waiting in the car looks quite ill.
The shoppers, with many packages balanced on their arms, hurried out of the store.
Have you heard the new album that Lady Gaga produced?
This gift, received from an unknown source, contains something rather heavy.
The season I like best is summer because I can go swimming every day.
I'd like to have my car repaired by tomorrow, if that's possible.

Quotation Marks

A quote is *direct discourse* shown in written form. Most quotations are introduced by a verb such as **say**, **ask**, or **reply**. If the quote follows one of these or similar verbs, a comma precedes the quote. The quote is surrounded by quotation marks. For example:

> **Direct discourse:** "I don't want to live in New York anymore."
> **Quote:** John said, "I don't want to live in New York anymore."
> **Direct discourse:** "Are you taking a vacation this year?"
> **Quote:** Ms. Garcia asked, "Are you taking a vacation this year?"
> **Direct discourse:** "I think this play is boring, too."
> **Quote:** Someone replied, "I think this play is boring, too."

If the quotation precedes an introductory clause with **say**, **ask**, **reply**, or similar verb, a comma is not used. The punctuation of the quotation is used and stands inside the quotation marks. If that punctuation is a period, it changes to a comma.

> **Direct discourse:** "I hate this weather!"
> **Quote:** "I hate this weather!" shouted Mary.
> **Direct discourse:** "Who gave you that information?"
> **Quote:** "Who gave you that information?" asked the judge.
> **Direct discourse:** "I'll give you my answer tomorrow."
> **Quote:** "I'll give you my answer tomorrow," she replied.

Titles of magazine articles and songs are written within quotation marks. For example:

> "Obama's First Term"
> "A Plan for Roe v Wade"
> "White Christmas"
> "Yellow Submarine"

If titles of magazine articles or songs appear within a quotation, the *double quotation marks* are changed to *single quotation marks*.

> The teacher asked, "Have you read **'Obama's First Term'** for today's class?"
> "I didn't learn much from the article **'A Plan for Roe v Wade'** in this magazine," said Maria.
> Bill said, "My grandmother never heard of **'White Christmas.'**"
> She replied, "I can play **'Yellow Submarine'** for you."

Colons

The colon is most commonly used to separate hours from minutes in telling time. For example:

6:05	*six o five, five after six*
10:30	*ten thirty, half past ten*
2:45	*two forty-five, a quarter to (of) three*
12:00	*twelve o'clock, noon (midnight)*

A colon at the end of a sentence indicates that more information is following. If that information is a single sentence, the first word in the sentence is not capitalized. If more than one sentence follows, both sentences are capitalized.

The prisoner came into the courtroom: his eyes were lowered, his face was gaunt, and he wore an orange jumpsuit.
The crowd screamed and cheered at the news: Their candidate had won! The tyrant had been defeated!

In an informal letter, the greeting is followed by a comma. In a formal or business letter, the greeting is followed by a colon. For example:

Informal	**Formal**
Dear Maria,	Dear Ms. Holmes:
Dear Mom and Dad,	To Whom It May Concern:

Semicolons

It was pointed out in Chapter 13 that a semicolon is used to precede the conjunctions **accordingly**, **however**, **indeed**, and **therefore**. These conjunctions are followed by a comma and the concluding clause. For example:

This is a wonderful dance; **however**, my feet need a rest.
The baby was a newborn; **indeed**, she was a mere two hours old.
A terrible storm is brewing; **therefore**, we're canceling the trip across the lake.
John's neighbor threatened to sue; **accordingly**, John consulted a lawyer immediately.

Use a semicolon to separate a series, especially when the elements are rather long or contain a comma that makes the meaning of the sentence hard to understand. For example:

> James spent many hours waiting in long lines; filling out applications, disclaimers, and other documents that made little sense to him; and being interviewed by officers who cared nothing about his background or education.
>
> They plan to build factories in Peoria, Illinois; Grand Rapids, Michigan; and Lincoln, Nebraska.

When two sentences are closely linked in meaning or intent, they can be written as one sentence separated by a semicolon.

> Jean was a superb musician; her skill on the piano was matched by her skill with the harp.
>
> The soldiers marched triumphantly into the village; their puffed-up chests and broad smiles revealed their pride in the victory.

Apostrophes

You discovered in Chapter 9 how the apostrophe is used in forming contractions. For example:

cannot	can't	nothing is	nothing's
I am	I'm	they are	they're
we have	we've		

The apostrophe is also used extensively in forming English **possessive nouns**. Most singular nouns form the possessive by adding -'s. The meaning derived from this ending is similar to *of*; it shows ownership. For example:

boy	boy's	*of the boy*
horse	horse's	*of the horse*
girl	girl's	*of the girl*
parent	parent's	*of the parent*

Even if a noun ends in -s, an apostrophe is added to form the possessive.

boss	boss's	*of the boss*
Mr. Jones	Mr. Jones's	*of Mr. Jones*

Plural nouns form their possessive by adding -s'.

dogs   dogs'   *of the dogs*
teams   teams'   *of the teams*
bosses   bosses'   *of the bosses*

If a noun has an irregular plural form, it is treated like a singular noun; the possessive is -'s: **men's**, **children's**, **women's**, and so on.

Oral Practice

Read each sentence aloud, paying attention to the use and form of the possessive nouns.

Jean's hair color seemed to change every day or two, according to her mood.

The officers' commands and the soldiers' responses to them confused everyone.

Although the star's role was enormous, the other actors' parts had been reduced nearly to nothing.

The animal's left side was injured, but having spotted the hunter's hiding place, the creature limped off into the woods.

The girls' new tree house had been built by Lois's father.

During the storm's final hour, the Browns' house was damaged by lightning.

Whose overcoat is this? Bill's or Mr. Callahan's? It's not mine.

Should I buy Tom's moped or my cousins' motorcycle?

IDIOMS DEMYSTIFIED

Possessives can be found in several idioms. Two such idioms are:

on someone's behalf = *do something for someone or in place of another person*
I'll conduct the meeting on the boss's behalf. He's been delayed.

a stone's throw from = *near to, not far from*
We can walk to the café. It's only a stone's throw from here.

Written Practice 15-3

Review each sentence and correct the punctuation by inserting the appropriate punctuation marks.

1. She said Get out and never come back

_____

2. The childs temperature was over 103 indeed he was burning up

_____

3. Behind the garage we found some old tools and a wheelbarrow

_____

4. Does this umbrella belong to you he asked with a smile

_____

5. The volunteers meeting was canceled and a party began instead

_____

QUIZ

Choose the letter of the word, phrase, or punctuation mark that best completes each sentence.

1. We entered the _____ of Russia and soon saw Red Square.
   A. capital
   B. fortress
   C. Country
   D. Moscow

2. Our plane landed exactly at 9:55 _____.
   A. evening
   B. morning
   C. a.m.
   D. later

3. The president is commander-_____-chief of the military.
   A. in
   B. In
   C. the
   D. The

4. Jack is living in Warsaw and speaks a little _____.
   A. Polish
   B. the language
   C. words
   D. slow

5. I never want to see you again _____

    A. .   C. ,

    B. !   D. ;

6. My aunt asked, "Can you come for a visit next week _____"

    A. .   C. ?

    B. !   D. :

7. Did you see the _____ new car?

    A. man   C. governors

    B. Garcias'   D. someone's

8. I won't listen to anymore _____ therefore, this conversation is over.

    A. .   C. !

    B. ;   D. ?

9. On _____ behalf, I would like to thank all of you for this honor.

    A. my family's   C. men's

    B. they're   D. our teams

10. This is the United States _____ America.

    A. in   C. of

    B. In   D. Of

PART THREE TEST

Choose the letter of the word, phrase, or punctuation mark that best completes each sentence.

1. **I have been going to this school _____ August.**
   A. like
   B. since
   C. assuming
   D. cope with

2. **He doesn't know where the children were _____.**
   A. of
   B. on
   C. at
   D. N/A

3. **She wanted to try to drive home _____.**
   A. of the summer
   B. beneath the highway
   C. during the blizzard
   D. N/A

4. **_____ just ordering a pizza for dinner?**
   A. Should I
   B. Does he want
   C. Are we able to
   D. How about

5. **Americans have a very strong belief _____ freedom and fairness.**
   A. of
   B. from
   C. in
   D. upon

6. **_____ stop by for a visit next week.**
   A. Maybe can
   B. Do
   C. Let
   D. Don't let

7. **Don't _____ your brother know that you have the keys to the car.**
   A. speak
   B. be
   C. worry
   D. let

8. **Let's _____.**
   A. we should help them
   B. not discuss it anymore
   C. the neighbors try it
   D. you should go get a job

9. Try _____.

    A. as they often visit us   C. don't you think

    B. to get along with James   D. not today

10. _____ the good dishes, please!

    A. Don't use   C. Why don't you

    B. Let someone else   D. Let's

11. I'd like to go on the trip with you, _____ I just can't get away from work.

    A. well   C. but

    B. for   D. therefore

12. There's nothing to eat or drink, and _____.

    A. where is everything now   C. someone needs to go shopping

    B. can find nothing to eat anywhere   D. is an embarrassment

13. I have no idea _____ this machine will work.

    A. surely   C. although

    B. suppose   D. whether

14. We're impressed because she's such a hard worker; _____, we want her to manage this department.

    A. because   C. given

    B. therefore   D. neither

15. Where are the applications _____?

    A. that is so important   C. which was written by them

    B. we sent you yesterday   D. when I signed them

16. We _____ yet finished repairing the dishwasher.

    A. have   C. can't

    B. won't   D. hadn't

17. I ordered _____ from your store.

    A. no   C. not ever

    B. never   D. nothing

18. My family doesn't want _____ advice from you.

    A. any   C. no one

    B. none   D. anybody

19. _____ his suggestion not be wrong? Why is he so confident?

    A. Might   C. Won't

    B. Does   D. May not

20. _____ you and I discussed this many times?

    A. Didn't   C. Had not

    B. Could   D. Haven't

21. Our bus arrived about 11:45 _____.

    A. evening   C. p.m.

    B. morning   D. later

22. Abdul was born in Egypt but is now an _____.

    A. American   C. English language

    B. citizen   D. Immigrant

23. Leave this house and never come back _____

    A. .   C. ,

    B. !   D. ;

24. My aunt asked, "Can you come for a visit next week _____"

    A. .   C. ?

    B. !   D. :

25. The _____ new house is out in the suburbs.

    A. woman   C. mayors

    B. Browns'   D. someone's

Part Four

The Final Details

chapter **16**

Passive Voice

In this chapter you will encounter the passive voice as it is contrasted with the active voice. The static passive will also be introduced and compared with the regular passive voice.

CHAPTER OBJECTIVES

In this chapter you will learn about:

- The difference between the active voice and the passive voice
- The formation of the passive voice
- The tenses of the passive voice
- How the passive voice and the static passive differ

Forming the Passive Voice

The passive voice can be formed from transitive verbs used in the active voice. A sentence that has a subject and a transitive verb followed by a direct and/or indirect object is said to be in the active voice. For example:

Subject	Transitive Verb	Direct and/or Indirect Object
The men	are building	a house.
We	gave	her a gift.
Someone	has stolen	my wallet.

? Still Struggling

Intransitive verbs, which include linking verbs and verbs of motion, cannot be used to form the passive voice. For example:

be   fly
become   go
die   run

Intransitive verbs do not have direct or indirect objects.

The normal pattern of an active voice sentence is **subject + transitive verb + object**. These elements are retained in the passive voice, but each one functions somewhat differently. Consider the active voice sentence: **The man buys a new tie.** In the passive voice, the three elements (**subject + transitive verb + object**) change.

The subject **The man** becomes the object of the preposition **by**: **by the man.**
The verb **buys** becomes a past participle introduced by the auxiliary **be** in the same tense as the verb in the active sentence: **is bought.**
The direct object **a new tie** becomes the subject of the passive voice sentence: **A new tie.**

The completed passive voice sentence is: **A new tie is bought by the man.** Any adjectives, adverbs, or prepositional phrases in the active voice sentence accompany the elements they modify in the passive voice sentence.

The meaning of a passive voice sentence is essentially the same as that of a sentence with the same elements arranged in the active voice. However, the original subject is now *in a passive position* as the object of a preposition.

Let's look at another active voice sentence and observe how it becomes a passive voice sentence: **She will design a large house.**

The subject **She** becomes the object of the preposition **by**: **by her.**
The verb **design** becomes a past participle introduced by the auxiliary **be** in the same tense as the verb in the active sentence: **will be designed.**
The direct object **a large house** becomes the subject of the passive voice sentence: **A large house.**

The completed passive voice sentence is: **A large house will be designed by her.**

Oral Practice

Read each sentence aloud, noting the difference between the active voice and passive voice sentences.

> My brother found someone's wallet.
> Someone's wallet was found by my brother.
> He invited our cousin from Philadelphia to the dance.
> Our cousin from Philadelphia was invited by him to the dance.
> The parents of the team members eagerly support the soccer team.
> The soccer team is eagerly supported by the parents of the team members.
> Will foreign tourists purchase tickets to this opera?
> Will tickets to this opera be purchased by foreign tourists?
> Have they delivered the new television set yet?
> Has the new television set been delivered by them yet?

Let's look at how a passive voice sentence changes in the various tenses. Note that the past participle is not changed as the tense changes. Only the auxiliary **be** changes. First, let's review the tenses of the verb **be**.

> **Present:** he is
> **Past:** he was
> **Present perfect:** he has been
> **Past perfect:** he had been
> **Future:** he will be
> **Future perfect:** he will have been

Notice how the same conjugation of **be** occurs in the passive voice in the example sentence: **The book is stolen by him.**

> **Present:** The book is stolen by him.
> **Past:** The book was stolen by him.
> **Present perfect:** The book has been stolen by him.
> **Past perfect:** The book had been stolen by him.
> **Future:** The book will be stolen by him.
> **Future perfect:** The book will have been stolen by him.

You learned in Chapter 4 that the future perfect tense is sometimes avoided when it becomes cumbersome and contains a long string of verbs. This awkwardness in phrasing can occur in the passive voice. If the passive voice sounds awkward, the active voice is preferred.

Written Practice 16-1

Reword each sentence in the tenses indicated.

1. Present: The toy is broken by the little boy.

   Past: _____

   Present perfect: _____

   Past perfect: _____

   Future: _____

2. Present: _____

   Past: The dog was washed by Thomas.

   Present perfect: _____

   Past perfect: _____

   Future: _____

3. Present: _____

   Past: _____

   Present perfect: Has the silverware been polished by your husband?

   Past perfect: _____

   Future: _____

4. Present: _____

   Past: _____

   Present perfect: _____

   Past perfect: It had been discovered by a scientist from England.

   Future: _____

5. Present: _____

   Past: _____

   Present perfect: _____

   Past perfect: _____

   Future: The group will be led by a museum guide.

Omitting the Prepositional Phrase

The passive voice comes in handy when the speaker or writer wishes to make the *doer of the action* anonymous. There may be a variety of reasons for this: wishing to keep the doer's identity a secret; not knowing who the doer is; or simply wanting to form a less complex sentence. Compare the following pairs of sentences.

> The money was taken by the city's mayor during the night.
> The money was taken during the night.
> Corn and wheat are grown in this region by the local farmers.
> Corn and wheat are grown in this region.
> Was this article written for a large newspaper by a reporter?
> Was this article written for a large newspaper?

When an active voice sentence has a *vague subject* (a subject that does not represent a precise doer of the action), it is often omitted in the passive voice sentence. Vague subjects are words such as **one**, **they**, **people**, and **many**. Let's look at some active voice sentences and see how they change to the passive voice and omit the subject of the active voice sentence.

> **They** manufactured airplanes here during the war.
> Airplanes were manufactured here during the war.
> Does **one** irrigate these fields regularly?
> Are these fields irrigated regularly?
> **People** will sometimes shun strangers and foreigners.
> Strangers and foreigners will sometimes be shunned.
> **Many** carried swords and shields into battle.
> Swords and shields were carried into battle.

Written Practice 16-2

Retaining the tense of the active voice verb, reword each active voice sentence in the passive voice. Then reword the passive voice sentence, omitting the prepositional phrase introduced by **by**. For example:

> Mark kissed all the girls.
>
> *All the girls were kissed by Mark.*
>
> *All the girls were kissed.*

1. Someone burned down the old barn last night.

_____

2. My brother had purchased a little cottage on the lake.

_____

3. Will the owners build a new factory here?

_____

_____

4. All the people love the queen very much.

_____

_____

5. They have done more and more every day.

_____

_____

6. I discovered a small cave in the park.

_____

_____

7. Will the farmer drive the cattle into the pasture?

_____

_____

8. His wife has milked the cows.

_____

_____

9. The teachers tested the juniors and seniors regularly.

_____

_____

10. No one noticed his strange behavior.

_____

_____

An Action in Progress

English has two conjugational forms in all the tenses: the habitual or completed form and the incomplete or progressive form. For example:

Complete	In Progress
he sells	he is selling
he sold	he was selling
he has sold	he has been selling
he had sold	he had been selling
he will sell	he will be selling
he will have sold	he will have been selling

When an active sentence has a verb that shows an action in progress, that form of conjugation must also appear when the sentence is stated in the passive voice. This is particularly true of the present and past tenses. The perfect and future tenses can sound awkward and cumbersome; therefore, the progressive form is avoided in those tenses. The auxiliary for the progressive form is not the verb **be** alone but the verb phrase **be being** (**am being, is being, are being, was being, were being**). Compare the following pairs of sentences.

They punish him for his actions.
He **is punished** for his actions.
They are punishing him for his actions.
He **is being punished** for his actions.
The man helped the injured woman.
The injured woman **was helped** by the man.
The man was helping the injured woman.
The injured woman **was being helped** by the man.

Active voice sentences in the perfect tenses in the progressive form use the completed or habitual form of a verb *in the past tense* in the passive voice. For example:

They have been building a school.
A school **was being built**.
Someone had been painting the garage.
The garage **was being painted**.

The progressive form of the future tense is avoided in the passive voice and is replaced by the completed or habitual future tense conjugation.

People will be sending postcards to all of them.
Postcards **will be sent** to all of them.

Oral Practice

🔘 Track 49

Read each sentence aloud, paying attention to the form and meaning of the passive voice.

The thief was being taken to jail by a policewoman.
Several photographs had been taken by a local journalist.
Will the children be guided through the museum by their teachers?
Money is being spent on foolish things every day.
My mother has been driven to the airport by one of our neighbors.
The snow is being cleared from the highway by a team of snowplow operators.
Traffic was being directed by an officer with a loud whistle.
The patient was wheeled to the operating room on a gurney.
The town residents are being asked once again to pay higher taxes.
All our bills have been paid in advance through February.

Modal Auxiliaries

The modal auxiliaries were introduced in Chapter 8. The same auxiliaries can be used with sentences in the passive voice. However, *the progressive conjugational form is avoided* because it sounds awkward. When a modal is added to a passive voice sentence, it is the modal that is conjugated, and it is followed by a *passive voice infinitive*. A passive voice infinitive is composed of **be** and a past participle. The structure is: **modal + be + past participle**. Let's look at a passive voice sentence: **The store is cleaned by a janitor**. The list that follows shows how the sentence changes when modal auxiliaries are added.

The store **must** be cleaned by a janitor.
The store **can** be cleaned by a janitor.
The store **is supposed to** be cleaned by a janitor.
The store **might** be cleaned by a janitor.
The store **has to** be cleaned by a janitor.
The store **needs to** be cleaned by a janitor.

The meaning of the passive voice sentence changes according to the meaning of the modal that is added.

Remember that not all modals have a form for every tense. Review the tense patterns shown in Chapter 8; then consider the example sentences that follow.

Present: The damage can be repaired.
Past: The damage could be repaired.
Present perfect: The damage has been able to be repaired.
Past perfect: The damage had been able to be repaired.
Future: The damage will be able to be repaired.
Future perfect: (*extremely awkward and to be avoided*)

Whenever a sentence sounds awkward or contains many verb forms, change to a less complex tense. For example:

He **has been supposed to be punished** for his behavior. (*awkward*)
He **was supposed to be punished** for his behavior. (*better*)

Written Practice 16-3

Reword each passive voice sentence by adding the modal auxiliaries given in parentheses. Retain the tense of the original sentence. For example:

John is urged to run for political office.

(should) _John should be urged to run for political office._

1. The ailing boy is rushed to the hospital.

   (must) _____

   (need to) _____

2. The old house has been sold by the owners.

   (has to) _____

   (be supposed to) _____

3. Will you be educated in England?

   (want to) _____

   (be able to) _____

4. The problem is investigated by our committee.

   (should) _____

   (can) _____

5. The new constitution was completed by the end of the year.

(have to) _____

(need to) _____

Idioms that contain a transitive verb can be stated in the passive voice. The verb **fire** is a transitive verb and is used idiomatically to mean *release from a job or position*, or *sack*. In the active voice it is used like this: **The boss fired our manager for coming in late.** Now consider the following passive voice examples.

Our manager <u>was fired</u> for coming in late.
No one in this department <u>will be fired</u>.

Another verb that is used idiomatically is **answer**. It often means *to respond to a knock on the door or the ringing of a telephone*. In the active voice, it is used like this: **The eager children answered the door.** Now consider the following passive examples.

The door <u>was answered</u> by the eager children.
Your call <u>will be answered</u> by the first available agent.

Oral Practice

🔘 Track 50

Read each sentence aloud, paying attention to the various passive voice forms.

This kind of problem cannot be solved overnight.
You should be rewarded for your heroism and courage.
Will my mother be able to be released from the clinic today?
The contracts must be prepared and ready for signing before the end
   of the day.
Michael is being trained to compete in the Iron Man race.
Wasn't this clock supposed to be repaired yesterday?
The aircraft has been refueled and is ready for takeoff.
The Florida Everglades had been infested with nonnative snakes.
I shall be sworn in as the representative from my district tomorrow morning.
We knew that lies were being told by the witness for the defense.

Indirect Objects

The active voice sentences used thus far in this chapter have contained direct objects. Active voice sentences with indirect objects can also be changed to the passive voice, and there are two ways of accomplishing this. If there is an indirect object in a sentence, there will also be a direct object. However, if the direct object is made the subject of the passive voice sentence, the indirect object becomes the object of the preposition **to** or **for**. For example:

> **Active:** Bill gave the girl a birthday present.
> **Passive: A birthday present** was given **to the girl** by Bill.
> **Active:** Someone is sending me flowers.
> **Passive: Flowers** are being sent **to me.**

If the indirect object is made the subject of the passive voice sentence, the direct object remains the direct object of the passive voice verb.

> **Active:** Bill gave the girl a birthday present.
> **Passive: The girl** was given **a birthday present** by Bill.
> **Active:** Someone is sending me flowers.
> **Passive: I** am being sent **flowers**.

Sentences that use the indirect object as the subject of a passive voice sentence can sound awkward. Use this construction carefully, or form passive voice sentences with the direct object as the subject.

Get

The verb **get** is used in so many ways. One of those ways is the formation of a *colloquial* passive voice form. It has both a completed/habitual form and an incomplete/progressive form. **Gets** and **is getting** are replacements for **is** and **is being**. For example:

> My car **gets** washed every Thursday. (*is washed*)
> My car **is getting** washed right now. (*is being washed*)
> The roof shingles **got replaced** after the storm. (*were replaced*)
> The roof shingles **were getting replaced** because of the damage. (*were being replaced*)

Written Practice 16-4

Reword each sentence by replacing the passive auxiliary with a form of **get**. For example:

He was injured in a fall.

He got injured in a fall.

1. The car was being repaired at Jim's Garage.

_____

2. My uncle was kicked by that old mule.

_____

3. The bride is being made up for her wedding day.

_____

4. The boy is caught stealing an apple.

_____

5. We were being drenched by the sudden rainstorm.

_____

Static Passive

The static (or stative) passive is sometimes confused with the regular passive voice because both are expressed by combining **be** and a past participle. It was pointed out in Chapter 5 that past participles can act as adjectives. For example:

The **injured** man hurried to the clinic.
Tom had to replace the **broken** window.
The **written** word sometimes speaks more loudly than the **spoken** word.

When the verb **be** is followed by a past participle, the participle can act as either a passive voice structure or as an adjective. This capability is particularly notable in the complete/habitual conjugation of the verb and when a prepositional phrase introduced by **by** is omitted.

The tree limb was **broken** by a sudden gust of wind.
The tree limb was **broken**.

Your coat is **singed** by the fire.
Your coat is **singed**.
The village was **destroyed** by a terrible earthquake.
The village was **destroyed**.

How do you know what is intended? Is the past participle an adjective, or is it in a passive voice structure? A little test can help you answer those questions about intended meaning: replace the past participle with an adjective that might fit in the sentence. If the adjective makes sense, the participle *could* be in the static passive. If it makes no sense, the participle is in a passive voice structure. Consider the sentences just given, rewritten with adjectives.

The tree limb was **strong** by a sudden gust of wind. (*makes no sense/passive*)
The tree limb was **strong**. (*makes sense/could be static passive*)
Your coat is **blue** by the fire. (*makes no sense/passive*)
Your coat is **blue**. (*makes sense/could be static passive*)
The village was **quaint** by a terrible earthquake. (*makes no sense at all*) The
    village was **quaint**. (*makes sense/could be static passive*)

The adjectives that make sense in the sentence are described with *could be static passive*. The sentence could also be a passive voice sentence. Only the speaker or the writer knows the exact intent. When you use sentences like these, their meaning will be governed by *your intent*.

There is no problem when the auxiliary is conjugated in the incomplete/progressive form (**is being**). The static passive does not follow this form of the auxiliary. Let's compare some pairs of sentences that have a **by**-prepositional phrase in them with those that do not.

The house **is being painted** by three college students.
The house **is being painted**.
The soldiers **were being trained** by a drill sergeant.
The soldiers **were being trained**.
No one **is being fired** by Mr. Hughes.
No one **is being fired**.

If you use the test of a replacement adjective for the past participle, you will see that these sentences make no sense with most adjectives.

TAKE NOTE *When the doer of the action that follows the preposition* **by** *is an inanimate object, the preposition* **due to** *can replace* **by**. *If a cause is provided for the action instead of a doer of the action,* **due to** *is the preferred form.*

The house was destroyed by a hurricane.
The house was destroyed due to a hurricane.
The little boy was being scolded due to his bad behavior.

Oral Practice

Read each sentence aloud, identifying those that contain the actual static passive.

The older women were being helped into the carriages.
Several telephone poles were downed last night.
The clock was broken but is in fine repair now.
A new student was being led into our class by the principal.
Have you been given your passport and visa for the trip to China?
The stolen goods were placed in a secret location.
The president was being introduced to the audience by the speaker of the
    House of Representatives.
The Declaration of Independence was signed by the men we call *the
    Founding Fathers*.
The windshield is cracked, which is dangerous, and it must be replaced.
Should we be concerned that the stock market is going down again today?

QUIZ

Choose the letter of the word or phrase that best completes each sentence.

1. **This safe cannot _____ opened without the combination.**
   A. will be   C. was
   B. be   D. is being

2. **The orchestra is _____ by a conductor from Vienna.**
   A. directed   C. took
   B. played   D. being

3. You _____ be arrested for driving like that!
   A. were   C. want
   B. should   D. was able to

4. He was being convinced _____ a very eloquent man.
   A. by   C. to
   B. of   D. from

5. Someone _____ needed to work in the library tonight.
   A. will be   C. were being
   B. must   D. cannot be

6. The diplomas for the graduates had _____ on a table near the podium.
   A. being   C. waited
   B. be prepared   D. been placed

7. Our daughter was flunked _____ her miserable grades.
   A. being   C. by
   B. of   D. due to

8. Unfortunately, that toy _____.
   A. is being there   C. is going well
   B. was broken   D. will be selling

9. The novel _____ be read by the entire class.
   A. will be   C. will need
   B. is able   D. must

10. The horse _____ exercised before the upcoming race.
    A. will   C. wanted to be
    B. are   D. was being

chapter **17**

Subjunctive Mood

This chapter will introduce you to the subjunctive mood. The conjugational patterns of the subjunctive mood will be described and opportunities for practice will be provided.

CHAPTER OBJECTIVES

In this chapter you will learn about:

- The formation of the subjunctive from infinitives
- The formation of the subjunctive from the past tense
- The formation of the subjunctive with the auxiliary *would*
- The usage of the three forms of subjunctive

The subjunctive mood is a conjugational form that native speakers use automatically, often without realizing that it is a form somewhat different from indicative conjugations of verbs. Also, many native speakers of English simply avoid a subjunctive conjugation when it is needed because the indicative conjugation makes sense and is used regularly to replace the subjunctive by many throughout the English-speaking world.

There are rules for using the subjunctive, which will be provided here. In order to speak and write correctly and effectively, readers should become familiar with these rules.

The Present Subjunctive

One conjugational form of the subjunctive is derived from infinitives. It is sometimes called the *present subjunctive* because it resembles the present tense. This form is quite simple because all persons, singular and plural, use the same verb form. For example:

	Be	Go	Have	Do
I	be	go	have	do
you	be	go	have	do
he/she/it	be	go	have	do
we	be	go	have	do
they	be	go	have	do

If nouns are the subject of a sentence, both singular and plural nouns follow the same conjugational pattern in this subjunctive form.

the girl	be	go	have	do
the cats	be	go	have	do

This subjunctive conjugational pattern is obviously quite simple, but how is it used?

There is a short list of verbs that are the *signals* that this conjugational form will be required in the sentence. Some of the commonly used verbs in this list are:

ask	desire	order	request
command	determine	prefer	require
demand	insist	recommend	suggest

Now let's look at some example sentences that contain these verbs and the subjunctive formed from the infinitive. Because these subjunctive verbs resemble the familiar present tense, the subjunctive conjugation is not always obvious, especially in the first and second persons singular and plural and in the third person plural. The verb **be** is the only verb that is clearly in the subjunctive with all persons, singular and plural.

I **asked** that you all **be** here today to hear my proposal.
We **insist** that our soldiers **be** returned home as soon as possible.
I really **prefer** that I **be** allowed to sleep late on weekends.
How can you **demand** that we **pay** higher taxes in this economic downturn?
The boss **suggested** she **look** for another job.

? Still Struggling?

The conjunction **that** is used to introduce the clause that contains the verb in the subjunctive form. But **that** is optional and is often omitted.

I request **that** he remain home today.
I request he remain home today.

Some of the verbs previously listed have a noun or adjective form. Those nouns and adjectives, too, can act as the signals to use a subjunctive verb in the sentence. For example:

John was **insistent** that his wife **buy** a new winter coat.
The **order** was given that we **retreat** immediately.
She made the **suggestion** that Tom **spend** more time studying.

Oral Practice

Track 51

Read each sentence aloud, paying attention to the form and use of the subjunctive mood.

The president demanded that the diplomat cease making such statements.
Someone suggested that we all try to remain calm.
It is required in this club that you be on time for all meetings.
Someone requested that I apply for the job in accounting.
Why do you insist that my mother go to live somewhere else?
How can the landlord suggest that we pay that kind of rent?
The neighbors asked that our son play his music a bit less loudly.
We are determined that this project be completed on time.
It is our recommendation that every graduate student have access to this library.
Is it required that I show my ID each time I enter the courthouse?

Written Practice 17-1

Complete each sentence twice with clauses appropriate for the sentence. For example:

I suggest that <u>we hold a meeting once a month.</u>

I suggest that <u>you be our leader.</u>

1. It is still required that _____

   It is still required that _____.

2. The governor demands that _____.

   The governor demands that _____.

3. We have asked that _____.

   We have asked that _____.

4. It was my suggestion _____.

   It was my suggestion _____.

5. She insists that _____.

   She insists that _____.

6. It is desired by the committee that _____

   It is desired by the committee that _____.

7. He ordered that _____.

   He ordered that _____.

8. Do you prefer that _____?

   Do you prefer that _____?

9. I shall recommend that _____.

   I shall recommend that _____.

10. The state requires that _____.

    The state requires that _____.

Other Phrases that Introduce the Subjunctive

Among the handful of other phrases that are signals that a clause with a subjunctive verb is required are the following:

it is agreed   it is essential
it is important it is necessary

Let's look at some example sentences that include these phrases.

It was agreed that Ms. Barton **be** promoted to manager.
It is essential that no one **speak** about this to others.
Is it really important that I **be** a member of this committee?
It will be necessary that we **be** vigilant in this matter.

These phrases *do not have to* be used with a subjunctive verb. There is a difference between the use of phrases like these with verbs in the subjunctive and with verbs in the indicative. When an indicative verb is used, there is a slightly different meaning. Consider the following pairs of sentences.

It is agreed that Ms. Barton **be** promoted to manager.
It is agreed that Ms. Barton **is** promoted to manager.

The first sentence implies that there is a suggestion that this promotion take place. Perhaps a group has voted on just such a promotion. But Ms. Barton is not yet officially the manager.

The second sentence is not a suggestion for the future. It is what has already taken place. Perhaps a group has just voted, and Ms. Barton was thereby promoted to manager.

Is it really important that I **be** a member of this committee?
Is it really important that I **am** a member of this committee?

The first sentence implies that *I* am not yet a member of the committee. The question is whether it is important that *I* become a member of the committee in the future.

The second sentence says that *I* am already a member of the committee. The question is whether that fact is important.

When using phrases such as those illustrated, it is the speaker or writer who determines whether the verb should be subjunctive or indicative; it is the mood of the verb that determines the meaning of the sentence.

Oral Practice

Read each sentence aloud, paying attention to the verb form and the meaning of the sentence.

It is really absurd that you were fired from your job.
I find it absurd that Mr. Kelly has such poor manners.
It was quite important that the Wright brothers chose Kitty Hawk for their flights.
It will be essential that he have every opportunity to prove himself innocent.
It is essential that you be our candidate in the next election.
Why is it important that she take the driver's test today?
It was not important that Jack and his wife wanted to leave town.
Is it necessary that the boss's son be included in our discussions?
It is not wise that the solution to this problem is being delayed for so long.
She feels it is wise that our firm have more than enough money to make this purchase.

Written Practice 17-2

Complete each sentence twice: once with a verb in the subjunctive and once with a verb in the indicative. Consider how the two sentences differ in meaning. For example:

It is wise that _we be prepared for any bad weather._

It is wise that _you are taking your time with this project._

1. It was important that _____.

   It was important that _____.

2. I feel it is necessary that _____.

   I feel it is necessary that _____.

3. It is essential that _____.

   It is essential that _____.

4. Is it necessary that _____?

   Is it necessary that _____?

5. It was agreed that _____.

   It was agreed that _____.

The Past Subjunctive

The past subjunctive is derived from the simple past tense of a verb. All regular verbs will end in **-ed**, and all irregular verbs will appear with their irregular past tense stem. With the verb **be**, there is a difference between the singular and plural form of the past tense verb: **was** and **were**. Only the plural form is used in the subjunctive. Let's look at the past subjunctive conjugation with three irregular verbs and one regular verb.

	Be	Go	Have	Help
I	were	went	had	helped
you	were	went	had	helped
he/she/it	were	went	had	helped
we	were	went	had	helped
they	were	went	had	helped

If nouns are the subject of a sentence, both singular and plural nouns follow the same conjugational pattern in the past subjunctive.

the girl	were	went	had	helped
the cats	were	went	had	helped

The past subjunctive is used in a sentence that describes something *wished for*. Such a sentence often begins with **if only**.

If only my wife could have seen our daughter today.
If only you had a bit more time to spend with us.
If only our son were a little more ambitious.
If only the sun would come out today.
If only she had money for the taxi fare.

Notice that each of these sentences is a *wish*. You can test such sentences by changing **if only** to **a person wishes**. If the sentence makes sense with **a person wishes**, it is a true wish-clause and requires a past subjunctive verb. For example:

I wish my wife could have seen our daughter today. (*a true wish*)
We wish our son were a little more ambitious. (*a true wish*)
She wishes she had more money. (*a true wish*)

Notice that a sentence that uses the verb **wish** also requires a past subjunctive verb.

Oral Practice

Read each sentence aloud, paying attention to the past subjunctive verb and the meaning of a wish.

If only their dog would stop barking for a while.
If only you were healthy enough to go back to work.
If only our neighbors would make a few repairs to their home.
If only the private school would lower its tuition.
If only someone would stop by our house for a visit this evening.
If only I had received their letter before I went on vacation.
If only you had paid that bill on time.

Written Practice 17-3

Complete each sentence with any appropriate **wish**-clause.

1. If only you had _____.

2. If only I could _____.

3. If only he were _____.

4. If only my boss would _____.

5. If only my parents were _____.

6. If only she _____.

7. If only I _____.

8. If only the children _____.

9. If only their music _____.

10. If only the cost of groceries _____.

Conditions and Results

The conjunction **if** is also used in a dependent clause. That clause *sets a condition* and is followed by an independent clause that describes the *result* that will be observed if the condition is met. In both clauses, a past subjunctive verb is required. For example:

Condition	Result
If you got home before six,	we could go to a movie.
If the baby were not so sick,	I would be able to go back to work.

If it were not so terribly cold outside,   the children would go out to play.
If I had enough for a big down payment,   I would buy a house in this
neighborhood.

It is possible to place the dependent clause at the end of the sentence.

I would be able to go back to work if the baby were not so sick.
The children would go out to play if it were not so terribly cold outside.

When a sentence is in the subjunctive mood, it is not in an actual tense. However, by using a perfect tense structure, it is possible to imply that a condition met *in the past* would result in a certain condition, also *in the past*. When the perfect tense structure is not used, it's implied that the condition is being set in the present or future. For example:

If he **had been** here (*yesterday*), he **would have helped** me (*yesterday*).
If he **were** here (*today or tomorrow*), he **would help** me (*today or tomorrow*).

When no other auxiliary is in the independent clause, the auxiliary **would** introduces a perfect tense structure or an infinitive. For example:

If it became colder, it **would snow.**
If it had become colder, it **would have snowed.**

If another auxiliary is in the independent clause, **would** is not used.

If it became colder, it **could snow.**
If it had become colder, it **might have snowed.**

Oral Practice

🔘 Track 52

Read each sentence aloud, paying attention to the condition-result meaning.

If my husband got a raise, we would save for a vacation in Alaska.
If Europe were not so far, I would travel there by steamer.
If my brother had not borrowed so much money, I could have bought
a new car.
Will you spend some time with my cousin if I introduce you to her at
the party?

If that were true, it could cause a scandal.

Raj would have passed the exam if he had studied harder.

If you wanted to work at this firm, you would have learned programming.

Would you have attended the lectures if the topics hadn't been
so boring?

If I went to the opera with you, you would have to go to a rock concert
with me.

If Michael had known how to salsa, he could have danced with Alicia.

OMITTING THE CONJUNCTION *IF*

The conjunction **if** can be omitted in the if-clause, and the same meaning will be achieved. This form of the sentence, however, sounds formal and old-fashioned. The omission of **if** occurs primarily with the verbs **have** and **be.**

If she had had the money, she would have paid the rent.

Had she had the money, she would have paid the rent.

If Tom were here, he would help.

Were Tom here, he would help.

Could, Might, Should, Would

The past tense of **can, may, shall,** and **will** is given, respectively, by **could, might, should,** and **would.** Like other past tense verbs, the past tense forms are also the past subjunctive forms. Several examples of their usage in the subjunctive have already been presented.

The same subjunctive auxiliaries are also used in colloquial expressions that show a variety of emotions. These expressions tend to be independent clauses with the dependent if-clauses omitted but understood.

If he had studied, he could have passed that test.

He could have passed that test. (*colloquial statement expressing regret*)

Other colloquial statements similar to this are emotional statements but are not necessarily associated with a dependent if-clause. These statements can stand alone and have meaning on their own.

Our candidate should have been elected. (*disappointment*)

That hat would have looked better in blue. (*disapproval*)

Someone might have helped me carry my luggage. (*complaint*)

You couldn't have bought a less becoming dress. (*negativity*)

When these auxiliaries are combined with other perfect tense structures, the meaning implies a certain point of view. For example:

She **should have made** a good president. (*She became president, but for some reason, she did not perform well in office.*)

She **would have made** a good president. (*Despite her qualifications, she did not become president.*)

She **might have made** a good president. (*There was the possibility that she might have done well as president, but this did not happen.*)

She **could have made** a good president. (*Despite the belief of many that she could be a good president, she was not elected.*)

Oral Practice

Read each sentence aloud, paying attention to the emotion implied in each.

I should have painted the bedroom a brighter color.
No one had predicted that the hurricane would cause so much damage.
You might have told me that my blouse was ripped.
My brother should have been captain of the football team.
Would you have been one of the supporters of our protest march?
No one should have tried to capture that old bear alone.
Robert could not have been more helpful to us during our move.
I think Granny might have made a roast for dinner tonight.
The manager wouldn't have fired everyone in our department.

As if

The conjunction **as if** introduces a clause that requires a past subjunctive verb. This conjunction is sometimes replaced by **as though**. Let's look at some example sentences.

John acted **as if** he knew exactly what that document meant.
The elderly woman spoke **as if** she had kept that secret all her life.
Tom checked the map again **as if** he were afraid that he was lost again.
Susan looked at me **as if** she had never seen me before.
The professor stopped suddenly **as though** the man before him were his enemy.

Clauses introduced by these conjunctions express *doubt* about the validity of a statement or the belief that the action described is *improbable*. When a verb or an auxiliary and an infinitive are in the past subjunctive, the clause can be preceded by a statement in any tense.

She **speaks/spoke/will speak** to me as if I were her student.
John **acts/acted/will act** as if he were able to understand German.

The introductory statement implies a similar tense meaning in the subjunctive clause. To ensure that those being addressed will understand that the subjunctive clause refers to something in the past, a perfect tense structure is used.

She **speaks/spoke/will speak** to me as if I **had been** her student.
John **acts/acted/will act** as if he **had been able** to understand German.

Written Practice 17-4

Complete each sentence with any appropriate subjunctive clause.

1. If I were you, _____.

2. The funny man was dancing as if _____.

3. If _____,
   I would have returned your tools sooner.

4. If _____,
   this would be a happier time together.

5. _____
   as if she were the guest of honor tonight.

6. The children's choir sang as if _____.

7. If we hadn't prepared our tax return in time, _____.

8. My girlfriend kissed me as if _____.

9. If _____,
   I could go to the park to play tennis.

10. Aunt Helen might bake a chocolate cake if _____.

11. The homeless man ate as if _____.

12. If Mr. Brown had been earning a paycheck, _____.

13. If his story were true, _____.

14. He should have _____!

15. The band played as though _____.

IDIOMS DEMYSTIFIED

Some idioms are expressed in the subjunctive. For example:

I wouldn't dream of it. = *Someone is certain that he or she would not do something.*
Me? Hurt the puppy? I wouldn't dream of it!
My daughter? Cheat on an exam? She wouldn't dream of it!

Other idioms that are expressed in the indicative can be used in a sentence that requires a subjunctive verb.

1. **to eat one's own words** = *Someone acknowledges having been wrong.*
   If you made a promise like that, you would have to eat your words.

2. **to get over someone or something** = *no longer interested in someone or something and trying to move on with life*
   William should have gotten over Maria by now. Why is he so sad?

3. **to know (all) the ropes** = *be well trained and to know the correct procedures*
   The new programmer acts as if he knew all the ropes already.

QUIZ

Choose the letter of the word or phrase that best completes each sentence.

1. _____ that all the members be loyal to their oath.
   A. If it were necessary   C. Had I known
   B. It is important   D. If there were an agreement

2. Grandpa laughed and joked _____ he were trying to be the life of the party.
   A. if   C. that
   B. as if   D. though

3. If you had been kinder, you _____ more friends.
   A. should have   C. could be wanting
   B. might like   D. would have had

4. Is it really necessary that _____ the night here again?
   A. she spend   C. we are sleeping
   B. it happens   D. they have had

5. If _____, I would gladly have come by to help.
   A. it had been important   C. your husband had known
   B. you are working so hard   D. you had said you had so much cleaning to do

6. The stranger glared at me as if _____ something of me.
   A. she knows   C. she will wonder
   B. he suspected   D. he can discover

7. It would have been better _____ you had stayed away.
   A. that   C. as if
   B. if   D. as though

8. _____ she known about that earlier, she could have saved everyone a lot
   of grief.
   A. If   C. Would
   B. As if   D. Had

9. That would never happen! We would _____!
   A. never dream of it   C. if you would
   B. have been there   D. as if we were to blame

10. _____ that Ms. Patel would be our candidate in the next election.
    A. If you would like   C. Had we heard about it
    B. It was finally agreed D. It is over

chapter **18**

Impersonal Pronouns and Numbers

This chapter deals with impersonal pronouns and how they function in sentences. In addition, numbers and their various forms and functions are introduced.

CHAPTER OBJECTIVES

In this chapter you will learn about:

- How **it** functions as an impersonal pronoun
- How **there** functions as an impersonal pronoun
- Commonly used impersonal expressions
- Numbers and their various forms and uses

The Impersonal Pronoun *It*

The personal pronoun **it** is a replacement for an inanimate noun. It requires a verb conjugated for the third person singular

Noun	Pronoun
The house is located on Main Street.	**It** is located on Main Street.
Why did you buy **that car**?	Why did you buy **it**?
The castle's walls are tall and thick.	**Its** walls are tall and thick.

Besides being the neuter personal pronoun, **it** is an *impersonal pronoun*. An impersonal pronoun is not a replacement for a noun or any other grammatical element. Its function is to be the subject of a sentence, but *that subject has no concrete meaning*. It refers to no one and nothing.

The impersonal pronoun **it** is used to describe weather events with verbs such as **rain** or **snow** and with **be** followed by an adjective. Here are a few of the many examples of such sentences.

It rains every morning.	Why is **it** so cold?
It was snowing.	I prefer a day when **it's** sunny.
It will be hot tomorrow.	**It's** always warmer in the South.

The impersonal pronoun **it** is used in the same way with other words that describe weather events, such as: **hail, thunder, drizzle, sleet,** and **fog up.** For example:

Drive carefully. **It's fogging up.**
It thundered so loudly that the children were frightened.

Impersonal **it** is also used with **get, become,** or **turn** and adjectives. For example:

It is getting **hot.**
It was becoming very **uncomfortable.**
It will turn **humid** again tomorrow.
Is **it** getting **icy**?
Does **it** often get **rainy** in the tropics?

TAKE NOTE *Although* ***lightning*** *deals with weather, it is not a verb and is not used with* ***it***. *Instead, it is stated with* ***there is/was***.

There was lightning all around us.
Don't go under a tree when **there's lightning**.

When identifying a person or an object, the impersonal pronoun **it** and the verb **be** are used again. For example:

Who was at the door?	**It** was our neighbor.
Who is **it**?	**It's** me, Uncle Robert.
Who won the prize?	**It** was Ms. Gardner.
What was on the windshield?	**It** was another ticket!
What is **it**?	**It's** my new invention.

When describing distances, use the impersonal pronoun **it** and the verb **be**.

How far is **it** to the capital?	**It's** about forty miles from here.
Is **it** nearby?	Yes, **it's** only about two more blocks.
Was **it** a long distance to drive?	No, **it** was just about five kilometers.

Oral Practice

Track 53

Read each sentence aloud, paying attention to which ones contain the impersonal pronoun **it**.

It won't take long to get to Union Station from here.
I hate it when it's warm in the morning and then turns cold in the evening.
Maria put the soup on the stove to heat it.
If it rains on Friday, we'll postpone the picnic until Saturday.
It looks like a storm is coming.
You can't wear the blue suit because I sent it to the cleaner yesterday.
If it's more than a five-minute walk, I don't want to go along.
It was getting cloudy, and we knew that it would start to rain very soon.
That's an antique bicycle. It belongs to my Uncle Joseph.
It stopped snowing, but I'll bet it's going to be a cold and windy night.

Use the impersonal **it** to tell what time it is or what day, month, or year it is. For example:

What time is **it**?	I think **it's** three o'clock.
Is **it** already **10 p.m.**?	No, **it's** still quite early.
Yesterday was **Monday**.	No, it was **Tuesday**.
Were you in China in **March**?	Yes, **it** was March 10th.
When did World War II end?	**It** was in 1945.

Written Practice 18-1

Respond to each question with a sentence that includes the impersonal pronoun **it**.

1. How much farther is it to the beach?

    _____

2. What time was it when you got home?

    _____

3. When will the next Olympics be held?

    _____

4. Is it drizzling again?

    _____

5. There's someone at the door. Who is it?

    _____

6. Is today Saturday?

    _____

7. Is it getting chilly in here?

    _____

8. What year was Barack Obama first elected president?

    _____

9. Is it finally getting warmer in the bedroom?

    _____

10. Who is winning the race?

    _____

It for an Indirect Meaning

There are times when a speaker or writer who wants to make a statement would like to do so *indirectly*. To avoid making the speaker or writer the subject of the sentence, one uses the impersonal **it** to introduce a phrase that is followed by the statement. Compare the following pairs of sentences.

Direct Statement	Indirect Statement
I think a library should be built here.	**It is important** to build a library here.
The mayor says that taxes must be raised.	**It is clear** that taxes must be raised.
I believe the speed limit should be lowered.	**It seems** that the speed limit should be lowered.

There are several *introductory phrases* that can be used to make an indirect statement. Nearly all can be followed by the optional **that** and a clause. For example:

It is assumed that	It is important that
It is worth noting that	It is (im)possible that
It is to be expected that	It can be argued that
It can be assumed that	It is clear that
It is (un)likely that	It is significant that
It is suggested that	It is surprising that
It is difficult to say that	It is evident that
It is for that reason that	It seems that
It is essential that	

Naturally, statements that begin with an introductory phrase can be made in the negative and with modal auxiliaries: **It cannot be assumed that, It must be surprising that, It is not suggested that, It should not be argued that.**

The list of indirect statements is not final. Other such phrases can be made with the impersonal **it**. For example.

John hopes that he can find work in the city.
It is hoped that he can find work in the city.

There are a few phrases that follow an indirect statement that are not followed by the conjunction **that**. For example: **it is easy, it is hard**. They can be followed by prepositional phrases or infinitives. The conjunction **that** and its clause can end the sentence, but other phrases can be used as well.

It is easy for us to say **that** housing costs will go down.
It is hard to know **why** the fire broke out.

Oral Practice

Read each sentence aloud, paying attention to the introductory indirect statement.

It was essential that the people rallied around their leaders at this time.
Is it really so surprising that the exhausted workers needed time for rest?
It is for that reason that I must decline your offer to join your firm.
It was quite hard for us to say good-bye to our relatives.
Why was it always impossible to get a straight answer from that politician?
It seems that we are finally on the path to success.
It cannot be assumed that our team will win every game.
It was only to be expected that the unruly boy would rebel again.
It is quite evident that you have no wish to tell the entire truth.
It will be important to recognize that not every goal will be met.

Written Practice 18-2

Reword each sentence by changing the subject and direct statement to it and an indirect statement. For example:

I expect that you will work very hard.

It is expected that you will work very hard.

1. We suggest that you find enough time to finish the job today.

   _____

2. The governor thinks that more people are finding jobs.

   _____

3. I believe we should help the needy and the old.

   _____

4. My boss hopes that sales will finally increase.

   _____

5. John mentioned that rents in this town are still very high.

   _____

6. I assume you know how to operate this machinery.

   _____

7. We believed that the play would be a success in New York.

_____

8. Ms. Garcia stated in her memo that she is calling a meeting for Tuesday.

_____

9. My mother had difficulty in saying good-bye to me.

_____

10. The teacher thought the boy's writing skills were still weak.

_____

The Impersonal Pronoun *There*

The impersonal **there**, like **it**, is not a replacement for a specific noun. Instead, it is the subject of the verb **be** that introduces a noun. The usual meaning for **there** as an adverb is *in or at a place—the location of someone or something.*

Where is Anna?	She's **there**.
Where do you live?	**There**, in that white house.

The impersonal **there** tells of the *existence* of someone or something. When the adverb is combined with **be**, the sentence can be in any tense. For example:

There is a problem here.	**There had been** a problem here.
There was a problem here.	**There will be** a problem here.
There has been a problem here.	

The meaning of the present tense example is: **A problem exists here.**

As with other verbs, the verb **be** in this impersonal expression can be accompanied by modal auxiliaries: **there can be**, **there should be**, and so on.

Oral Practice

🔘 Track 54

Read each sentence aloud, paying attention to the use and meaning of the impersonal **there**.

There was no way out of the building except for the front entrance.
Is there anyone here who understands French or Spanish?

There have been a few mistakes made by this company.
Will there be a test on what we're discussing today?
There should be larger signs to direct people to the stadium.
There is really no reason for you to get so upset.
There must be something that we can do to help that poor woman.
Can there be any justification for such bad behavior?
Has there been a flu epidemic like this before?
I think there are several ways that we can solve this problem.

The most frequently used verb with the impersonal **there** is **be**. However, a few other verbs exist that form an impersonal expression with **there**. Just as with **be**, the meaning is impersonal, and the verb introduces a noun that is the potential subject of a direct statement. Compare the following pairs of sentences and note how they differ as indirect and direct statements.

There existed a plan to improve the city's schools.
A plan to improve the city's schools **existed**.
There arose a terrible uproar about the plan to raise taxes.
A terrible uproar about the plan to raise taxes **arose**.
There developed a story about a little girl who saved her mother's life.
A story **developed** about a little girl who saved her mother's life.

The noun that follows the impersonal expression determines how the verb is conjugated. For example:

There **is one book** on the table.	There **exists** only one way to react.
There **are two books** on the table.	There **exist** several ways to react.

Written Practice 18-3

Reword each string of words as a sentence introduced by the impersonal **there**. For example:

man/at the door

There is a man at the door.

1. several magazines/on the floor

_____

2. three burglaries/this neighborhood

_____

3. arguing/in the Senate/about housing

_____

4. exists/peace and quiet/in the country

_____

5. a few problems/computers

_____

6. arose/loud noises/factory

_____

7. no milk/refrigerator

_____

8. a gift/for you/table

_____

9. four children/ill

_____

10. nothing/do/for the man

_____

IDIOMS DEMYSTIFIED

Some idiomatic phrases can be used in an impersonal expression begun with **there**. One such example is **red tape**.

red tape = *complicated procedures and forms used by businesses and government that are responsible for delays or inaction*
It was hard to get a loan. There was so much red tape.
If there's going to be a lot of red tape, I won't apply for the job.

Numbers

Numbers are actual *amounts* of something. They are the concepts that describe *how many* persons or things are being discussed. *Numerals* are the symbols that describe numbers in writing. Written English uses Arabic numerals to describe amounts. For example: **2 boys, 5 apples, 10 cars.**

In some cases, Roman numerals are used in place of Arabic numerals. You will often find Roman numerals on clock faces; in addition, they are used to distinguish two relatives of the same name, in certain expressions that have become traditional, and in outlines. For example:

I, II, III, IV, V, VI, VII, VIII, IX, X, XI, *and* **XII** *on a clock face*
William Shaw I *and his grandson* **William Shaw II** (*The names are said with an ordinal number: William Shaw* **the first** *and William Shaw* **the second**.)
Super Bowl XLVII *traditional designation of a Super Bowl game*
My Vacation *an outline*

    I. Seeing the sights of Colorado
      A. Hiking on mountain trails
      B. Fishing and swimming in chilly rivers

    II. Camping in the wilderness
      A. Nighttime sounds in the forest
      B. Breakfast cooked over a fire on a frosty morning

Any number that begins a sentence should be spelled out. Small numbers should nearly always be spelled out, but longer numbers should be written as Arabic numerals. If the longer number begins a sentence, it should be spelled out.

He bought **300** sheep at the auction.
Three hundred sheep now graze the pastures of his farm.

If a phrase has a combination of a large number and a small number, both should be written in the same way, including when one of them begins a sentence.

There were **80 guests and just 7** waiters for the large group.
Four score and seven years ago
The Girl Scouts collected **$20,000** in donations.
Twenty thousand dollars was a record amount.

In English, a comma is used to separate thousands:

2,450   12,600   650,000   2,900,045

Use a period to separate decimal amounts:

65.5   1,010.55
2.675   15.01

Amounts that are shown with the thousands separated by a comma or the decimal amount separated by a period (decimal point) should not be written as a word. If such an amount occurs at the beginning of a sentence, *reword the sentence* to avoid having to write the amount as a word.

$2,000 is the down payment. = The down payment is $2,000.

TAKE NOTE *When writing and saying amounts of money or other quantities, there is sometimes more than one version that you may encounter. Be aware that large numbers are generally not spelled out. For example:*

twenty thousand dollars	8 million homes
$20,000	8M homes
$20K	sixty-five cents
eight million homes	$0.65
8,000,000 homes	65¢

Dates are most often written with the day and the year shown in numerals. For example:

October 31, 2012, was my son's first Halloween.
Do you have a family dinner planned for January 1, 2014?
Our granddaughter was born on April 12, 2010.

If the year is omitted from the date, the day can be written as a word. If the day precedes the month, it is written as a word.

Today is May first.
They arrived in America on the tenth of August 1889.

Numbers and Arithmetic

The four basic areas of arithmetic are **addition**, **subtraction**, **multiplication**, and **division**. Each one has a symbol that indicates what kind of mathematical action is taking place. In addition, a plus sign is used to show that two or more numbers should be made a *sum*. For example:

6 + 1 = 7   or   6
                      +1
                       7

When numbers being added appear in a line across a page, the equal sign (=) indicates that the number that follows is the sum of the other numbers.

The plus sign in writing can be said as either **plus** or **and**. The equal sign can be either **equals** or **is**. For example:

Six plus one equals seven.   Six plus one is seven.
Six and one equals seven.   Six and one is seven.

In these example sentences, the verb is shown as a singular (**equals** and **is**) because the mathematical statement (**Six plus one**) is considered a *single concept*. It is possible to use **equal** and **are** in the plural, particularly when **and** is used in the mathematical statement.

Six and one equal seven.
Six and one are seven.

The symbol used in subtraction is the minus sign.

$$6 - 1 = 5 \quad \textit{or} \quad \begin{array}{r} 6 \\ -1 \\ \hline 5 \end{array}$$

This mathematical statement is spoken as follows:

Six minus one equals five.
Six minus one is five.

The symbol used in multiplication is the **times sign**.

$$6 \times 2 = 12 \quad \textit{or} \quad \begin{array}{r} 6 \\ \times 2 \\ \hline 12 \end{array}$$

This mathematical statement is spoken as follows:

Six times two equals twelve.
Six times two is twelve.

A mathematical statement for multiplication appearing in a line across a page can use a **multiplication dot** in place of the times sign.

$$6 \cdot 2 = 12$$

The symbol used in division is the **division sign**:

$$6 \div 2 = 3 \quad or \quad \frac{6}{2} = 3$$

This mathematical statement is spoken as follows:

Six divided by two equals three.
Six divided by two is three.

A mathematical statement for division in a straight line can use a **division slash** in place of a division sign.

$$6/2 = 3$$

Oral Practice

🔘 Track 55

Read each sentence aloud, paying attention to the kind of numbers used.

The Ravens won Super Bowl XLVII.
The queen of England is Elizabeth II.
We have finally saved $15,000 and hope to make a down payment on a house soon.
The salary for this job is $2,250 a month plus benefits.
Thirty-five children are crammed into this little classroom.
The final chapter in this book is Chapter 20.
Five years ago, my parents came to this country from Poland.
Two candy bars will cost $1.80.
Could you lend me 50¢ so I can buy some gum?
The city government has announced that the municipal debt has risen to $45 million.
The Declaration of Independence was signed on July 4, 1776.

Ordinal Numbers

Whereas the cardinal numbers describe an *amount*: **eleven boys, three old cars, nine magazines**, the **ordinal numbers** show the *order* or *rank* of people and things.

The fourth boy in line was Phillip.
She was born on the ninth of June.

Most cardinal numbers can be changed to ordinal numbers by adding the suffix **-th**. For example:

Cardinal	Ordinal
four	fourth
eleven	eleventh
thirty	thirtieth
hundred	hundredth
thousand	thousandth

A few ordinal numbers have an irregular formation.

Cardinal	Ordinal
one	first
two	second
three	third
five	fifth
twelve	twelfth

When two or more numbers are combined, it is the last one that takes the ordinal form.

Cardinal	Ordinal
twenty-one	twenty-first
eighty-six	eighty-sixth

Written Practice 18-4

Give the ordinal form of each number. For example:

7 *seventh*

1. 13 _____

2. 22 _____

3. 30 _____

4. 1 _____

5. 43 _____

6. 75 _____

7. 12 _____

8. 100 _____

9. 66 _____

10. 50 _____

QUIZ

Choose the letter of the word, number, or phrase that best completes each sentence.

1. I think _____ rained last night.
   - A. he
   - B. being
   - C. they
   - D. it

2. Is _____ any money left to buy some groceries?
   - A. she
   - B. there
   - C. exist
   - D. it

3. Was _____ in 1914 that World War I began?
   - A. there
   - B. here
   - C. the year
   - D. it

4. There _____ a rumor that Dr. Smith was no physician at all.
   - A. arose
   - B. is being
   - C. exist
   - D. develop

5. Who won the contest? _____ Mr. Kelly again?
   - A. There are
   - B. Was it
   - C. Who is
   - D. Why was

6. _____ girls showed up for soccer practice at the wrong field.
   - A. 6
   - B. Four
   - C. How many
   - D. Was it clear

7. Today is _____ of September.
   - A. the second
   - B. thirtieth
   - C. 8
   - D. on the eighth

8. Ten _____ four is forty. Am I correct?

A. times

B. plus

C. divided

D. divided by

9. Last year the company earned _____ and the year before just $900,000.

A. $3,500,000

B. two years

C. over 100 employees

D. in 2013

10. The sum of all the numbers _____ eighty-three.

A. plus

B. are

C. equals

D. times

chapter 19

Phrasal Verbs

This chapter deals with the combinations of verbs, adverbs, and prepositions called *phrasal verbs*. Their special function and meaning will be introduced, with examples and practice provided.

CHAPTER OBJECTIVES

In this chapter you will learn about:

- The adverbs and prepositions that combine with verbs
- The function and meaning of phrasal verbs
- The difference between separable and inseparable phrasal verbs

The Meaning of Phrasal Verbs

When a commonly used verb is combined with adverbs or prepositions, it can take on a completely new meaning. Not only does the meaning change, but prepositions that accompany the verb often no longer function as prepositions but become adverbs that modify the verb. The name for any such structure is **phrasal verb**.

Most phrasal verbs are formed from the many Anglo-Saxon verbs that still exist in modern English. Just as in other Germanic languages, in English, verbs can add prefixes that are derived from adverbs and prepositions and that change the meaning of the verb. For example:

Base Verb	Verb with Prefix
come	become
get	forget
see	oversee
stand	understand

Something similar happens to phrasal verbs, but the adverbs and prepositions are not added as prefixes. Instead, these modifiers follow the verb, and the new combination of words changes the meaning of the original verb. For example:

Base Verb	Phrasal Verb	Meaning
bring	bring up	*mention; educate, nurture*
come	come to	*regain consciousness, become alert*
get	get along with	*cooperate, have a friendly relationship*
lay	lay off	*temporarily dismiss from a job*

In this chapter, a list of base verbs will be provided. Following each base verb will be two or more phrasal verbs that have been formed from the base verb. The meaning of each phrasal verb will be described and illustrated in an example sentence.

Act

The following phrasal verbs are formed from the base verb **act**:

1. act (up)on = *take action to solve a problem or correct a mistake*
   Are you going to act on the suggestion I gave you?
   The police acted on the information they received about the crime.

2. act up = *have a tantrum or behave very badly*
   My son sometimes acts up when we have guests in the house.
   Uncle John had too much to drink and began to act up.

Ask

Three regularly used phrasal verbs formed with the verb **ask** are:

1. ask (someone) out = *invite someone on a date*
   I really liked Bill and hoped he would ask me out on a date.
   I think I'm going to ask Maria out.

2. **ask (someone) up to** = *request that someone come for a visit or meeting*
   Mr. Carlson asked me up to the boardroom for a meeting.
   His girlfriend never asks him up to her apartment.

3. **ask around** = *look for information from several people*
   We asked around, but no one had ever heard of the Jones family.
   You might ask around in school to see if anyone has found your coat.

Take note that some of the prepositions in the example sentences function as adverbs: **act up**, **ask out**, and **ask around**. This is made clearer in the example sentence **His girlfriend never asks him up to her apartment**. The word **up** is an adverb that modifies **asks**. The word **to** is a preposition followed by the object of that preposition **her apartment**.

Be

Three high-frequency phrasal verbs are formed with the verb **be**:

1. **be in/out** = (with **in**) *be at the office or at home*/(with **out**) *not be at the office or at home*
   Ms. Patel is not in today. She'll be back in the office tomorrow at nine o'clock.
   You always seem to be out when I come by for a visit.

2. **be onto (something)** = *discovering a clue to a mystery or an important idea or thing*
   The formula is working! I really think we're onto something.
   The author of this article about pollution is onto something big.

3. **be up to (something)** = *act in a way that causes suspicions; have evil intentions*
   That man hiding in the shadows seems to be up to something.
   Their children are often up to no good.

Break

The verb **break** combines with various adverbs and prepositions to form phrasal verbs. Five high-frequency phrasal verbs are provided here.

1. **break down** = *stop functioning (machinery); succumb to one's emotions*
   That old car broke down in the middle of the freeway.
   Mr. Boyd saw his daughter getting off the plane and broke down in tears.

2. **break (someone) in** = *train someone for a new activity or job*
   The foreman is breaking in the new drill press operator.
   The choreographer wants to break us in on the new dance routine.

3. **break out (of)** = *escape; escape (from a particular place)*
   The prisoner was going mad and had to break out soon.
   Using a piece of wire as a key, he finally broke out of his cell.

4. **break out (with)** = *exhibit signs of a disease on the skin (from a specific disease)*
   There is a rash breaking out on my arm.
   I think John broke out with the hives.

5. **break up with** = *end a romantic relationship with someone*
   Jean said she wants to break up.
   Last year she broke up with a friend of mine.

Catch

The verb **catch** can combine with the prepositions **at** and **from** to form two distinctly different meanings.

1. **catch at** = *discover someone doing something wrong*
   Father caught Tom at lying again.
   The teacher caught the girl at her old tricks.

2. **catch from** = *contract a disease from someone or something*
   I think I caught a virus on that crowded flight.
   The baby caught a cold from her mother.

Clean

When the adverbs **out** and **up** and the prepositions **of** and **on** are combined with **clean**, two new meanings are made.

1. **clean out (of)** = *remove unwanted people or things from a place; gamble and win all the money; remove unwanted things from the inside of an object*
   The voters cleaned out city hall, ousting the crooked politicians.
   She cleaned us out of every penny at the poker game last night.
   Clean out every bit of dust from those filters.

2. **clean up (on)** = *make someone or something clean again; profit from someone in business or gambling*
   The members of the team went to the locker room to clean up.
   We cleaned up on that deal. We'll make hundreds in profit.

Oral Practice

🔘 Track 56

Read each sentence aloud, paying attention to the use and meaning of the phrasal verbs.

> The company is having financial problems and will lay off fifty workers.
> Why must you act up like that when your friends come over?
> I asked around the whole school, but no one knew who had taken my bike.
> If you ask Susan out, we can go to the movies on a double date.
> The dishwasher broke down again, and I had to wash the dishes by hand.
> Don't mention the accident to Mary. She might break down again and cry.
> The burglars came while we were shopping and cleaned us out.
> The teacher thought she had caught someone cheating on the exam.
> That's quite the invention. You're really onto something important.
> Professor Murray was out all week with the flu.
> We have to act on this problem before it gets worse.

Do

The verb **do** is a transitive verb and a frequently used auxiliary verb. It combines with the adverbs **over** and **away** and the preposition **with** to form two phrasal verbs.

1. **do (something) over** = *do again, repeat; do in a new form*
   Those figures don't match the ones in the other tables. Please do them over in metrics.
   Do that piano piece over again. It's really sounding good.

2. **do away with** = *discard*
   The Russian Revolution did away with the czarist regime.
   Mr. Ling said we can do away with these old documents.

Remember that phrasal verbs are verbs. They have tenses and conjugations. They can be used like any other verb. Consider these examples in the various tenses.

Present: I do the drawing over.   Tom is acting up again.
Past: I did the drawing over.   Tom was acting up again.

Present perfect: I have done the drawing over.

Past perfect: I had done the drawing over.

Future: I will do the drawing over.

Tom has been acting up again.

Tom had been acting up again.

Tom will be acting up again.

Written Practice 19-1

Reword each sentence four times, using the tenses indicated in each numbered item.

1. Present: _____

   Past: They did away with the old rules.

   Present perfect: _____

   Past perfect: _____

   Future: _____

2. Present: _____

   Past: _____

   Present perfect: Shopping has cleaned me out.

   Past perfect: _____

   Future: _____

3. Present: _____

   Past: _____

   Present perfect: _____

   Past perfect: Had Tanya and Bob broken up?

   Future: _____

4. Present: _____

   Past: _____

   Present perfect: _____

   Past perfect: _____

   Future: I will ask your sister out.

5. Present: She catches us cheating.

Past: _____

Present perfect: _____

Past perfect: _____

Future: _____

Drive

The word **off** is often used as a preposition, but when combined with **drive**, it is used as an adverb. This is also true when **on** forms a phrasal verb with **drive**. That phrasal verb also includes the preposition **to**.

1. **drive off** = *depart for a destination in a vehicle; repulse or chase away someone or something*
   With a little wave, Mary drove off into the mist.
   The raccoons come every night. We just can't drive them off.

2. **drive on (to)** = *continue traveling by vehicle*
   It was early, so she drove on for a couple more hours.
   We decided to drive on to the next town.

Eat

When **eat** appears in a phrasal verb, it continues to have the basic meaning of *consuming*, but it's used in a slightly different form.

1. **eat away (at)** = *rust, cause to decompose*
   The metal chair, which had been left outdoors over the very humid summer, got badly rusted.
   That chemical will eat away all the grease and mildew.

2. **eat in/out** = *have a meal at home/in a restaurant*
   I don't want to go out. Let's eat in tonight.
   When he travels, he has to eat out every day.

End

When the adverb **up** is used with the verb **end**, the meaning now involves a *conclusion to something, often with negative implications.*

1. **end up** = *eventually deciding in favor of something*
   Robert ended up getting his own apartment.
   Mary and I ended up just renting a couple movies.

2. end up (with) = *having to accept less than what was desired*
I hoped for a two-bedroom apartment but ended up with a small studio.
Carol wanted to dance with Felipe but ended up with Jorge.

Most phrasal verbs are accompanied by a direct object or the object of the preposition in the phrasal verb. Those objects can be anything the speaker or writer desires. For example:

My little sister ended up with **a bad cold**.
My little sister ended up with **a small check** from Aunt Mary.
We cleaned up **the children** and got them ready for bed.
We cleaned up **the kitchen** and got ready for bed.
I had to do **the calculations** over.
I had to do **my nails** over.
Our boss brought up **a subject** that we dreaded.
Our boss brought up **the raises** that we had hoped for.

Written Practice 19-2

Complete each sentence with two phrases that appropriately complete each one. For example:

The rust ate away at *the fender*.
The rust ate away at *the lawn furniture*.

1. The frustrated citizens did away with

_____

The frustrated citizens did away with

_____

2. Tina doesn't want to break up with

_____

Tina doesn't want to break up with

_____

3. The authorities acted on

_____ they received from

a citizen.

The authorities acted on

_____ they received from
a citizen.

4. The boss is asking _____
up to his office for a talk.

The boss is asking _____
up to his office for a talk.

5. How did I end up with

_____?

How did I end up with

_____?

Figure

When the adverb **out** is added to the verb **figure**, the idea of a strict calculation
is lost and the idea of *coming to an understanding* replaces it.

> **figure (someone or something) out** = *seek understanding of someone or
> something*
> These forms are complicated. I can't figure them out.
> My brother still can't figure out why his girlfriend left him.

Fill

When the verb **fill** is paired with **out**, it has two distinct meanings. Notice that
only the verb that means *complete something* has a direct object.

> 1. **fill out** = *put on some weight, look less thin*
>   After a long illness, Jack is finally filling out again.
>   You've really filled out since the last time I saw you.
>
> 2. **fill (something) out** = *complete something in written form, provide written
>   information*
>   I filled out four job applications today but still have no work.
>   Please fill out the top half of the questionnaire.

Get

The verb **get** has a variety of meanings when it stands alone in a sentence. It
changes even more as a phrasal verb with the addition of adverbs and prepositions.

1. **get behind** = *support or promote someone or some activity*
   We got behind Sara Richards in the mayoral race.
   Why would anyone get behind these horrible tax proposals?

2. **get behind in** = *lag behind in performing a task or doing a job*
   Bill is getting behind in his work again.
   She got behind in her fitness training and put on a little weight.

3. **get off** = *depart from one's job; clear someone of a criminal charge*
   If my husband gets off early from work, we often go out to dinner.
   The clever attorney got the accused man off with a small fine.

Hang

The adverb **out** and the preposition **of** modify the meaning of **hang** in the phrasal verb. When the preposition **with** is added to the verb, a new, colloquial meaning is derived.

1. **hang out (of)** = *protrude or fall out of something*
   There's a handkerchief hanging out of your purse.
   Why is that man hanging out the window? That's dangerous.

2. **hang out (with)** = *spend casual time at a place or with someone*
   Let's meet at the gym and hang out for a while.
   I really enjoy hanging out with Jim and his friends.

Keep

When the adverb **up** is combined with **keep**, the meaning of *maintain posses-sion* is lost. The new phrasal verb has an entirely new meaning.

keep (some task) up = *continue doing something at the same rate*
Keep up the good work!
If you keep those study habits up, you should earn a scholarship.

Let

Two very different phrasal verb meanings are derived by adding **down** and **in** to the verb **let**.

1. **let someone down** = *disappoint or fail to support and help someone*
   I needed Bill to stay and help me, but he let me down.
   She let us down when we really needed a loan from her.

2. let someone in = *let someone enter or join an organization*
The doorman won't let anyone in because the building is closed.
Mr. Garcia was let in the club as soon as he had paid the initiation fee.

Make

The verb **make** can be combined with various adverbs and prepositions. It can be used to form several phrasal verbs. Three of the most commonly used ones are formed with **of**, **up**, and **up (for, to, with)**.

1. make (something) of = *interpret someone or something; become a success*
What do you make of this letter? Is it a confession?
Maria wants to make something of herself; she plans to become
a lawyer.

2. make up (for) = *lie; compensate for something negative or unpleasant*
Why did that man make up those horrible stories about me?
It's going to be hard for you to make up for such bad behavior.

3. make up (to, with) = *compensate; reconcile*
He promised to make the loss up to me, but I never heard from him
again.
I hope Ashley will make up with me, but I think she's still angry.

Oral Practice

Track 57

Read each sentence aloud, paying attention to the use and meaning of the phrasal verbs.

Keep up your work on pronunciation.
We did away with the last of his letters and put the past behind us.
One of the girls asked me to hang out with her and her friends.
Unfortunately, they drove off this morning without noticing that one
of the tires was low on air.
I believe you made up everything in the article you wrote. Is none
of it true?
Their youngest son hung out with the wrong crowd and ended up
in prison.
If you get too far behind in your studies, you'll never catch up.

His memories of his deceased mother ate away at his heart.

You're deep in debt, and you've let everyone, including yourself, down again.

Why should it be so hard to figure out how much federal tax I owe?

Pass

With the adverbs **away** and **out**, the verb **pass** forms two phrasal verbs that have distinctly different meanings.

1. **pass away** = *die*
   During the night, the elderly gentleman passed away peacefully.
   When I pass away, remember that I had a long and happy life.

2. **pass out** = *faint*
   Smoke filled the room, and Jane knew she would soon pass out.
   I feel dizzy. I think I'm going to pass out.

Put

The verb **put** combines with several adverbs and prepositions to form phrasal verbs. A few of them are **down**, **off**, **together**, and **up with**.

1. **put down** = *place something on a surface; insult or ridicule someone; write down*
   I put my pencil down and listened more closely to the lecture.
   Why do you always put me down? Do you think you're superior?
   Someone should put down our comments and type them up for the benefit of those who missed the meeting.

2. **put off** = *postpone, delay*
   The party was put off until next Saturday.
   We had to put off the start of the play for ten minutes.

3. **put together** = *assemble*
   I can't put this jigsaw puzzle together.
   Jim put together a group of people to work on the problem.

4. **put up with** = *endure, tolerate*
   How do you put up with that dog's barking?
   I'm not going to put up with your lying anymore.

Run

The verb **run** forms three high-frequency phrasal verbs with **across**, **down**, and **into**.

1. **run across** = *unexpectedly meet someone or find something*
   I ran across a book of Shakespeare's sonnets.
   Did you happen to run across your college roommate when you
      visited the university for the reunion?

2. **run down** = *become unwound and stop working; criticize someone or something; go somewhere that is not too distant*
   This old clock has run down again. Please wind it up.
   You shouldn't run down the manager like that. She's doing her best.
   I'll run down to the deli and get some bread and cheese.

3. **run into** = *encounter someone; bump something*
   While in Los Cabos, my husband and I ran into Carlos.
   The room was dark, and I ran into the coffee table.

Show

The adverb **off** is used with **show** to describe someone who behaves boastfully

   show off = *act out, pretend to be special, be an exhibitionist*
   When guests are in the house, our daughter likes to show off.
   You don't dance as well as you think. Don't try to show off at the party.

Stand

Several phrasal verbs are formed from the verb **stand**. Two of them are combined with **by** and **for**. Other phrasal verbs formed with **stand** can be used with various prepositions. Take note of how the meaning changes with each preposition.

1. **stand by** = *wait; support someone in a difficult time*
   Please stand by. We may be able to find you table in a few minutes.
   We stood by Jack when everyone else believed the lies about him.

2. **stand for** = *tolerate; be the symbol for something*
   I refuse to stand for any more of your rude behavior.
   The American flag stands for liberty and democracy.

3. **stand in for** = *be the substitute for someone or something*
   When Ellen was sick, Jane stood in for her at the meetings.

4. **stand out (from, against)** = *be highly noticeable; be prominent in comparison to someone or something; be prominent against a background*
   That large neon sign really stands out.
   Maria's essay stood out from all the others I read.
   Her white dress stood out against the darkening sky.

5. **stand up (against, for, to)** = *fail to keep an appointment; endure a challenge; defend someone or something; make a defense against a challenge*
   Why didn't you come to the restaurant? Why did you stand me up?
   People need to stand up against corruption in government.
   Michael stood up for me when I was accused of cheating.
   Although Mr. Kelly was powerful, the woman stood up to him and
   made sure he was held accountable.

Separable and Inseparable Verbs

Perhaps you have noticed that the position of the direct object with certain phrasal verbs is not constant. Some transitive phrasal verbs have two positions for the adverb: one position is following the verb and the other is following the direct object noun. For example:

   I put **down** my pencil and listened.
   I put my pencil **down** and listened.

When the direct object is a pronoun, the adverb follows the direct object.

   I put it **down** and listened.
   I liked that hat and just had to put it **on**.

Many phrasal verbs have this pattern. Among them are:

   I ask her **out**. I ask Mary **out**.
   They bring him up. They bring **up** the child.
   They lay us **off**. They lay **off** the whole department.
   He broke me **in**. He broke **in** the new employee.
   She cleaned herself **up**. She cleaned **up** the living room.
   We couldn't drive them **off**. We couldn't drive **off** the attackers.
   Who figured it **out**? Who figured **out** the problem?
   Bill filled it **out**. Bill filled **out** the forms.

Keep it **up**. Keep **up** the good work.

Don't let me **down**. Don't let **down** the team.

She put it **off**. She put **off** the party.

I'll put it **together**. I'll put **together** the new bike.

Why does he run **us** down? Why does he run **down** his own relatives?

Any future phrasal verbs in this chapter that have a separable adverb will be identified by (*separable*).

Written Practice 19-3

Reword each sentence twice with any appropriate noun. Place the adverb in each sentence in a different position. For example:

Please put it down.

Please put the box down.

Please put down the box.

1. Fill them out before leaving.

_____

_____

2. We brought her up to be polite.

_____

_____

3. Can you put it together for me?

_____

_____

4. The workers are cleaning them up.

_____

_____

5. You won't be able to figure them out.

_____

_____

Take

The verb **take** combines with several adverbs and prepositions. Three of these are **after**, **apart**, and **back**.

1. **take after** = *resemble, be like another person*
   She's very pretty. She takes after her mother.
   He's a good athlete; in other words, he takes after me.

2. **take apart** (*separable*) = *remove each part from a device; break into pieces*
   Why did you take the radio apart?
   Jimmy took apart his sister's doll just to be mean.

3. **take back** (*separable*) = *return something; withdraw something that was said*
   You should have taken all the books back to the library.
   He'd better take back what he said about my father.

Turn

The verb **turn** can form several phrasal verbs. Notice how the meaning of **turn out** changes as the prepositions used with that verb (**to, for**) change.

1. **turn in (to)** = *go to bed; hand someone over to the authorities; change into a different kind of person or thing*
   It's late. I'm going to turn in.
   My brothers caught the thief and turned him in to the police.
   With help from his wife, he turned himself into a respectable person again.

2. **turn off/on (to)** (*separable*) = *stop or start functioning (as machinery); switch something off or on to cause it to stop functioning; interest or stimulate someone*
   Why was the music suddenly turned off?
   Please turn the television set on.
   I turned on the lights and found an empty room.
   Classical music just doesn't turn me on.

3. **turn out** (*separable*) (**for**) = *end in a certain way; switch off; come to a place for a certain event*
   My calculations turned out wrong.
   I'll turn out the lights after you go upstairs.
   A large crowd turned out for the governor's speech.

Use

When combined with **up**, the verb **use** maintains its basic meaning but implies that the action is complete.

> **use up** (*separable*) = *exhausted the supply of something*
> We already used up all the toothpaste.
> If you use it up, I'll buy some when I go shopping.

Wear

The verb **wear** forms two high-frequency phrasal verbs with the separable adverbs **off** and **out**.

> 1. **wear off** (*separable*) = *cease to function; become degraded*
>   My perfume has worn off. I need a quick dab on my neck.
>   The expensive coating on my glasses is starting to wear off.
>
> 2. **wear out** (*separable*) = *exhaust someone or something; become damaged or tattered from use*
>   That long tennis match has worn me out.
>   My running shoes are worn out and need to be discarded.

Work

Two high-frequency phrasal verbs are formed with the verb **work**. Notice how the prepositions make a difference in the meaning of the phrasal verb even though the idea of **work** is maintained.

> 1. **work out** = *discover, come to a conclusion; exercise*
>   When I finally work out what's wrong with this engine, I'll get it to start.
>   We needed to work out, so we went to the gym for a while.
>
> 2. **work up** (*separable*) = *develop*
>   I've worked up some drawings that will give you an idea of how the house will look.
>   You should work up a study schedule before next week's exam.

IDIOMS DEMYSTIFIED

Phrasal verbs occur in many idioms. The verb **brush** combines with the adverb **up**. Both **brush** and **get** use the preposition **on** to introduce a prepositional phrase.

brush up on = *study something again; refresh one's memory of a subject*
Before I take geometry, I should brush up on algebra.
You need to brush up on your Spanish before the trip.

get on the ball = *improve; approach something seriously*
Your work is very sloppy. Get on the ball!
You need to get on the ball and do something with your life.

Written Practice 19-4

Using the string of words provided, create a complete sentence. For example:

lay off/workers

Mr. Brown says the company will not lay off any workers.

1. make up with/my husband

   _____

2. my son/let down/family

   _____

3. winter coat/wear out

   _____

4. no one/put off/examination

   _____

5. hang out with

   _____

6. pass away

   _____

7. in India/run across/friends

   _____

8. what/stand for

_____

9. put together/it

_____

10. break in/new employee

_____

QUIZ

Choose the word or phrase that best completes each sentence.

1. I was told _____ up the good work.
   A. run   C. put off
   B. to keep   D. to stand

2. I _____ for over an hour and I'm exhausted.
   A. will stand for   C. have worked out
   B. broke   D. asked out

3. I want to _____ French before we go to that fancy restaurant.
   A. eat away at   C. fill out
   B. brush up on   D. run down

4. How did you figure out _____?
   A. that   C. it
   B. what to do   D. all of them

5. You look healthier now that you've filled _____ a little.
   A. out   C. up with
   B. up   D. down

6. We can find out where they live if we _____ around.
   A. ask   C. keep up
   B. pass   D. clean up

7. Did you _____ from someone at work?

    A. let him down   C. catch a cold

    B. drive off   D. hang out

8. Tom thinks he really _____ on that investment he made a month ago.

    A. cleaned up   C. passed away

    B. put together   D. has run

9. Don't wear that suit. It's _____.

    A. hung out   C. put off

    B. stood for   D. worn out

10. It's still early. I don't want to _____ in yet.

    A. turn   C. break

    B. pass   D. figure

chapter 20

Writing Demystified

This chapter will provide you with a variety of writing activities that offer practice in achieving control of content and structure. The goal is to make this chapter a forum for your creative use of the topics you encountered in the preceding chapters.

CHAPTER OBJECTIVES

In this chapter you will:

- Complete sentences with phrases of your choice
- Write sentences with nouns and pronouns in various forms
- Write sentences with verbs in various conjugations
- Provide the lines missing from a brief story
- Create original sentences

Anyone who learns a new language begins with developing *speaking and understanding skills.* After these basic skills have been acquired, the learner turns to *reading* and eventually *writing.* Writing is the most difficult skill to develop because it requires an intermediate level of fluency when speaking and the ability to apply grammar and vocabulary in original sentences.

If you have successfully completed the practice exercises in other chapters in this book, you are ready to apply your skill to writing. This chapter will continue to guide you in the direction your writing should take, but you will be in control of content and vocabulary. If you are not satisfied with the outcome of one of the sections, refer to the chapters that discussed the topics found in the section and then repeat the section.

Sentence Completions

The exercises in this section are incomplete because they are missing certain necessary elements. Provide the appropriate words or phrases to make whole sentences.

Written Practice 20-1

Complete each sentence with any pronoun or noun phrase that makes good sense. For example:

There were only <u>two or three boys</u> playing baseball in the park.

1. If _____ rains again today, I'm going to scream.

2. I really like _____, but they don't seem interested in me.

3. _____ were born last night.

4. In 1776 _____ signed the Declaration of Independence.

5. Can _____ fix the car by tomorrow?

6. _____ wasn't able to control the speeding car.

7. You look as though _____ had seen a ghost.

8. According to _____, we're going to have a hot summer.

9. I always enjoyed spending time in

_____.

10. While I made the campfire,

_____ put up the tent.

11. I need help. Where is

_____?

12. Mom said that the scissors are in

_____.

13. _____ sat at the head of

the table, and the young prince sat across from her.

14. Some students were having a party inside

_____.

15. _____ got on the bus

without her purse or wallet.

Written Practice 20-2

Complete each sentence with any verb phrase that makes good sense. For
example:

Around noon Mr. Smith _came home for lunch_.

1. After the rain stopped, we

_____.

2. Please _____ before your
father comes home.

3. While I _____, John got
the campfire going.

4. Despite all her complaining, Jean

_____.

5. Someone _____, "Watch
out for that car!"

6. When Juanita _____,
everyone ran to embrace her.

7. _____ you

_____ before it gets
too late?

8. Uncle Robert _____ to
   his son in the army.

9. Tina _____, but there
   wasn't enough snow on the ground.

10. The Smiths _____ nor
    watch much TV.

11. We finally found the puppy that

    _____

12. The children can't go to the park unless it

    _____

13. Professor Gold is not only intelligent; he

    _____

14. Although _____, I still
    waited to buy a new car.

15. We can go to the pool for a swim if it

    _____

Written Practice 20-3

Reword each sentence twice, completing each new sentence with a phrase of
your choosing. For example:

Tom was dancing with _____.

Tom was dancing with the girl from Argentina.

Tom was dancing with the women who had no dates.

1. _____ is the best time of the year to visit the mountains.

   _____

   _____

2. When we were in Berlin, we met _____.

   _____

   _____

3. Who _____ while I was asleep?

_____

_____

4. How many times have you _____?

_____

_____

5. I'd like to introduce the man that _____.

_____

_____

6. Several _____ during the night.

_____

_____

7. Although _____, Maria decided to stay in San Francisco.

_____

_____

8. Did Mr. Cole get a letter from _____?

_____

_____

9. If you helped me today, _____.

_____

10. The old church is being _____.

_____

_____

11. My boss, who _____, is in Toronto visiting his daughter.

_____

_____

12. The newlyweds are trying to save some money; however, _____.

_____

_____

13. The police officer asked, "_____?"

_____

_____

14. Frank's neighbor suggested that he _____.

_____

_____

15. The woman _____, but no one heard her.

_____

_____

Written Practice 20-4

Give two replacements for the word or words underlined in each sentence.
For example:

I sent <u>those women</u> flowers.

my new girlfriend

your mother and her sister

1. I've always liked <u>working in this store</u>.

_____

_____

2. <u>During the summer</u>, several students take jobs on farms.

_____

_____

3. My son will finish his education <u>by the end of next year</u>.

_____

_____

4. Why <u>are you lying</u> under the car?

_____

_____

5. <u>Because of the rainstorm</u>, several houses were damaged.

_____

_____

6. My family <u>has been living</u> in this town for many years.

_____

_____

7. <u>A large branch</u> fell from the tree in the windstorm.

_____

_____

8. I think you <u>should have</u> spent more time with your parents.

_____

_____

9. We had a picnic <u>alongside</u> a slowly moving stream.

_____

_____

10. <u>Beautifully dressed</u> women danced with the young officers.

_____

_____

11. Jane was able to type <u>more quickly</u> than Phillip.

_____

_____

12. <u>Working as your colleague</u> has always been a pleasure.

_____

_____

13. That woman <u>won't bother</u> you anymore.

_____

_____

14. The boys decided to take a nap <u>under a huge elm tree</u>.

_____

_____

15. <u>The bear growled</u> and looked menacingly at us.

_____

_____

Written Practice 20-5

Reword each sentence twice, completing each new sentence with a clause of your choosing. For example:

When <u>the sun was rising</u>, I looked out at the lake.

When <u>I heard a rooster crow</u>, I looked out at the lake.

1. Although _____, I never had enough money to go there.

_____

_____

2. The committee recommended that _____.

_____

_____

3. Laura finally bought the coat that _____.

_____

_____

4. Our soccer team finally won a game, which _____.

_____

_____

5. Our flight arrived at 9:45 p.m., but _____.

_____

_____

6. One of the hikers walked as if _____.

_____

_____

7. _____, nor do I care for rude language.

_____

_____

8. While the teenagers danced in the basement, _____.

_____

_____

9. As soon as we arrived in the big, open field, _____.

_____

_____

10. _____ because it had finally begun to snow.

_____

_____

11. _____; therefore, we cannot attend your wedding.

_____

_____

12. Please stop arguing about helping, and _____.

_____

_____

13. _____, or you are a very naïve person.

_____

_____

14. Ashley wants to become a scientist, so _____.

_____

_____

15. My best friend, who _____, has enlisted in the navy.

_____

_____

Written Practice 20-6

Write a sentence, using the tense indicated, in each of the blanks. If a tense form does not exist for a verb, write N/A.

1. Present: The senators are voting on the bill.

   Past: _____

   Present perfect: _____

   Future: _____

2. Present: _____

   Past: My in-laws were able to spend a week with us.

   Present perfect: _____

   Future: _____

3. Present: _____

   Past: _____

   Present perfect: Has she had to have corrective surgery?

   Future: _____

4. Present: _____

   Past: _____

   Present perfect: _____

   Future: Thomas won't discuss money with me.

5. Present: Do we meet at a party?

   Past: _____

   Present perfect: _____

   Future: _____

6. Present: _____

   Past: That old book cost nine dollars.

   Present perfect: _____

   Future: _____

7. Present: _____

    Past: _____

    Present perfect: Her fiancé has been living in Maryland.

    Future: _____

8. Present: _____

    Past: _____

    Present perfect: _____

    Future: Lightning strikes will be rare.

9. Present: Can you arrange a meeting with him for me?

    Past: _____

    Present perfect: _____

    Future: _____

10. Present: _____

    Past: Did Jorge want to go on the hike?

    Present perfect: _____

    Future: _____

11. Present: _____

    Past: _____

    Present perfect: His grandparents have always drunk red wine.

    Future: _____

12. Present: _____

    Past: _____

    Present perfect: _____

    Future: Why will the detective follow her?

13. Present: The wedding guests are painting the town red.

    Past: _____

    Present perfect: _____

    Future: _____

14. Present: _____

Past: I had to borrow your car.

Present perfect: _____

Future: _____

15. Present: Why must he buy so many shirts and ties?

Past: _____

Present perfect: _____

Future: _____

Story Completions

The exercises in this section feature stories that are missing necessary elements. Provide appropriate words or phrases to complete these little narratives.

Written Practice 20-7

Where indicated, give a phrase or sentence that is appropriate to the story.

Alone on the River

When I was on vacation in Michigan, I rented a boat (1) _____

_____. I wasn't good at it, but I loved to

fish. I set off down the river, but around noon I began to feel tired and

(2) _____. The wind picked

up when I was sleeping, and (3) _____

_____ (4) _____ When

I awoke, the boat was heading (5) _____

_____. Straight ahead I saw (6) _____

_____. (7) _____

The danger was over. I rowed to shore and (8) _____

_____. My brother looked at me and said,

"(9)_____." I knew he was

right. I never (10) _____.

Written Practice 20-8

Where indicated, give a phrase or sentence that is appropriate to the story.

The Experiment

Mary was always interested in science and (1) _____

_____. She loved to (2) _____

_____. Her friend suggested she try to make

(3) _____, so Mary (4) _____

_____. When the test batch was done,

she rubbed (5) _____. But it

didn't smell good. It smelled (6) _____

_____. Mary didn't know what had gone wrong. (7) _____

_____ Then she noticed that her

hand was turning green. (8) _____

_____ When she took another look at the ingredient she had used, she

saw (9) _____. She quickly

added the correct substance, and (10) _____

_____.

Written Practice 20-9

Where indicated, give a phrase or sentence that is appropriate to the story.

A Message in the Wind

After the snowstorm ended, Claudia and her friends went to the park

(1) _____. The hill was long and

steep. Just perfect for (2) _____.

Jim came up to her and asked, "Can I join you? I don't have a sled." Claudia

liked Jim. He was (3) _____,

so, of course, she agreed. They climbed the hill together, pulling the sled

behind them. When they arrived at the top, (4) _____

_____. Finally (5) _____

_____. Claudia sat in the front of the sled, and Jim

(6) _____. He put his arms

(7) _____. He pushed the sled

off, and down they rushed (8) _____

_____. The wind was whistling in Claudia's ears, and Jim was leaning

near her head. She thought she heard him say, "(9) _____

_____." Or was it her imagination? She liked

Jim, and (10) _____.

Written Practice 20-10

Where indicated, give a phrase or sentence that is appropriate to the story.

The Genie

Billy and Sally were twins and just seven years old. They lived

(1) _____. In the attic of the

house, they found (2) _____.

They loved discovering things together and were overjoyed when

(3) _____. It was made of

brass but dull from age. When Billy accidentally rubbed it, (4) _____

_____. Sally gasped and said,

"(5) _____." But it was true.

The little man said that he was a genie, and (6) _____

_____. Billy and Sally were afraid at first, but the genie

(7) _____. So they made a

wish, and (8) _____ appeared

there in the attic. It whinnied and clomped and made lots of noise. So the

genie (9) _____. "What else do

you wish?" he asked. As the children were about to make their wish,

(10) _____. It was all a dream.

But how could both twins have dreamed the same thing?

Creating Original Sentences

The exercises in this section provide prompts for you to create your own sentences.

Written Practice 20-11

Use the subject phrase, provided in bold, to create original sentences; in each numbered item, use the grammatical form given in parentheses. For example:

the mother

(subject) *The mother of the bride was sobbing.*

(indirect object) *Someone gave the mother a cup of tea.*

a broken lamp

1. (subject) _____

2. (direct object) _____

3. (object of preposition *by*) _____

4. (subject of a passive voice sentence) _____

5. (antecedent of a relative pronoun) _____

6. (possessive) _____

7. (object of preposition *of*) _____

8. (direct object in a relative clause) _____

9. (subject of a clause begun with *as if*) _____

10. (direct object in a clause begun with *although*) _____

Written Practice 20-12

With the phrase provided in bold, create original sentences using the phrase in the form given in parentheses.

our new neighbors

1. (subject) _____

2. (indirect object) _____

3. (object of preposition *about*) _____

4. (object of *by* in a passive voice sentence) _____

5. (antecedent of a relative pronoun) _____

6. (possessive) _____

7. (direct object) _____

8. (subject of a passive voice sentence) _____

9. (antecedent of relative pronoun *whose*) _____

10. (direct object in a clause begun with *when*) _____

Written Practice 20-13

With the phrase provided in bold, create original sentences that use the phrase in the form given in parentheses.

another illness

1. (subject) _____

2. (direct object) _____

3. (object of preposition *due to*) _____

4. (object of *by* in a passive voice sentence) _____

5. (antecedent of a relative pronoun) _____

6. (object of preposition *like*) _____

7. (subject of a passive voice sentence) _____

8. (subject of verb *could have*) _____

9. (antecedent of possessive relative pronoun *the cause of which*)

_____

10. (direct object in a clause begun with *while*) _____

Written Practice 20-14

With the phrase provided in bold, create original sentences that use the phrase in the form given in parentheses.

that strange man

1. (subject) _____

2. (indirect object) _____

3. (object of preposition *according to*) _____

4. (object of *by* in a passive voice sentence) _____

5. (antecedent of a relative pronoun) _____

6. (possessive) _____

7. (direct object of verb *suspect*) _____

8. (subject of a passive voice sentence) _____

9. (subject of a present perfect tense verb) _____

10. (indirect object in a clause begun with *if*) _____

Written Practice 20-15

With the phrase provided in bold, create original sentences that use the phrase in the grammatical form given in parentheses.

several foreign tourists

1. (subject) _____

2. (indirect object) _____

3. (object of preposition *for*) _____

4. (object of *by* in a past passive voice sentence) _____

5. (antecedent of a restrictive relative pronoun) _____

6. (possessive) _____

7. (direct object) _____

8. (subject of a future passive voice sentence) _____

9. (antecedent of relative pronoun *whose*) _____

10. (direct object in a clause begun with *before*) _____

Final Exam

Choose the letter of the word or phrase that best completes each sentence.

1. This door cannot _____ opened without a key.

   A. will be   B. be   C. was   D. is being

2. Close your eyes. I have _____ surprise for you.

   A. the   B. an   C. a   D. any

3. Jane _____ be given a reward.

   A. were   B. should   C. want   D. was able to

4. I had been swindled _____ a very clever man.

   A. by   B. of   C. to   D. from

5. The children _____ naughty again.

   A. will   B. must   C. were being   D. is able to be

6. The diplomas for the graduates had _____ on a table near the podium.

   A. being   B. be prepared   C. waited   D. been placed

7. The letter was returned _____ lack of postage.

   A. being   B. of   C. by   D. due to

391

8. I _____ to phone my parents before ten o'clock.

    A. have   B. must   C. should   D. be able

9. The novel _____ be purchased in most bookstores.

    A. will be   B. is able   C. will need   D. can

10. The goat _____ fed in the barn.

    A. will   B. are   C. want to be   D. was being

11. _____ that all the guests be comfortable at the reception.

    A. If it were necessary   C. Had I known

    B. It is essential   D. If there were an agreement

12. Marie had _____ when someone knocked on the door.

    A. been reading   C. found the remote

    B. noticed   D. sitting and waiting

13. If you had been kinder, you _____ more friends.

    A. should have   C. could be wanting

    B. might like   D. would have had

14. Is it really necessary that _____ with us again?

    A. the baby sleep   C. we are sleeping

    B. it happens   D. he had come

15. You really _____ be in such a hurry.

    A. never   C. anywhere

    B. needn't   D. nowhere

16. Have you _____ here long?

    A. wait   C. been waiting

    B. be waiting   D. have to wait

17. We entered the _____ of London and soon saw Buckingham Palace.

    A. capital   B. fortress   C. city   D. country

18. _____ she known about that earlier, she could have saved everyone a lot of grief.
    A. If   B. As if   C. Would   D. Had

19. That would never happen! We would _____!
    A. never dream of it
    B. have been there
    C. if you would
    D. as if we were to blame

20. _____ that Ms. Patel would be our candidate in the next election.
    A. If you would like
    B. It was finally agreed
    C. Had we heard about it
    D. It is over

21. _____ going to dinner in the city tonight?
    A. Should we
    B. Does he want
    C. Are you able to
    D. How about

22. Is _____ any money left to buy some groceries?
    A. she   B. there   C. exist   D. it

23. Was _____ in 1914 that World War I began?
    A. there   B. here   C. the year   D. it

24. The freight train began to move even _____ than before.
    A. now   B. more slowly   C. yesterday   D. least

25. _____ you have strong writing skills, we plan to offer you an editing job.
    A. Inasmuch as   B. Whether   C. Concerning   D. As if

26. Your politics _____ yet become a problem for our party.
    A. doesn't   B. haven't   C. wasn't   D. weren't

27. Today is _____ of September.
    A. the second   B. thirtieth   C. 8   D. on the eighth

28. Of all the guests, Charles always arrives _____.
    A. lately   B. the end of the party   C. more punctual   D. the earliest

29. Last year the company earned _____ and the year before just $900,000.

    A. $3,500,000   B. two years   C. over 100 employees   D. in 2013

30. Don't _____ anyone try to talk you out of buying this car.

    A. speak   B. be   C. worry   D. let

31. _____ it snow a lot last year?

    A. Does   B. Was able to   C. Did   D. Can

32. My sister _____ is older than my sister Helen.

    A. who is not any younger   C. whichever she needs

    B. that works in Boise, Idaho,   D. I want to meet someday

33. To _____ mistaken for a movie star was a compliment.

    A. wasn't   B. being   C. have been   D. will be

34. How did you figure out _____?

    A. that   B. what to do   C. it   D. all of them

35. I hope to learn something from _____.

    A. who will study with me   C. which you tried to explain to me

    B. they are the officers of the bank   D. whomever the governor sent

36. Michael and Tina have known _____ all their lives.

    A. each   B. themselves   C. one another   D. oneself

37. Did you _____ from someone at work?

    A. let him down   B. drive off   C. catch a cold   D. hang out

38. Tom thinks he really _____ on that investment he made a month ago.

    A. cleaned up   B. put together   C. passed away   D. has run

39. Don't wear that suit. It's _____.

    A. hung out   B. stood for   C. put off   D. worn out

40. I like how you think; _____, I want you to begin writing my speeches.

    A. because   B. therefore   C. given   D. neither

Choose the letter of the sentence that illustrates the correct use of the word or phrase in bold.

41. *a happy man*: Indirect object.
   A. He knows he is a happy man.
   B. What makes a happy man so happy?
   C. What more could you give a happy man?
   D. A happy man makes others happy.

42. *his red boat*: Direct object.
   A. I think Jack has lost his red boat.
   B. When did his red boat go missing?
   C. His red boat is under the bed.
   D. Can his red boat really float?

43. *that*: Restrictive relative pronoun.
   A. A man that lies is not to be trusted.
   B. Did you know that she is from Spain?
   C. That strange man followed me home.
   D. If you said that, you were wrong.

44. *broken*: Used in the static passive.
   A. You could have broken your arm.
   B. It was broken by that little boy.
   C. A broken glass can be a danger.
   D. This watch is broken again.

45. *his*: Pronoun.
   A. Is his in the kitchen or the living room?
   B. I haven't met his family yet.
   C. Are his parents from Alabama?
   D. She likes all his novels.

46. *working*: Gerund.
   A. The clock isn't working again.
   B. Will you be working on Sunday?
   C. I truly like working with you.
   D. How are things working out with Jane?

47. *up*: Prepositional usage.
   A. I saw the man coming up the hill.
   B. She ended up with someone else.
   C. Tom doesn't want to break up with her.
   D. You need to clean up before supper.

48. *a few friends*: Object of a preposition in a passive voice sentence.
   A. She was helped by a few friends.
   B. I got this from a few friends.
   C. Can you give this to a few friends?
   D. He called Jim instead of a few friends.

49. *be*: **In the subjunctive mood.**

    A. Be here on time tomorrow.

    B. Will you be able to lend me some money?

    C. My cousin won't be in town then.

    D. I suggest you be more alert.

50. *it*: **In an impersonal expression.**

    A. It has fleas and needs a bath.

    B. Who put it on the kitchen table?

    C. Its location is somewhere in Asia.

    D. Tina said, "It's almost five o'clock."

Appendix

International Phonetic Alphabet (IPA)

Consonants

IPA	Examples
b	bad, tab
d	did, body
f	find, if
g	give, drag
h	his, hello
j	yarn, yellow
k	cat, back
l	leg, little
m	man, rumor
n	no, ten
ŋ	sing, finger
p	pet, map
r	red, try
s	sun, miss
ʃ	she, trash
t	tea, letting

Vowels

IPA	Examples
ʌ	up, luck
ɑː	arm, father
æ	sat, black
e	met, bed
ə	away, area
ɜːʳ	turn, learn
ɪ	hit, winning
iː	see, meat
ɒ	hot, rock
ɔː	call, four
ʊ	look, would
uː	blue, food
aɪ	dive, eye
aʊ	now, out
eɪ	play, eight
oʊ	go, home

Consonants

IPA	Examples
tʃ	chin, church
θ	think, both
ð	this, mother
v	very, five
w	wet, window
z	zoo, hazy
ʒ	pleasure, decision
dʒ	just, cage

Vowels

IPA	Examples
ɔɪ	toy, boil
eəʳ	where, hair
ɪəʳ	near, here
ʊəʳ	pure, tourist

Answer Key

Sample answers are given for subjective exercises.

CHAPTER 1

Written Practice 1-1
1. father ð   2. faith θ   3. think θ   4. thumb θ   5. together ð   6. bath θ
7. bathe ð   8. mother ð   9. thank θ   10. mathematics θ

Written Practice 1-2
1. gather V   2. bags V   3. bitter V   4. clocks VL   5. pace VL   6. size VL
7. most VL   8. quiz V   9. special VL   10. painter VL

Written Practice 1-3
1. laughing f   2. kneel S   3. bought S   4. flight S   5. knead S   6. rougher f
7. slaughter S   8. kept k   9. although S   10. kicking k

Written Practice 1-4
1. tough f   2. row r   3. white S   4. who h   5. when w   6. fix x   7. through S
8. tower w   9. store t   10. why w

QUIZ
1. (dʒ)judge   2. (ð)then   3. (eɪ)snake   4. (ɜːʳ)father   5. (ʊ)book   6. (ʃ)sharp
7. (ɒ)rock   8. (æ)nap   9. (ŋ)sing   10. (ɪ)Tim

CHAPTER 2

Written Practice 2-1
1. Martin   2. Rebecca   3. Juan   4. Robert Joseph   5. Zelinski   6. Adams
7. Smith   8. Kenneth Michael Barnes   9. Patel   10. Obama

399

Written Practice 2-2
1. James   2. William   3. Judith   4. Ronald   5. Samuel

Written Practice 2-3
1. a   2. a   3. The   4. a, an   5. the

Written Practice 2-4
1. Whose   2. Which   3. Whose   4. What, Which, Whose   5. What, Which   6. What, Which
7. Whose   8. What   9. What   10. Whose

Written Practice 2-5
1. this   2. these   3. that   4. these, those   5. These   6. those   7. that   8. that   9. this, that
10. those

Written Practice 2-6
1. my   2. their   3. our   4. its   5. your   6. her   7. his   8. our   9. their   10. his

Written Practice 2-7
1. Few students can recite the Gettysburg Address from memory.   2. A few of these e-mails are from our cousin in Guatemala.   3. The few gymnasts that can do that trick often get injured.

Written Practice 2-8
1. first   2. third   3. hundredth   4. fifth   5. *Twelfth*   6. thirty-first   7. fiftieth   8. second
9. eighth   10. nineteenth

QUIZ
1. b   2. a   3. d   4. c   5. a   6. c   7. a   8. a   9. a   10. b

CHAPTER 3

Written Practice 3-1
1. We have a lot of fun.   2. He has a lot of fun.   3. My friends and I have a lot of fun.   4. I learn a new language.   5. You learn a new language.   6. They learn a new language.   7. She is in an unpleasant situation.   8. They are in an unpleasant situation.   9. I am in an unpleasant situation.
10. You want to order another glass of soda.   11. He wants to order another glass of soda.   12. The little girl wants to order another glass of soda.   13. It hides out of fear.   14. Maria and I hide out of fear.   15. One hides out of fear.

Written Practice 3-2
1. Some are yours.   2. These are yours.   3. This is yours.   4. Each looks hungry.   5. Many look hungry.   6. A couple look hungry.   7. Are a few yours?   8. Is this yours?   9. Are some yours?
10. Is one yours?

Written Practice 3-3
1. My friend sometimes works for his girlfriend's father.   2. My friend often works for his girlfriend's father.   3. My friend works for his girlfriend's father during summer vacation.   4. Mother brings me

hot soup when I'm ill.   5. Mother usually brings me hot soup.   6. Mother brings me hot soup on a cool afternoon.   7. Do you play the piano once a day?   8. Do you always play the piano?   9. John runs a couple laps around the track before his first class.   10. John regularly runs a couple laps around the track.

Written Practice 3-4
1. dropping   2. holding   3. sending   4. approving   5. following   6. making   7. saying   8. drinking   9. hitting   10. getting

Written Practice 3-5
1. helps   2. drinks   3. run   4. are doing   5. is walking

Written Practice 3-6
1. These boys can look for the misplaced wallet.   2. These boys want to look for the misplaced wallet.
3. You should join a health club downtown.   4. You need to join a health club downtown.   5. Martin is supposed to be building something in the garage right now.   6. Martin may be building something in the garage right now.   7. We must live on the food we grow ourselves.   8. We are able to live on the food we grow ourselves.   9. I need to get my car fixed as soon as possible.   10. I can get my car fixed as soon as possible.

Written Practice 3-7
1. Habitual: Ms. Delgado spoke with Dr. Keller. Progressive: Ms. Delgado was speaking with Dr. Keller. Emphatic: Ms. Delgado did speak with Dr. Keller.   2. Habitual: The girls cooperated. Progressive: The girls were cooperating. Emphatic: The girls did cooperate.   3. Habitual: I practice the piano. Progressive: I was practicing the piano. Emphatic: I did practice the piano.   4. Habitual: The lawyer signed the contract. Progressive: The lawyer was signing the contract. Emphatic: The lawyer did sign the contract.
5. Habitual: Some boys relaxed in the shade of a tree. Progressive: Some boys were relaxing in the shade of a tree. Emphatic: Some boys did relax in the shade of a tree.

Written Practice 3-8
1. Did the little boy make his bed for the first time?   2. Was Jack supposed to help me pick apples?
3. Were the soldiers were getting tired and hungry?   4. Did Mr. Patel want to rent the apartment again?
5. Did a strange man come up to my desk?   6. Who slipped on the ice and fell?   7. What did the girls' soccer team win?   8. Where did Tom find his wallet?   9. Why was the boy crying?   10. How did she glare at the rude man?

QUIZ
1. b   2. d   3. a   4. c   5. d   6. a   7. b   8. b   9. c   10. a

CHAPTER 4

Written Practice 4-1
1. My parents have dined at a very nice restaurant. My parents had dined at a very nice restaurant.
2. Someone has wanted to dance with you. She had wanted to dance with you.   3. We have never traveled by rail. We had never traveled by rail.   4. A friendly dog has followed me home. A friendly dog had followed me home.   5. My wife has always brushed her hair before bed. My wife had always brushed her hair before bed.   6. Have you talked to your neighbors? Had you talked to your neighbors?

7. Has Sara closed all the windows? Had Sara closed all the windows?   8. Has the rain damaged the fragile plants? Had the rain damaged the fragile plants?   9. That boy has sometimes copied my homework. That boy had sometimes copied my homework.   10. Bill has joined a fitness club. Bill had joined a fitness club.

Written Practice 4-2

1. sung   2. understood   3. come   4. gone   5. eaten   6. drunk   7. knelt   8. sent
9. said   10. taught   11. grown   12. held   13. brought   14. let   15. drawn

Written Practice 4-3

1. Tom has been taking the dog for a walk. Tom had been taking the dog for a walk.   2. Maria has bought an expensive sweater. Maria had bought an expensive sweater.   3. My grandparents have always drunk only tea. My grandparents had always drunk only tea.   4. Phillip has been speaking with Mr. Jackson. Phillip had been speaking with Mr. Jackson.   5. Have you seen a lunar eclipse? Had you seen a lunar eclipse?   6. Has the team been traveling out of state? Had the team been traveling out of state?
7. The children have been very naughty. The children had been very naughty.   8. Why have those men been following us? Why had those men been following us?   9. Dr. Schwartz has been giving lectures on smoking. Dr. Schwartz had been giving lectures on smoking.   10. I have finally been spending less money. I had finally been spending less money.

Written Practice 4-4

1. I have not been writing a novel.   2. Jack does not speak only of his former girlfriend.   3. Your daughter had already received my gift.   4. The temperature is not very high today.   5. Jean has been receiving her magazines.   6. I have always trusted you.   7. Carla does have an idea what that word means.   8. Jim has not been dating someone from Africa.   9. A large tree had not fallen near the garage.
10. No one has been slamming the door.

Written Practice 4-5

1. My professor is speaking about evolution next week. My professor will be speaking about evolution next week.   2. My wife drives to Connecticut tomorrow. My wife will drive to Connecticut tomorrow.
3. Are you leaving on vacation on Monday? Will you be leaving on vacation on Monday?   4. My son is spending the summer at a camp in Michigan. My son will be spending the summer at a camp in Michigan.
5. The foreign tourists arrive around 4 p.m. today. The foreign tourists will arrive around 4 p.m. today.

Written Practice 4-6

1. Who will be riding in the convertible? Who is going to be riding in the convertible?   2. My in-laws will be traveling to Guatemala. My in-laws are going to be traveling in Guatemala.   3. Shall I borrow more money from him? Am I going to borrow more money from him?   4. Bob will send her an important e-mail. Bob is going to send her an important e-mail.   5. The ambassador will speak with the other diplomats. The ambassador is going to speak with the other diplomats.

Written Practice 4-7

1. Bob will be walking for two hours. Bob will have been walking for two hours by day's end.
2. Mr. James will pay off the loan. Mr. James will have paid off the loan before the end of the year.
3. That girl will dance with every boy. That girl will have danced with every boy by midnight.   4. Will you write a lot of poems? Will you have written a lot of poems before the month ends?   5. I will perfect my English. I will have perfected my English before the close of the semester.   6. Sophia will be living with her grandmother for a month. Sophia will have been living with her grandmother for a month by April.

7. He will get a bad cold. He will have gotten a bad cold before the cold weather ends.   8. My brother will find a job in the city. My brother will have found a job in the city soon after arriving there.   9. The dolphins will chase the shark away. The dolphins will have chased the shark away before it can approach their young.   10. The young chemist will develop a new formula. The young chemist will have developed a new formula by autumn.

Written Practice 4-8

1. I have been able to understand his philosophy. I have been able to repair that old car.   2. Mary will have to spend more time studying. Mary will have to explain the solution to the puzzle.   3. No one had wanted to keep all the puppies. No one had wanted to raise eight little pups.   4. Will you need to volunteer at the hospital? Will you need to arrange for John's transportation to the airport?   5. The tourists had wanted to go out sightseeing. The tourists had wanted to visit the beautiful old cathedral.

QUIZ

1. b   2. a   3. d   4. c   5. b   6. a   7. d   8. b   9. b   10. c

CHAPTER 5

Written Practice 5-1

1. stale   2. red   3. That   4. my   5. a dozen   6. weekly   7. downtown   8. tiny   9. interesting   10. ripped

Written Practice 5-2

1. My neighbor is such a thoughtful person.   2. I try to be generous during the holidays.   3. I'm told that the surgery you're scheduled to have is rather painless.   4. You need to wash your dirty hands and face.   5. The lake is very deep in the middle.   6. These baseball cards are very collectible.   7. My son likes mechanical toys.   8. A gruesome accident took place on Highway 41.   9. I won't tolerate such childish behavior.   10. Why must you always be so negative?

Written Practice 5-3

1. That traffic light   2. a sports arena   3. the morning newspaper   4. My e-mail inbox   5. a television antenna   6. The soccer field   7. your credit card   8. the airline schedule   9. an ice cream parlor   10. the light switch

Written Practice 5-4

1. adverb   2. adjective   3. adjective   4. adjective   5. adverb   6. adjective   7. adjective   8. adjective   9. adjective   10. adverb

Written Practice 5-5

1. very slowly   2. rather quietly   3. somewhat boring   4. unusually rapidly   5. quite frantically   6. quite terrible   7. quite gently   8. utterly shattered   9. very unexpected   10. extremely boldly

Written Practice 5-6

1. sooner, sooner   2. brighter, more brightly   3. darker, more darkly   4. more frightful, more frightfully   5. more special, more specially   6. lovelier, more lovely   7. more boring, more boringly   8. more envious, more enviously   9. shallower, more shallowly   10. more logical, more logically

Written Practice 5-7

1. My two sisters work harder than my older brother.   2. Is Mr. Taylor older than his wife?
3. I sometimes drive faster in my sports car than in my SUV.   4. We painted the house more quickly than three years ago.   5. Yesterday's storm was more violent than the one we had last week.

QUIZ

1. b   2. a   3. a   4. d   5. c   6. b   7. a   8. b   9. c   10. d

PART ONE TEST

1. c.   2. a   3. b   4. a   5. d   6. c   7. a   8. a   9. a   10. b   11. b   12. c   13. d
14. c   15. c   16. b   17. a   18. d   19. a   20. b   21. c   22. a   23. d   24. c   25. b

CHAPTER 6

Written Practice 6-1

1. I like to spend the evenings reading.   2. Are you happy with your new apartment?   3. He wants to go out on a date with Sonja.   4. She is starting to take classes at the junior college.   5. It is impossible to understand a word you're saying.   6. Shall we all go into the living room?   7. They borrowed the lawn mower again.   8. One should speak with carefully chosen words.   9. Who knows what the future holds?   10. What did you send to your mother?

Written Practice 6-2

1. I   2. me   3. him/her   4. him/her/them   5. she   6. her   7. It   8. it   9. us   10. us
11. they, them   12. them   13. one   14. whom   15. What

Writing Practice 6-3

1. My sister lends her/him a jacket.   2. My sister lends it to her/him.   3. Will you give him these tools?
4. Will you give them to him?   5. Bill finally found her the perfect gift.   6. Bill finally found it for her.
7. The governor assigned her a difficult task.   8. The governor assigned it to her.   9. Mr. Patel often sends them postcards from America.   10. Mr. Patel often sends them to them.   11. Grandmother always tells them interesting stories.   12. Grandmother always tells them to them.   13. We were writing them long letters.   14. We were writing them to them.   15. I will sell them my old car.   16. I will sell it to them.

Written Practice 6-4

1. The children were playing with the dogs, whose kennel is in the barn.   2. My husband, who is out of town, still works at the mill.   3. I sat through an opera, which lasted nearly four hours.   4. This is Mr. Hughes, whom you met in St. Louis.   5. The actress about whom I wrote in an essay will star in a play.   6. This is the woman I mentioned, for whom I have worked for several years.   7. That's a rather good restaurant, whose menu/the menu of which is extensive.   8. I was born in a village, which was severely damaged during the war.   9. We're going to visit our uncle, for whom we bought this fruit basket.
10. This is a letter from my cousin, to whom I recently sent tickets for the ballet.

Written Practice 6-5

1. was built in the nineteenth century   2. plans to become a lawyer someday   3. you were telling me about   4. I picked up in Rome   5. I found an old diary   6. I rarely get a response   7. live in that apartment   8. won the award   9. I never talk about   10. we invited to our party

Written Practice 6-6

1. I won $2,000, which helped me pay off the loan.   2. My father's heroism was publicly acknowledged, which brought tears to my mother's eyes.   3. All the flights back home are canceled, which means two more days of vacation.   4. Tom gave her a big hug and a kiss, which took her breath away.   5. Marco's parents returned to Europe, which changed Marco's life forever.

Written Practice 6-7

1. Whoever pays the most gets to sleep in the biggest room.   2. Whatever may happen between us, I will not betray our friendship.   3. I will probably vote for whomever my friends recommend.
4. The little boy wanted whichever whistle would make the most noise.   5. Whomever you accept as your leader, the others will also follow.   6. Whoever wins the lottery should share the money with the family.
7. I always agree with whatever the boss says.   8. Whichever mushroom he eats, he will surely get sick.
9. Whomever the students like the most will be crowned prom queen.   10. This is a gift for whoever shoveled the snow from my driveway yesterday.

QUIZ

1. b   2. a   3. d   4. b   5. b   6. d   7. c   8. a   9. d   10. b

CHAPTER 7

Written Practice 7-1

1. yourselves   2. myself   3. herself   4. She   5. ourselves   6. himself   7. They   8. itself
9. himself   10. yourself

Written Practice 7-2

1. You shame yourself with such talk.   2. She hurt herself during the soccer match.   3. My teammates pride themselves on their fairness.   4. Ms. Ling can seat herself here alongside me.   5. We really enjoyed ourselves at the reception.   6. Jack and I covered ourselves with leaves and hid.   7. Several guests amused themselves at the piano.   8. I promised myself to quit smoking.   9. It was frightened and hid itself in a dark corner.   10. You have all perjured yourselves.   11. Dr. Ravel cut himself/herself with a scalpel.   12. Someone bumped himself on the corner of the table.   13. The frog protected itself from the hot sun.   14. My grandmother bundled herself up in a warm shawl.   15. Each of you has to control himself better.

Written Practice 7-3

1. Tom himself drank a bit too much at the party.   2. The contestants themselves were dressed in the latest fashion.   3. I myself can speak three languages.   4. We ourselves have been in both Europe and Africa.
5. You yourself suggested that we visit that museum.   6. Anna herself graduated from college early.

7. Do you yourselves eat in this restaurant regularly? 8. He himself wanted to join the Marine Corps. 9. The lamp itself cost more than the sofa. 10. They themselves lived on a beautiful mountainside.

Written Practice 7-4

1. The lawyer and the judge do not trust one another/each other. 2. Jill and Karen knit sweaters for one another/each other. 3. My father and mother bought cameras for one another/each other. 4. My children and I love one another/each other. 5. Do the boys and the girls want to dance with one another/each other? 6. Jim and Bill help one another/each other with the cleaning. 7. The actor and the singer are jealous of one another/each other. 8. Larry and Laura have written poems for one another/each other. 9. They (he and she) never visit one another/each other. 10. The governor and the senator supported one another/each other in the campaign.

Written Practice 7-5

1. Whom did my relatives from Brazil visit last week? 2. Which wallet do I/you really like? 3. How do they plan to get to Washington? 4. Where do our/your neighbors have a summer house? 5. When does the engaged couple hope to go to Hawaii? 6. Why will we/you drive to Pittsburgh? 7. Why does he save a hundred dollars every week? 8. From whom did Jean receive a large bouquet? 9. Whose late father left him a large sum of money? 10. Which puppy does her daughter want?

Written Practice 7-6

1. Where did the boys find the treasure? Do you know where the boys found the treasure? 2. How many cars can park in this parking lot? Someone asked me how many cars can park in this parking lot. 3. With whom was Jill dancing on the balcony? Did you see with whom Jill was dancing on the balcony? 4. Whose dog is hiding under the porch? I wonder whose dog is hiding under the porch. 5. What kind of books does she have hidden there? Jim asked her what kind of books she has hidden there. 6. When will the rest of the guests arrive? Can you tell me when the rest of the guests will arrive? 7. Which suit should I wear to their wedding? I don't care which suit I/you wear to their wedding. 8. How long should the tablecloth be that he wants for the party? Help me decide how long the tablecloth that he wants for the party should be. 9. What did Laura send them for their anniversary? Sara asked what Laura sent them for their anniversary. 10. Why is the TV set still broken? Did you tell him why the TV set is still broken?

QUIZ

1. a　2. a　3. d　4. b　5. c　6. a　7. b　8. b　9. d　10. a

CHAPTER 8

Written Practice 8-1

1. Present: I am not careless with my tools. Past: I was not careless with my tools. Present perfect: I have not been careless with my tools. Future: I will not be careless with my tools. 2. Present: Raj is writing an essay on climate change. Past: Raj was writing an essay on climate change. Present perfect: Raj has been writing an essay on climate change. Future: Raj will be writing an essay on climate change. 3. Present: Is she spending time in Poland? Past: Was she spending time in Poland? Present perfect: Has she been spending time in Poland? Future: Will she be spending time in Poland? 4. Present: The lawyers are not at the meeting. Past: The lawyers were not at the meeting. Present perfect: The lawyers have not been at the meeting. Future: The lawyers will not be at the meeting. 5. Present: We are roasting a turkey for

Thanksgiving dinner. Past: We were roasting a turkey for Thanksgiving dinner. Present perfect: We have been roasting a turkey for Thanksgiving dinner. Future: We will be roasting a turkey for Thanksgiving dinner.

Written Practice 8-2

1. Present: The bride has a new wardrobe. Past: The bride had a new wardrobe. Present perfect: The bride has had a new wardrobe. Future: The bride will have a new wardrobe.   2. Present: My girlfriend brings soda for the picnic. Past: My girlfriend brought soda for the picnic. Present perfect: My girlfriend has brought soda for the picnic. Future: My girlfriend will bring soda for the picnic.   3. Present: I am having parties all winter. Past: I was having parties all winter. Present perfect: I have been having parties all winter. Future: I will be having parties all winter.   4. Present: Is he singing in the opera chorus? Past: Was he singing in the opera chorus? Present perfect: Has he been singing in the opera chorus? Future: Will he be singing in the opera chorus?   5. Present: It becomes cold every evening. Past: It became cold every evening. Present perfect: It has become cold every evening. Future: It will become cold every evening.

Written Practice 8-3

1. Present: What do you do most evenings? Past: What did you do most evenings? Present perfect: What have you done most evenings? Future: What will you do most evenings?   2. Present: Do you take the subway to work? Past: Did you take the subway to work? Present perfect: Have you taken the subway to work? Future: Will you take the subway to work?   3. Present: I am doing charity work at the hospital. Past: I was doing charity work at the hospital. Present perfect: I have been doing charity work at the hospital. Future: I will be doing charity work at the hospital.   4. Present: Tom does not like broccoli. Past: Tom did not like broccoli. Present perfect: Tom has not liked broccoli. Future: Tom will not like broccoli. 5. Present: John did a drawing of our cats. Past: John did a drawing of our cats. Present perfect: John has done a drawing of our cats. Future: John will do a drawing of our cats.

Written Practice 8-4

1. The tour guide wanted to speak about the unusual painting. The tour guide was supposed to speak about the unusual painting.   2. We have to be going home now. We should be going home now.   3. Maria will be able to help you tomorrow. Maria will need to help you tomorrow.   4. It might rain every day in the spring. It can rain every day in the spring.   5. May she borrow money from you? Is she able to borrow money from you?   6. I ought to escort the woman down the street. I need to escort the woman down the street.   7. Why must you always argue with me? Why do you always want to argue with me?   8. You will have to show your passport at immigration. You will need to show your passport at immigration. 9. Daniel has been able to juggle for a long time. Daniel has wanted to juggle for a long time.   10. No one is supposed to be here. No one can be here.

QUIZ

1. d   2. b   3. a   4. a   5. a   6. b   7. c   8. c   9. c   10. b

CHAPTER 9

Written Practice 9-1

1. We're driving through a beautiful forest.   2. I'm very pleased with your behavior.   3. Who's that beautiful woman in the living room?   4. Are you from Mexico or Cuba?   5. What's Mary carrying under her arm?   6. No one's allowed in the laboratory today.   7. Is she an acquaintance of yours?

8. He's supposed to be a great soccer player.   9. They're rather silly questions.   10. Am I strong enough to lift that log?   11. Are you able to get around on your crutches?   12. Someone's watching us from across the street.   13. It's terribly windy today.   14. Is it supposed to snow again tomorrow?   15. They're able to pull down the old fence.

Written Practice 9-2

1. We didn't develop a new programming language. Didn't we develop a new programming language?
2. I don't know you. Don't I know you?   3. Indira didn't forget her purse again. Didn't Indira forget her purse again?   4. We don't spell the words correctly. Don't we spell the words correctly?   5. Someone didn't lock the door. Didn't someone lock the door?/Didn't anyone lock the door?   6. She doesn't start each day with a good breakfast. Doesn't she start each day with a good breakfast?   7. You didn't dance with the two foreigners. Didn't you dance with the two foreigners?   8. We don't belong to the same organization. Don't we belong to the same organization?   9. It didn't snow. Didn't it snow?   10. They didn't trick him again. Didn't they trick him again?

Written Practice 9-3

1. We wouldn't prefer to sit outside.   2. I won't drive you to work every day.   3. He can't stay in a hotel.   4. She hasn't time.   5. They mustn't stay in the basement.   6. Laura shouldn't dress for a business meeting.   7. Tom hadn't spent a lot of time in the library.   8. We haven't been to Pakistan twice.   9. This part of the audience can't see the stage.   10. Who hasn't seen that movie?

Written Practice 9-4

1. coats   2. noses   3. worries   4. bankers   5. neckties   6. bellies   7. kisses   8. marches
9. dishes   10. cherries

Written Practice 9-5

1. alumni/alumnae   2. cargoes   3. crisis   4. scissors   5. barbers   6. watch   7. sanitariums/ sanitaria   8. deer   9. parentheses   10. foreman   11. IDs   12. focus   13. '80   14. scholars
15. vetoes

QUIZ
1. d   2. a   3. c   4. d   5. b   6. a   7. b   8. d   9. a   10. d

CHAPTER 10

Written Practice 10-1

1. To be spending time alone is what she needed.   2. To be working from home made more sense.
3. To be borrowing so much money will get you in trouble.   4. To be seeking fame is a superficial goal.
5. To be traveling with Jack would have made the journey more fun.   6. To be conversing with the governor seemed unreal.   7. To be learning English from Mr. Jones means success.   8. To be watching television instead of studying is a bad idea.   9. To be sleeping late yet again was a serious mistake.
10. To be shopping with Aunt Mary will be fun.

Written Practice 10-2

1. to have learned this difficult language; To have learned this difficult language was a real achievement.
2. to have borrowed money from him; To have borrowed money from him was foolish.   3. to have traveled in Mexico; To have traveled in Mexico was part of my education.   4. to have interviewed the famous actor; To have interviewed the famous actor would have meant a lot to her.   5. to have cleaned the floor; [For you] to have cleaned the floor would have saved Mother time.   6. to have shoveled the driveway; To have shoveled the driveway would have given access to the garage.   7. to have rushed him to the hospital; To have rushed him to the hospital would have saved his life.   8. to have followed the suspect; To have followed the suspect would have been dangerous.   9. to have impressed the woman; To have impressed the woman might have proved to be expensive.   10. to have photographed the president; To have photographed the president gave her much pride.

Written Practice 10-3

1. to be hidden in the garage   2. to be struck by a wonderful idea   3. to be surrounded by great friends
4. to be embraced by her mother   5. to be thanked for their military service

Written Practice 10-4

1. to have been hidden in the garage   2. to have been introduced by the host   3. to have been escorted about the museum   4. to have been given medals   5. to have been elected governor

Writing Practice 10-5

1. Having enough money is important to me. Finding a good job is important to me.   2. My daughter is interested in living in Spain. My daughter is interested in writing novels.   3. Working in Chicago has changed my life. Marrying Maria has changed my life.   4. They really like spending time with us. They really like swimming in the river.   5. Why does your family prefer living in the country? Why does your family prefer dining out?   6. Having luxuries doesn't always make you happy. Knowing important people doesn't always make you happy.   7. People say that smoking cigarettes can harm your health. People say that eating fast food can harm your health.   8. The boys love working out. The boys love studying in the new library.   9. Camping in the woods reminds me of my childhood in Africa. Sharing a meal with good friends reminds me of my childhood in Africa.   10. Being allowed to go on the trip depends on your earning some money. Being allowed to go on the trip depends on your getting a passport.

Writing Practice 10-6

1. Being a good friend is not always easy. To be a good friend is not always easy.   2. I like speaking with Henry. I like to speak with Henry.   3. Is hiking safe around here? Is it safe to hike around here?
4. Swimming a long distance takes practice. To swim a long distance takes practice.   5. I prefer climbing in the Alps. I prefer to climb in the Alps.

QUIZ

1. c   2. b   3. a   4. a   5. d   6. b   7. c   8. b   9. a   10. d

PART TWO TEST

1. a   2. b   3. a   4. c   5. d   6. a   7. a   8. b   9. b   10. d   11. d   12. a   13. a
14. b   15. b   16. d   17. a   18. d   19. a   20. d   21. c   22. a   23. b   24. c   25. a

CHAPTER 11

Written Practice 11-1

1. The boys were roughhousing inside the gymnasium.   2. What do you know about plane geometry?
3. This article is concerned with clean water in Africa.   4. According to the weather forecast, it will
probably rain tomorrow.   5. The robber slipped the rings into his pocket.   6. Barbara stayed in bed
because of a terrible cold.   7. My grandmother came for a visit without her purse and glasses.
8. A group of protesters assembled outside city hall.   9. We could see tropical fish below the surface of
the water.   10. I usually have a day off between Sunday and Wednesday.

Written Practice 11-2

1. On account of their cranky dog, they rarely had visitors. We stayed at home on account of the heat wave.
2. He's a very strong man, like his father. I think Jane looks like her.   3. You are as nice as you are pretty.
I wrote as quickly as I could.   4. According to this article, winter will be mild this year. I should get better
grades, according to my teacher.   5. The governor spoke in place of the mayor. A garage will be built here
in place of the garden.   6. I saw him as he was jumping from the roof. The favorite tripped as the horses
were leaving the starting gate.   7. What is this poem about? It's about how painful and wonderful love can
be.   9. There's a lump of something underneath the carpet. What's underneath that blanket?
10. I baked a cake instead of a pie. Jan helped me instead of Laura.

Written Practice 11-3

1. Wagner was a contemporary of Brahms. Was Franklin a contemporary of Jefferson?   2. Assuming you
understand the terms, you may now sign here. Assuming the dress fits, we can have it ready in a week.
3. He differs so much from his brother. Differing from other people is no crime.   4. Provided there are
witnesses, we can proceed with the wedding. Provided you have a license, you can hunt in this area.
5. You have to trust in your parents. He seems to trust in no one.   6. Jack was injured during the game.
During my visit to the museum, I saw a collection of arrowheads.   7. Depending on the time of day, you
can often see Mount Rainier. I don't like depending on my parents.   8. You should dress more like him.
This tiny room is like a prison.   9. His mastery of the sword made him a feared man. With the mastery
of Chinese, you can travel the country alone.   10. This is a book of poems. That man is the father of
the bride.

QUIZ

1. b   2. d   3. a   4. c   5. a   6. b   7. d   8. a   9. b   10. c

CHAPTER 12

Written Practice 12-1

1. Learn how to tie your shoes before you start school.   2. Study very hard to pass your tests.   3. Don't
bring your laptop home, Jack.   4. Be careful whenever you use a sharp knife.   5. Make a huge chocolate
cake for the party.   6. Don't wait for me. Keep walking.   7. Try not to smile when Mary comes through
the door.   8. When Daddy sits at the table, give him a kiss.   9. Be as quiet as possible.   10. Paint the
eaves, repair the shutters, and clean out the gutters.

Written Practice 12-2

1. Stand up straight and salute. Please stand up straight and salute. Stand up straight and salute, please.
2. Pronounce this word correctly. Please pronounce this word correctly. Pronounce this word correctly, please.   3. Grow vegetables and flowers in your garden. Please grow vegetables and flowers in your garden. Grow vegetables and flowers in your garden, please.   4. Cook something wonderful for us. Please cook something wonderful for us. Cook something wonderful for us, please.   5. Be careful. Please be careful. Be careful, please.

Written Practice 12-3

1. Do spend some time with the children. Let your mother spend some time with the children. Let's spend some time with the children.   2. Do write Aunt Sally a thank you note. Let me write Aunt Sally a thank you note. Let's write Aunt Sally a thank you note.   3. Do help him find the keys. Let the boys help him find the keys. Let's help him find the keys.   4. Do not rent that action movie for tonight. Don't let the children rent that action movie for tonight. Let's not rent that action movie for tonight.   5. Do pour some wine into each glass. Let the server pour some wine into each glass. Let's pour some wine into each glass.   6. Do use the flashlight in that dark cave. Let the guide use the flashlight in that dark cave. Let's use the flashlight in that dark cave.   7. Do prepare some lunch for the girls. Let your husband prepare some lunch for the girls. Let's prepare some lunch for the girls.   8. Do plant some tulips near the porch. Let the gardener plant some tulips near the porch. Let's plant some tulips near the porch.   9. Do coach the wrestling team. Let Mr. Ortega coach the wrestling team. Let's coach the wrestling team.   10. Do sing that old song. Don't let Mary sing that old song. Let's not sing that old song.

QUIZ
1. c   2. a   3. b   4. d   5. a   6. b   7. d   8. b   9. b   10. a

CHAPTER 13

Written Practice 13-1

1. My uncle is in the army, and my aunt has a job on the army base.   2. The summers are very hot here, but in winter we have a lot of snow and it gets very cold.   3. Do you know how to swim well, or do you need to take lessons?   4. My parents don't like to watch television, nor do they like to attend plays.
5. The little boy stayed away from the water, for he knew the lake was quite deep.   6. The other boys ignored me, so I got on my bike and rode away.   7. Maria didn't show much interest in me, yet I think she found me appealing nonetheless.   8. We were going to go sailing, but we saw a storm brewing across the lake.   9. I don't like how you tell jokes, nor do I like the way you dance.   10. Stop annoying me, or I will be forced to call the police.

Written Practice 13-2

1. It is much too cold today; therefore, you should stay home and play in your room.   2. While my wife rested in the living room, I stayed in the kitchen and baked a cake.   3. I won't be going to the river unless the weather gets better.   4. I had to work late today because my department was behind in its work.
5. The wealthy woman spends little money on herself; however, she is very generous with her neighbors.
6. I think you're a lot smarter than Phillip and Jean.   7. After a vigorous tennis match, I like a long, hot shower.   8. I could understand you a lot better if you didn't talk and chew gum at the same time.

9. Although I had saved for weeks, I still didn't have enough money to buy the camera.   10. Once I knew that the children were safe, I closed my eyes and slept.

Written Practice 13-3

1. Both Jerry and his brother work in that factory.   2. Neither Father nor Mother came to my game.
3. Inasmuch as you now have your degree, I'd like to offer you a job.   4. Not only is Jane kind, she is also charming and friendly.   5. You can go on the bike trip provided you finish your chores.   6. Either you are hard of hearing or you are ignoring what I say.   7. Where young people congregate, there will be parties.   8. I can go to dinner with you as long as I'm home early.   9. You speak as though I know nothing about computers.   10. I made an early breakfast in order that the boys would be able to leave for school on time.

Written Practice 13-4

1. When the storm was finally over, we got back in the car and continued down the mountain.
2. The little girl acted as though she really understood the poem.   3. Considering Barbara's poor health, I feel she shouldn't try to travel right now.   4. The flight to Hawaii will not take place; however, you all will receive a refund.   5. In order that someone might be able to claim the lost bag, I placed it in the lost-and-found office.   6. You're welcome to go camping with us, provided you bring along your own sleeping bag.
7. While I set up the tent, you can get a fire going.   8. As long as you help us clean the house, we'll be happy to provide you with meals.   9. After I took a long, hot shower, I stretched out for a nap.
10. Regarding your poor grades in math, I have to warn you that your days at this school are numbered.
11. You can stay overnight if you don't mind sleeping in the attic.   12. I want you to take the puppy home, inasmuch as you love him so much.   13. According to the weather forecast, tomorrow we will finally have sunshine again.   14. I don't eat sushi, nor do I ever eat raw oysters.   15. Supposing that you can complete your degree this semester, you'll be able to look for a job in New York.

Written Practice 13-5

1. The ballerina, with whom my uncle wanted to chat, speaks little English.   2. An old friend from school, who used to live across the street, came by for a visit.   3. That nest, which took the sparrow so long to build, looks like it is ready to fall from the tree.   4. This floorboard, under which I keep some valuables, is intentionally loose.   5. Mr. Marconi, whose years in the navy were difficult, joined a veterans' organization recently.   6. I'm going to spend some time with my cousin, who is leaving for college next month.   7. The carpenters, whom we hired to build the garage, work so slowly.   8. I really like the house that your parents live in.   9. My family knows several sailors that served on the aircraft carrier that was in the news.   10. Have you found any books that we could sell at the rummage sale?   11. Where are the boxes that you got those letters from?   12. Words that rhyme and sound pretty aren't necessarily poetry.   13. A friend that just won the lottery may spend the winter in Puerto Rico.   14. We don't know any of the people that he claims to have worked with.   15. I want a laptop that is loaded with memory.

QUIZ

1. c   2. a   3. c   4. d   5. d   6. b   7. a   8. a   9. b   10. a

CHAPTER 14

Written Practice 14-1

1. We are not taking a ride out into the country. We aren't taking a ride out into the country.
2. Is that not your new car? Isn't that your new car?   3. My cousins were not in California last week. My cousins weren't in California last week.   4. Did your grandmother not speak English well? Didn't your grandmother speak English well?   5. The little girl was not playing in the sandbox. The little girl wasn't playing in the sandbox.   6. Was I not friendly enough to them? Wasn't I friendly enough to them?
7. My aunt does not keep her jewelry in a safe. My aunt doesn't keep her jewelry in a safe.   8. Will Robert not get home before supper? Won't Robert get home before supper?   9. We shall not lend him money again. We shan't lend him money again.   10. Do you not like living in the dormitory? Don't you like living in the dormitory?

QUIZ

1. c   2. a   3. a   4. d   5. d   6. b   7. a   8. a   9. d   10. b

CHAPTER 15

Written Practice 15-1

1. Someone Grove Street Bank   2. Do I Indiana University   3. No Friday   4. Jack London   5. We Paris France   6. My Ford Motor Company Detroit   7. Colonel James Hardy Fort Sheridan Illinois
8. Ms. Garcia   9. Our Golden Gate Savings Loan Company   10. He January   11. For Ford Fairlane
12. The American Marine Corps Band   13. Mayor Thompson   14. The White House   15. When Anne Latin Mr. Smith   16. John Miller   17. Dr. Keller   18. In Senator Rodriguez New Orleans
19. Is Uncle Thomas   20. Hundred-year-olds

Written Practice 15-2

1. During his life, my uncle owned a Buick, a Toyota, and a Cadillac.   2. They live in Brazil in the spring, in Maine in the summer, in Mexico in the fall, and in the Alps in the dead of winter.   3. We need a case of soda, four pizzas, and several bags of potato chips for the party.   4. On Sunday, I washed the car, my daughter made some lunch, and my son cleaned the garage.   5. My favorite books are *To Kill a Mockingbird*, *Catcher in the Rye*, and *The Great Gatsby*.

Written Practice 15-3

1. She said, "Get out and never come back!"   2. The child's temperature was over 103; indeed, he was burning up.   3. Behind the garage, we found some old tools and a wheelbarrow.   4. "Does this umbrella belong to you?" he asked with a smile.   5. The volunteers' meeting was canceled, and a party began instead.

QUIZ

1. a   2. c   3. a   4. a   5. b   6. c   7. b   8. b   9. a   10. c

PART THREE TEST

1. b   2. d   3. c   4. d   5. c   6. b   7. d   8. b   9. b   10. a   11. c   12. c   13. d
14. b   15. b   16. d   17. d   18. a   19. a   20. d   21. c   22. a   23. b   24. c   25. b

CHAPTER 16

Written Practice 16-1

1. Present: The toy is broken by the little boy. Past: The toy was broken by the little boy. Present perfect: The toy has been broken by the little boy. Past perfect: The toy had been broken by the little boy. Future: The toy will be broken by the little boy.   2. Present: The dog is washed by Thomas. Past: The dog was washed by Thomas. Present perfect: The dog has been washed by Thomas. Past perfect: The dog had been washed by Thomas. Future: The dog will be washed by Thomas.   3. Present: Is the silverware polished by your husband? Past: Was the silverware polished by your husband? Present perfect: Has the silverware been polished by your husband? Past perfect: Had the silverware been polished by your husband? Future: Will the silverware be polished by your husband?   4. Present: It is discovered by a scientist from England. Past: It was discovered by a scientist from England. Present perfect: It has been discovered by a scientist from England. Past perfect: It had been discovered by a scientist from England. Future: It will be discovered by a scientist from England.   5. Present: The group is led by a museum guide. Past: The group was led by a museum guide. Present perfect: The group has been led by a museum guide. Past perfect: The group had been led by a museum guide. Future: The group will be led by a museum guide.

Written Practice 16-2

1. The old barn was burned down by someone last night. The old barn was burned down last night.
2. A little cottage on the lake had been purchased by my brother. A little cottage on the lake had been purchased.   3. Will a new factory be built here by the owners? Will a new factory be built here?
4. The queen is loved by all the people very much. The queen is loved very much.   5. More and more has been done by them every day. More and more has been done every day.   6. A small cave was discovered by me in the park. A small cave was discovered in the park.   7. Will the cattle be driven into the pasture by the farmer? Will the cattle be driven into the pasture?   8. The cows have been milked by his wife. The cows have been milked.   9. The juniors and seniors were tested by the teachers regularly. The juniors and seniors were tested regularly.   10. His strange behavior was noticed by no one. His strange behavior was not noticed.

Written Practice 16-3

1. The ailing boy must be rushed to the hospital. The ailing boy needs to be rushed to the hospital.
2. The old house has had to be sold by the owners. The old house has been supposed to be/was supposed to be sold by the owners.   3. Will you want to be educated in England? Will you be able to be educated in England?   4. The problem should be investigated by our committee. The problem can be investigated by our committee.   5. The new constitution had to be completed by the end of the year. The new constitution needed to be completed by the end of the year.

Written Practice 16-4

1. The car got repaired at Jim's Garage.   2. My uncle got kicked by that old mule.   3. The bride is getting made up for her wedding day.   4. The boy gets caught stealing an apple.   5. We were getting drenched by the sudden rainstorm.

QUIZ

1. b   2. a   3. b   4. a   5. a   6. d   7. d   8. b   9. d   10. d

CHAPTER 17

Written Practice 17-1

1. It is still required that every driver have insurance. It is still required that we carry some form of ID.
2. The governor demands that the state senate pass the legislation now. The governor demands that children be inoculated against the disease.   3. We have asked that you join us in the ceremony. We have asked that a monument be erected in her honor.   4. It was my suggestion that Ms. Carter become our new director. It was my suggestion that we leave the matter for discussion at another time.   5. She insists that I be her dance partner. She insists that the party start at eight o'clock.   6. It is desired by the committee that meetings last no longer than three hours. It is desired by the committee that Mr. Kelly be in charge of refreshments.   7. He ordered that no one be allowed to leave the building. He ordered that the whole army stay away from the front.   8. Do you prefer that we order pizza? Do you prefer that I be the bartender tonight?   9. I shall recommend that this heroic woman get a medal. I shall recommend that his novel be marketed as a potential best seller.   10. The state requires that every city provide recreation for its citizens. The state requires that fresh water be available everywhere.

Written Practice 17-2

1. It was important that I be the new chairman. It was important that Wi-Fi was available throughout the area.   2. I feel it is necessary that our boss have a better office. I feel it is necessary that the company keep better records.   3. It is essential that Tom not smoke so much. It is essential that everyone remain calm.
4. Is it necessary that he argue with me? Is it necessary that he go to the races so often?   5. It was agreed that the proposition be submitted. It was agreed that having more fun was a great idea.

Written Practice 17-3

1. If only you had arrived a little earlier.   2. If only I could meet your new boyfriend.   3. If only he were able to join in the conversation.   4. If only my boss would give me more responsibility.
5. If only my parents were not so strict with me.   6. If only she had not become a politician.
7. If only I could find my passport.   8. If only the children would eat more vegetables.   9. If only their music weren't so loud.   10. If only the cost of groceries had not risen so fast.

Written Practice 17-4

1. If I were you, I wouldn't spend so much money.   2. The funny man was dancing as if he were a little drunk.   3. If I had known about your big project, I would have returned your tools sooner.   4. If there were no medical bills to worry about, this would be a happier time together.   5. My boss's wife acts as if she were the guest of honor tonight.   6. The children's choir sang as if we understood their language.
7. If we hadn't prepared our tax return in time, we would have had to pay a penalty.   8. My girlfriend kissed me as if she had really strong feelings toward me.   9. If the rain would ever stop, I could go to the park to play tennis.   10. Aunt Helen might bake a chocolate cake if we begged her a lot.   11. The homeless man ate as if he hadn't had a meal in a week.   12. If Mr. Brown had been earning a paycheck, his family wouldn't have been evicted.   13. If his story were true, he would be a hero to all of us.
14. He should have gotten a better education!   15. The band played as though the president had just entered the auditorium.

QUIZ
1. b   2. b   3. d   4. a   5. d   6. b   7. b   8. d   9. a   10. b

CHAPTER 18

Written Practice 18-1

1. It's only about five more blocks.   2. It was just after midnight when I came in the door.   3. I think it will be in 2016, in Brazil.   4. No, it's begun to rain very hard.   5. It's our neighbor from across the street.   6. Of course, it's Saturday.   7. Yes, it's getting quite cold.   8. It was 2008.   9. No, it's still very chilly.   10. It's the runner from Africa.

Written Practice 18-2

1. It was suggested that you find enough time to finish the job today.   2. It is believed that more people are finding jobs.   3. It is important to help the needy and the old.   4. It is hoped that sales will finally increase.   5. It was mentioned that rents in this town are still very high.   6. It's assumed that you know how to operate this machinery.   7. It was believed that the play would be a success in New York.
8. It was stated in the memo that Ms. Garcia is calling a meeting for Tuesday.   9. It was hard for her to say good-bye to me.   10. It was believed that the boy's writing skills were still weak.

Written Practice 18-3

1. There were several magazines lying on the floor.   2. There had been three burglaries in this neighborhood.   3. There was much arguing in the Senate about housing.   4. There exists far more peace and quiet in the country than in the city.   5. There were still a few problems with the new computers.
6. There arose loud noises from the factory.   7. There is no milk in the refrigerator.   8. There is a gift for you on the table.   9. Were there four children ill in that family?   10. There is nothing that we can do for the man.

Written Practice 18-4

1. thirteenth   2. twenty-second   3. thirtieth   4. first   5. forty-third   6. seventy-fifth
7. twelfth   8. hundredth   9. sixty-sixth   10. fiftieth

QUIZ

1. d   2. b   3. d   4. a   5. b   6. b   7. a   8. a   9. a   10. c

CHAPTER 19

Written Practice 19-1

1. Present: They do away with the old rules. Past: They did away with the old rules. Present perfect: They have done away with the old rules. Past perfect: They had done away with the old rules. Future: They will do away with the old rules.   2. Present: Shopping cleans me out. Past: Shopping cleaned me out. Present perfect: Shopping has cleaned me out. Past perfect: Shopping had cleaned me out. Future: Shopping will clean me out.   3. Present: Do Tanya and Bob break up? Past: Did Tanya and Bob break up? Present perfect: Have Tanya and Bob broken up? Past perfect: Had Tanya and Bob broken up? Future: Will Tanya and Bob break up?   4. Present: I ask your sister out. Past: I asked your sister out. Present perfect: I have asked your sister out. Past perfect: I had asked your sister out. Future: I will ask your sister out.   5. Present: She catches us cheating. Past: She caught us cheating. Present perfect: She has caught us cheating. Past perfect: She had caught us cheating. Future: She will catch us cheating.

Written Practice 19-2

1. The frustrated citizens did away with the corrupt officials. The frustrated citizens did away with the summer festival.   2. Tina doesn't want to break up with her boyfriend. Tina doesn't want to break up with the man she would like to marry.   3. The authorities acted on the report they received from a citizen. The authorities acted on the evidence they received from a citizen.   4. The boss is asking everyone up to his office for a talk. The boss is asking Mr. Kelly up to his office for a talk.   5. How did I end up with so little money? How did I end up with a bump on my head?

Written Practice 19-3

1. Fill the forms out before leaving. Fill out the forms before leaving.   2. We brought our daughter up to be polite. We brought up our daughter to be polite.   3. Can you put a model airplane together for me? Can you put together a model airplane for me?   4. The workers are cleaning them up. The workers are cleaning up the tools.   5. You won't be able to figure the secret codes out. You won't be able to figure out the secret codes.

Written Practice 19-4

1. I want to make up with my husband.   2. I'm ashamed that my son has let down the family.
3. My winter coat wore out after two seasons.   4. No one should put off his annual physical examination.
5. Tina hangs out with her friends at the mall.   6. The elderly patient passed away last night.   7. While in India, we ran across friends from college.   8. What do the stars and stripes of the flag stand for?
9. How did she put it together?   10. Bob has to break in the new employee.

QUIZ
1. b   2. c   3. b   4. b   5. a   6. a   7. c   8. a   9. d   10. a

CHAPTER 20

Written Practice 20-1

1. If it rains again today, I'm going to scream.   2. I really like the new family across the street, but they don't seem interested in me.   3. The twins were born last night.   4. In 1776 representatives of the first 13 states signed the Declaration of Independence.   5. Can your mechanic fix the car by tomorrow?
6. The teen driver wasn't able to control the speeding car.   7. You look as though you had seen a ghost.
8. According to the National Weather Service, we're going to have a hot summer.   9. I always enjoyed spending time in my aunt's cottage.   10. While I made the campfire, the other hikers put up the tent.
11. I need help. Where is the nearest hospital?   12. Mom said that the scissors are in the first drawer on the left.   13. Our new queen sat at the head of the table, and the young prince sat across from her.
14. Some students were having a party inside an old warehouse.   15. She got on the bus without her purse or wallet.

Written Practice 20-2

1. After the rain stopped, we ran out to play in the puddles.   2. Please get dinner started before your father comes home.   3. While I unpacked the car, John got the campfire going.   4. Despite all her complaining, Jean enjoyed her vacation in Canada.   5. Someone shouted to the man, "Watch out for that car!"   6. When Juanita came in the door, everyone ran to embrace her.   7. Can you bathe the children before it gets too late?   8. Uncle Robert was writing a letter to his son in the army.   9. Tina had hoped

to go skiing, but there wasn't enough snow on the ground.   10. The Smiths neither go to the movies nor watch much TV.   11. We finally found the puppy that had been lost for so long.   12. The children can't go to the park unless it gets a little cooler.   13. Professor Gold is not only intelligent, he is also funny and a great storyteller.   14. Although I had saved enough money, I still waited to buy a new car.   15. We can go to the pool for a swim if it gets a little warmer.

Written Practice 20-3

1. Late autumn; Right after a snowfall   2. the city's new mayor; a few students from New York   3. did the dishes; kept the children quiet   4. visited Mexico; tried to get a job there   5. saved my wife's life; works alongside me every day   6. accidents happened; fires took place   7. she cannot stand the climate; her boyfriend is returning to Colorado   8. our attorney; the owner of the antique store   9. I would help you tomorrow; you would feel better about yourself tomorrow   10. torn down; renovated by a team of artisans   11. hates to travel; never stays away from the office   12. they keep taking on new debts; they're worried that they might lose their jobs   13. Do you know how fast you were driving; May I see your identification, please   14. be a bit more aggressive with the dog; take better care of his lawn   15. called for help; shouted at the top of her voice

Written Practice 20-4

1. vacationing in Florida; shopping in this mall   2. When the school year is over; After the semester ends   3. before he turns twenty-two; around the end of May   4. is the cat hiding; have you put those tools   5. During the worst part of the hurricane; Because of the tornado   6. had resided; has been working   7. A tiny nest; Large seedpods   8. could have; might have   9. near; on the shore of   10. Several exotic-looking; Four German   11. less accurately; more speedily   12. Being one of your friends; Spending time chatting with you   13. can't harm; mustn't contact   14. after the difficult soccer match; inside one of the tents   15. The thief kicked the door shut; An armed man raised his gun

Written Practice 20-5

1. I had always wanted to visit India; my friends kept inviting me to visit them in Vancouver   2. you receive a medal for your valor; Martin be promoted   3. she had wanted for so long; Macy's had advertised so heavily   4. made everyone in our school so proud; was got us headlines in the local newspaper   5. we still missed our connection to Houston; there was no one there to meet us   6. he had injured his leg; she was in a terrible hurry   7. I neither like such jokes; I neither put up with bad behavior   8. the adults chatted in the living room; their parents played cards in the dining room   9. frightened birds flew into the sky; it began to rain cats and dogs   10. Little Tommy was overjoyed; The owner of the ski lodge smiled broadly   11. Our car was badly damaged in an accident; We didn't receive the invitation until yesterday   12. begin taking boxes out to the van; take your turn washing dishes   13. Either you are a bit dense; Either you are poorly informed   14. she has applied to M.I.T; she has enrolled in chemistry and physics courses   15. easily gets seasick; comes from a family of army men

Written Practice 20-6

1. Present: The senators are voting on the bill. Past: The senators were voting on the bill. Present perfect: The senators have been voting on the bill. Future: The senators will be voting on the bill.   2. Present: My in-laws are able to spend a week with us. Past: My in-laws were able to spend a week with us. Present perfect: My in-laws have been able to spend a week with us. Future: My in-laws will be able to spend a week with us.   3. Present: Does she have to have corrective surgery? Past: Did she have to have corrective surgery? Present perfect: Has she had to have corrective surgery? Future: Will she have to have corrective

surgery?   4. Present: Thomas doesn't discuss money with me. Past: Thomas didn't discuss money with me. Present perfect: Thomas hasn't discussed money with me. Future: Thomas won't discuss money with me. 5. Present: Do we meet at a party? Past: Did we meet at a party? Present perfect: Have we met at a party? Future: Shall we meet at a party?   6. Present: That old book costs nine dollars. Past: That old book cost nine dollars. Present perfect: That old book has cost nine dollars. Future: That old book will cost nine dollars. 7. Present: Her fiancé is living in Maryland. Past: Her fiancé was living in Maryland. Present perfect: Her fiancé has been living in Maryland. Future: Her fiancé will be living in Maryland.   8. Present: Lightning strikes are rare. Past: Lightning strikes were rare. Present perfect: Lightning strikes have been rare. Future: Lightning strikes will be rare.   9. Present: Can you arrange a meeting with him for me? Past: Could you arrange a meeting with him for me? Present perfect: N/A *or* Have you been able to arrange a meeting with him for me? Future: N/A *or* Will you be able to arrange a meeting with him for me?   10. Present: Does Jorge want to go on the hike? Past: Did Jorge want to go on the hike? Present perfect: Has Jorge wanted to go on the hike? Future: Will Jorge want to go on the hike?   11. Present: His grandparents always drink red wine. Past: His grandparents always drank red wine. Present perfect: His grandparents have always drunk red wine. Future: His grandparents will always drink red wine.   12. Present: Why does the detective follow her? Past: Why did the detective follow her? Present perfect: Why has the detective followed her? Future: Why will the detective follow her?   13. Present: The wedding guests are painting the town red. Past: The wedding guests were painting the town red. Present perfect: The wedding guests have been painting the town red. Future: The wedding guests will be painting the town red.   14. Present: I have to borrow your car. Past: I had to borrow your car. Present perfect: I have had to borrow your car. Future: I will have to borrow your car.   15. Present: Why must he buy so many shirts and ties? Past: N/A *or* Why did he have to buy so many shirts and ties? Present perfect: N/A *or* Why has he had to buy so many shirts and ties? Future: N/A *or* Why will he have to buy so many shirts and ties?

Written Practice 20-7

1. to go on a fishing trip   2. decided to take a little nap   3. The boat began to float down the river. 4. I must have drifted for more than a mile.   5. into rougher waters   6. rapids and huge boulders 7. I grabbed the oars and struggled and finally into calmer waters.   8. jumped to the dock in relief 9. I think you should leave boating to the sailors   10. went fishing again

Written Practice 20-8

1. enjoyed trying to invent new chemical compounds   2. add chemicals to different kinds of soap to make them smell better   3. a fragrant hand cream   4. began experimenting with various combinations 5. some of the cream on her hand and waited   6. musty and very unpleasant   7. She rubbed a little more of the cream on her hand and waited again.   8. Something was very wrong.   9. that she had chosen vinegar instead of a scented chemical   10. produced a pleasant-smelling hand cream

Written Practice 20-9

1. to go sledding   2. a rapid ride down the slope   3. a nice-looking man with a good sense of humor 4. they got in line behind a dozen others   5. it was their turn to put the sled on the edge of the hill 6. scooted in behind her   7. around her waist and leaned in close   8. through the crunching snow 9. I love you, Claudia   10. she hoped the half-heard message had not been the wind playing a trick on her

Written Practice 20-10

1. in a large house, built a hundred years ago   2. many treasures, including an old trunk   3. Sally found an old lamp at the bottom of the trunk   4. a puff of smoke came from the lamp followed by a little man in a strange green suit   5. If this is true, I don't like it   6. He told them that he was grateful to be released from the lamp   7. said there was nothing to fear and that he would grant them three wishes   8. a beautiful white pony appeared there in the attic   9. waved his hand, and the pony disappeared   10. they woke up with a start in their beds

Written Practice 20-11

1. A broken lamp lay on the floor next to the puppy.   2. Can anyone repair a broken lamp?   3. You can get cut by the sharp edges of a broken lamp.   4. A broken lamp is being sent back to the store for replacement.   5. Do you want to keep a broken lamp that cannot be fixed?   6. A broken lamp's electrical cord can still be used.   7. Who knows the cause of a broken lamp?   8. This is the man that fixed a broken lamp for us.   9. She laughed as if a broken lamp were no problem at all.   10. Although he found a broken lamp next to the window, there was no sign of a burglary.

Written Practice 20-12

1. Our new neighbors come from Kenya.   2. Mary brought our new neighbors an apple pie.   3. We know nothing about our new neighbors.   4. The apartment was rented by our new neighbors for only a month.   5. Our new neighbors, who seem to have a lot of children, have been here one week.   6. Our new neighbors' two cars look very expensive.   7. I invited our new neighbors to the block party.   8. Our new neighbors will be introduced by Ms. Garcia.   9. Our new neighbors, whose belongings are still on the lawn, don't seem to be home.   10. When I met our new neighbors, I knew I would like them.

Written Practice 20-13

1. Another illness has hit our family.   2. My mother can't endure another illness.   3. Due to another illness, our vacation is postponed again.   4. The elderly man was put back in bed by another illness.   5. Another illness, which is something we don't need right now, would be the worst thing for my husband.   6. Shingles is like another illness I had as a child.   7. Another illness is being considered by the doctors.   8. Another illness could have put him in the hospital.   9. Another illness, the cause of which is still unknown, has struck my parents.   10. While the doctor was treating another illness, my father came down with pneumonia.

Written Practice 20-14

1. That strange man stood on the corner all day.   2. Someone sent that strange man a secret message.   3. According to that strange man, the world will end tomorrow.   4. A statement made by that strange man gave me chills.   5. I spoke to that strange man, who seemed unaware of my presence.   6. That strange man's car looks very old.   7. The police suspected that strange man of a crime.   8. That strange man will have to be watched.   9. That strange man has made many phone calls from here.   10. If I gave that strange man some money, I think he would leave.

Written Practice 20-15

1. Several foreign tourists ended up in the hospital.   2. Mary gave several foreign tourists a tour of the church.   3. We have gifts for several foreign tourists.   4. The bridge is being photographed by several foreign tourists.   5. She met several foreign tourists that knew her brother in Korea.   6. Several foreign

tourists' passports were not stamped.   7. I liked several foreign tourists.   8. Several foreign tourists will be invited to the White House.   9. Several foreign tourists, whose relatives live in Canada, speak no English.   10. Before I met several foreign tourists, I had never met anyone born outside the United States.

FINAL EXAM
1. b   2. c   3. b   4. a   5. c   6. d   7. d   8. a   9. d   10. d   11. b   12. a   13. d
14. a   15. b   16. c   17. c   18. d   19. a   20. b   21. d   22. b   23. d   24. b   25. a
26. b   27. a   28. d   29. a   30. d   31. c   32. b   33. c   34. b   35. d   36. c   37. c
38. a   39. d   40. b   41. c   42. a   43. a   44. d   45. a   46. c   47. a   48. a   49. d
50. d